Try to describe the color of pure (still) water, my dear.

THEORETICAL PERFORMANCE

talented is sometimes not immediately apparent or hardly noticeable. 2) If the child is not registered as extremely talented, she can get bored in the company of average children, in an ordinary group. Because, where the others are still zealously occupied by solving an entered game / task, she has already solved it

/ that which remains a surprise for others is routine for her. And thus, a time gap is formed which she has an urge to fill with something – anything! But this

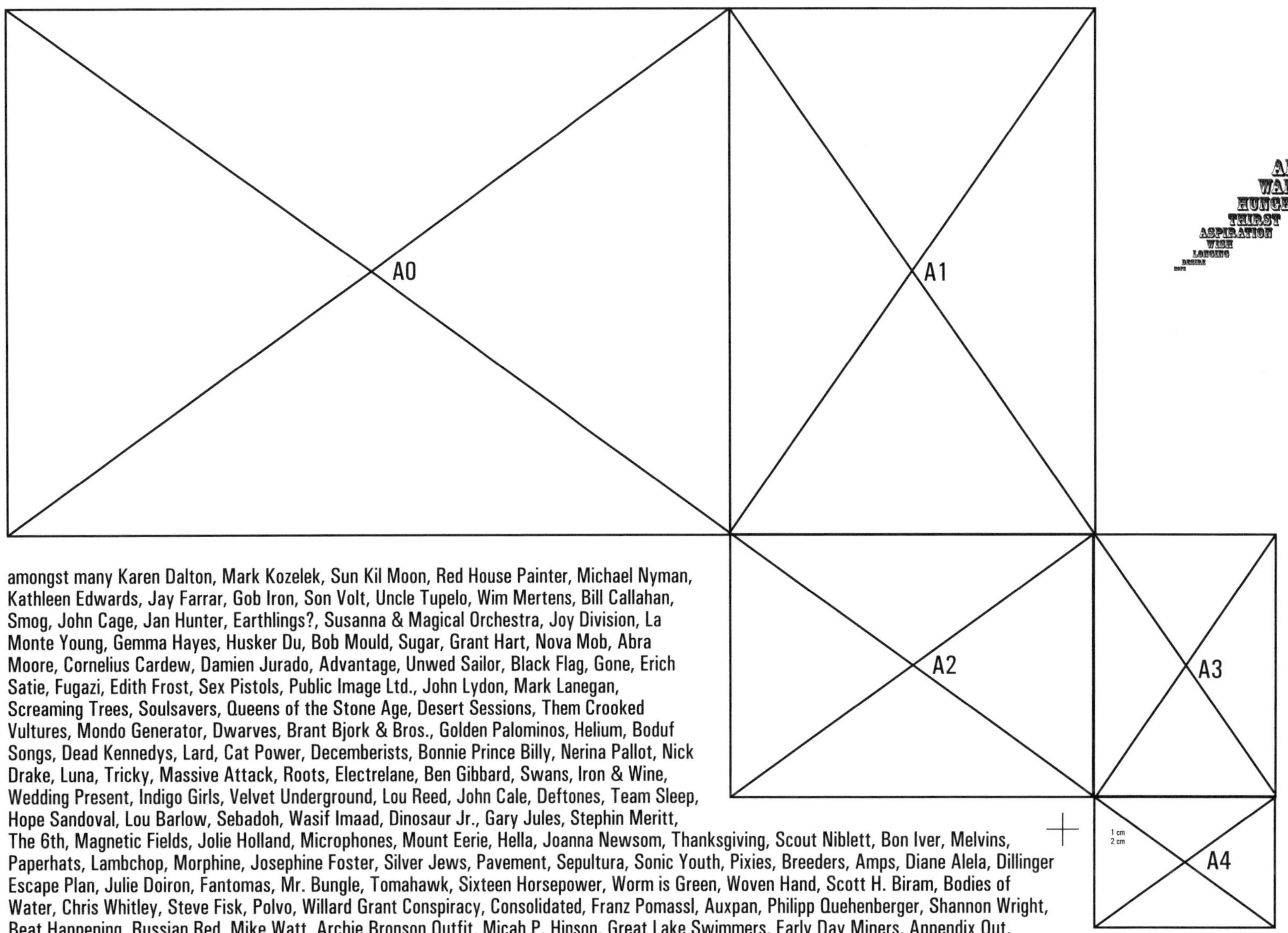

amongst many Karen Dalton, Mark Kozelek, Sun Kil Moon, Red House Painter, Michael Nyman, Kathleen Edwards, Jay Farrar, Gob Iron, Son Volt, Uncle Tupelo, Wim Mertens, Bill Callahan, Smog, John Cage, Jan Hunter, Earthlings?, Susanna & Magical Orchestra, Joy Division, La Monte Young, Gemma Hayes, Husker Du, Bob Mould, Sugar, Grant Hart, Nova Mob, Abra Moore, Cornelius Cardew, Damien Jurado, Advantage, Unwed Sailor, Black Flag, Gone, Erich Satie, Fugazi, Edith Frost, Sex Pistols, Public Image Ltd., John Lydon, Mark Lanegan, Screaming Trees, Soulsavers, Queens of the Stone Age, Desert Sessions, Them Crooked Vultures, Mondo Generator, Dwarves, Brant Bjork & Bros., Golden Palominos, Helium, Boduf Songs, Dead Kennedys, Lard, Cat Power, Decemberists, Bonnie Prince Billy, Nerina Pallot, Nick Drake, Luna, Tricky, Massive Attack, Roots, Electrelane, Ben Gibbard, Swans, Iron & Wine, Wedding Present, Indigo Girls, Velvet Underground, Lou Reed, John Cale, Deftones, Team Sleep, Hope Sandoval, Lou Barlow, Sebadoh, Wasif Imaad, Dinosaur Jr., Gary Jules, Stephin Meritt, The 6th, Magnetic Fields, Jolie Holland, Microphones, Mount Eerie, Hella, Joanna Newsom, Thanksgiving, Scout Niblett, Bon Iver, Melvins, Paperhats, Lambchop, Morphine, Josephine Foster, Silver Jews, Pavement, Sepultura, Sonic Youth, Pixies, Breeders, Amps, Diane Alela, Dillinger Escape Plan, Julie Doiron, Fantomas, Mr. Bungle, Tomahawk, Sixteen Horsepower, Worm is Green, Woven Hand, Scott H. Biram, Bodies of Water, Chris Whitley, Steve Fisk, Polvo, Willard Grant Conspiracy, Consolidated, Franz Pomassl, Auxpan, Philipp Quehenberger, Shannon Wright, Beat Happening, Russian Red, Mike Watt, Archie Bronson Outfit, Micah P. Hinson, Great Lake Swimmers, Early Day Miners, Appendix Out, Amalgamated Sons of Rest, Corrina Repp, Meredith Bragg, Rachael Cantu, and many others

MIRAGE AGOG
ANTICIPATION
DELUSION
EAGERNESS
ILLUSION
IMAGINATION BELIEF
EXPECTANCY
LUST DISAPPOINTMENT
PHANTASM
AWE ANTICLIMAX
BALK
ANXIETY
WANT
HUNGER
THIRST
ASPIRATION
WISH
LONGING
DESIRE
HOPE

Working,name, walking, peregrination, sitting, title, reading, hallucination, logo, writing, manual, waiting, identity, driving, culture, watching, idea, listening, sketch, drawing, construction, layout, univers condensed and other associated fonts, cleaning, negotiation, speaking, realisation, counting, distribution, measuring, pencil, swimming, pen, singing, notebook & notebook, travelling, handy, project, word, illustrator, photoshop, {quark}, pdf {.eps; .ai; .doc; .jpeg}, curves, corrections, email, attachment, download, power-point, screen-saver, live-act (sung, spoken, background), mp3 (sung, spoken, background), video {sung, spoken, background, animated}, print {billboard, poster, flyer, pamphlet, postcard, digital, ink-jet, laser, silkcreen, offset, xerox, plotter}, engraving, mural, joke, publication, poem?, object, text, installation, didactics, event, elementarism, speakers, exercise, headphones, lesson, projectors, class, "what?", monitors, learning, players, teaching, microphones, test, light, experiment, paint, example, brush, paint-roller, ruller, nails, screws, double-sided self-adhesive tape, biography, glue, therapy, unframed / framed, consideration, wall, floor, dislexia / graphomania, ceiling, representation, door, substitution, window, interpretation, staircase, pronunciation, lift, tonality, room, stage, auditorium, participants, garden, symposiarch & symposiasts, street, encomium, indoor / outdoor, colleagues, shelf, friends, table, competitors, sockle, visitors {readers, listeners, observers}, paper, institutions, fabric, supporters, vinyl, clients, visualisation, misunderstanding, dimension, lostness, illustrativeness, disappearance, size, edition {single / multiple}, economy, landscape / portrait, politics, colour, intuition, take-away, storage, concentration, home, selection, archive, do care / do not care, repetition, source, variability;

somewhere more than 1 piece on 1 sheet {just like this-one}; titles, descriptions on reverse sides.

context is not adjusted to the individual provision for alternative activities. Or, on contrary!: in order to teach her social adaptability, adjustment in the permanent diaspora of subjectivity, the requirement of simple waiting (and later, of meaningful waiting) – of knowing when to obey. This is still bearable in

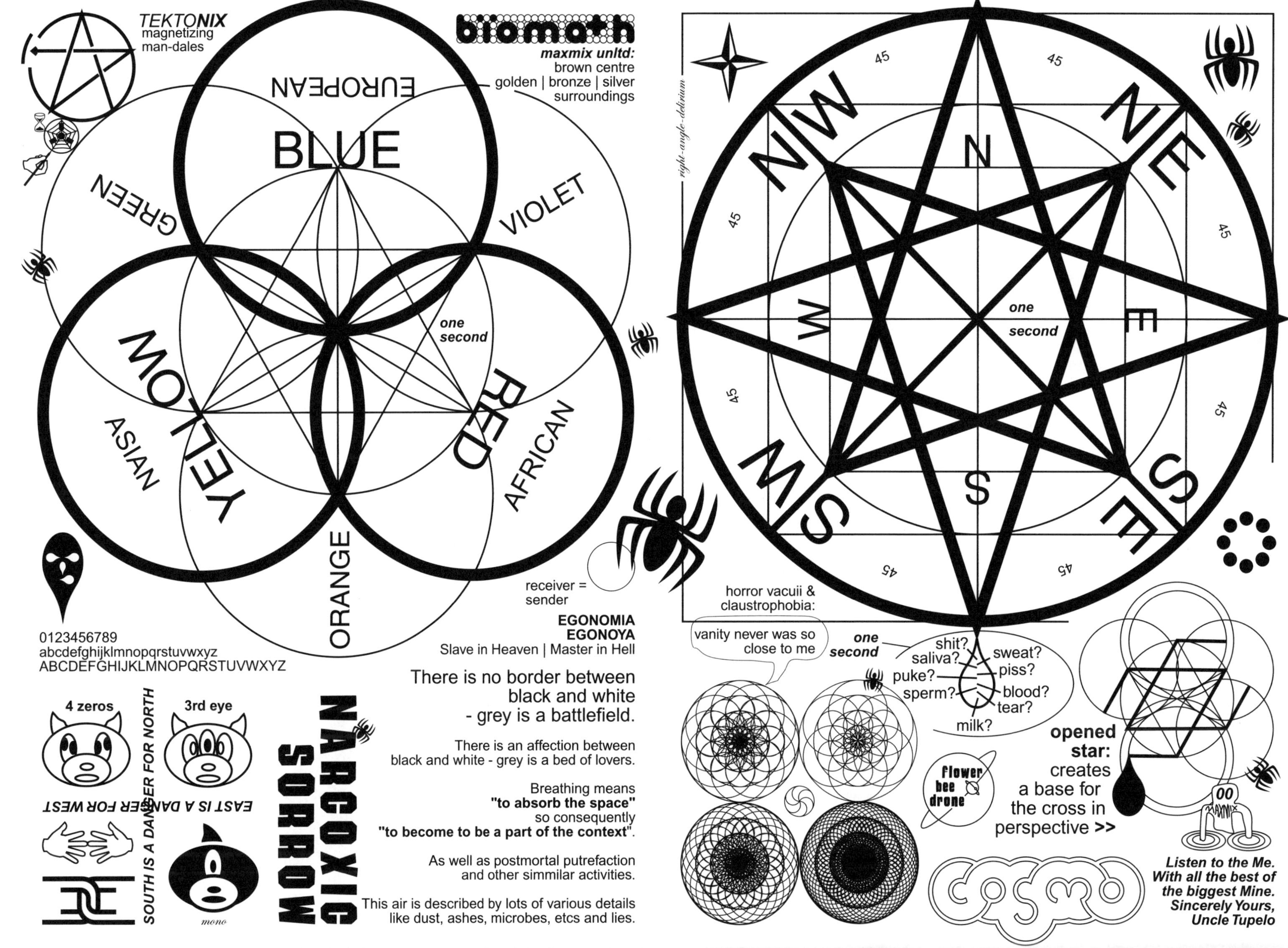

Boris Ondreička, *Delirium {Narcoxic series}*

kindergarten, but at grammar school it is unacceptable quantity-wise. Boredom is a substitute, manifestation of depression. 3) If bored, she creates "unfortunate"

parallel activities. When having unfilled redundant time, she is much more
inclined, due to a lack of centric focusing, to be a "victim" of manifold external

One comment to the page No. 53.

"A B C D E F G H I J K L M N O P Q R S T U V W X Y Z"

Fundamenty radikální poezie (The Fundaments of Radical Poetry) is a work created in 2007 by Boris Ondreička. It is made up of 26 elements – letters, graphemes, which in speech forms correspond to 26 phonemes – each one a distinctive vocal articulation. In the canonically arranged order above, the graphemes make up the Latin alphabet (there are also Arabian, Syrian, Cyrillic, Greek and Hebrew alphabets). An alphabet in which each element (each grapheme) corresponds to a specific sound made by the vocal tract is called an abjad.
This group of graphemes also creates the Fundament of this text, in spite of the fact that this text is not radical poetry. The question then arises what a person must know, be able to do, manage, experience, want, feel, suffer, in order to write radical poetry? What should one know to be a radical poet?

WHAT YOU SHOULD KNOW TO BE A POET

all you can about animals as persons.
the names of trees and flowers and weeds.
names of stars, and the movement of the planets
                                        and the moon.

your own six senses, with a watchful and elegant mind.

at least one kind of traditional magic :
divination, atsrology, the book of changes, the tarot ;

dreams.
the illusory demons and illusory shining gods ;

kiss the ass of the devil and eat shit ;
fuck his horny barbed cock,
fuck the hag,
and all celestial angels
                        and maidens perfum´d and golden –

& then love the human : wives husbands and friends.

Quoted from Gary Snyder, Premier chant du chaman et autres poemes, Orphée La Difference, Paris, 1992, p.58.

And because today (10.05.2011) the computer computes every combination of possibilities in tasks we give it with a speed of 1.7 petaflops (1 petaflop = over 10^15/1,000,000,000,000,000/ 1 quadrillion calculations per second) we take the following task as our starting point for arranging the graphemes and words of this text.
There are 26 elements: A, B, C, D, E, F, G, H, I, J, K, L, M, N, O, P, Q, R, S, T, U, V, W, X, Y, Z. The task is to compute all possible combinations of these 26 elements, in the course of which the elements can exist either individually or in clusters, and these clusters can exist in other clusters, while the clusters can be divided by the punctuation marks ! ? + " „ . : & (/) ÷ * , and while the group of punctuation marks cannot be considered as closed. The following symbols: 0123456789 can also be used, in the course of which these symbols can similarly be arranged in clusters and these clusters in further clusters. The length of the rows is not in any way determined in advance. End of task.
John Cage wrote about his composition Indeterminacy being an object inhuman rather than human, with the disquieting features of a Frankenstein monster. We could use the same characteristic for language. Language too is an object inhuman rather than human, with the disquieting features of a Frankenstein monster, but still allows for individualisation. Beginning with neologisms (in psychiatry, the term neologism is used to describe the use of words that have meaning only for the person who uses them, independent of their common meaning, while psychiatry uses neologisms as indicative symptoms of social pathology) language allows us to individualise some of its monstrous components and to create neologisms – from neologisms we could proceed further hierarchically – to combinations, Portmanteaux, abbreviations, acronyms, jargon...: feelosophia, anythinking, stereologue, verbalence, doomstyx, sabot:h, remembrane, lessness, a.b.solution, hard-correct, sextra, feminent, fee-mail, mediktat, alternazi, introlerance, modelirivm, U-Rope, Universüs, Antagonia, Bastardia, Resistika, Re)pub.lick, Empathex, Misantropolis, Miseraville, city.zen, Bionfó, Connot, Emot, Torpido, Chao, A)men, O)men, Utopsia, Gangel etc.
These neologisms are like freshly sprouting twigs of madness growing directly from the body of the Wittgenstein mysterium. And all of us – in the night, or in the early morning of our lives – sing, bellow, babble, gush, modulate, suffocate or give vent to our own Ursonatas. But the purpose of arranging the letters of this text is to follow the Collection of All Possible Texts, the title pointing to the solution of the task described above. Its solution however need not make anyone afraid. We press a (virtual) print key and experience a certain time lapse; that is, there is a discrepancy between the speed of the print and the speed of the computation – the process of printing is unquestionably slower than the print process. At first sight the texts dismay the reader, composing themselves from intimately known signs which are ordered into meaningless rows and you are actually thinking: "It's not so much that I'm dismayed, but incredibly bored when I see straightaway that there is no sense to this text, and it's long, and moreover I know that what I see printed in front of me here is only an unending fragment of something much longer, which is just as senseless as a whole," you think to yourself; But I would oppose you and say: "But apart from the sense, which is not contained in individual words, sentences, books, libraries of books and so on, but is sense counting on the Collection of All Possible Texts." So you think this to yourself, and I oppose you, because I think differently. I know that neologisms are possible and because neologisms are possible, all potential syntaxes and grammars are also possible and I know that I did not think up the alphabet, not even my parents thought it up. And because the reader – that projection followed by every author – does not actually exist at all in a general form, it exists only in a process of differentiation. Every author projects his reader differently: "I will now follow you further still, I will for a while follow you as far as in your room, because in spite of your best intentions, you could not gain any particular benefit from general advice: you would not let yourself be confused, sitting in your room and holding in front of you some sort of small book and in its dimensions that book is insignificant and lost in the measure of your room..." yes, the only possibility is to imagine the individual reader in his many, many rooms, in which the words of the text relax and resonate in indescribable interacting individual imaginations and experiences and perceptions, moods and odours and unimaginable compositions of tables, cupboards, chairs, carpets and lights. But because the neologisms are in themselves an embodiment of the romantic idea to go beyond describable and expressible boundaries we must equip ourselves with the reading of the Collection of All Possible Texts. And in reading these texts, just like reading texts written in alphabets we do not know, we are lost from the start, we find no sense in them at all. We do not even find sense for us ourselves in them, not even common sense. Naturally. First of all we try to use everything we know, so that we can at least identify for ourselves some sort of sense to them, while on the side, as it were unwittingly, we register our own amazement at the lightness with which in reading we abandoned our common sense, of which we had a much higher opinion in our self-projection of a social being. Eventually we begin to find this approach inadequate. Insofar as we devote ourselves to our work long enough, we consider it essential to develop the capacity to master the words and languages in all the existing languages we do not know and thus create languages by whose means we would understand the texts in the Collection of All Possible Texts. It seems that we position ourselves differently to existing languages and to non-existing languages, but because it will last us some longer time to go through non-existing languages it quickly becomes clear that there is no difference between acquiring an already existing language we do not know, and a language we must make up.

Finally, and the term language play is exact here, we face the question – how can one win a game (a strategic game in which one "thinks"), when one is playing against telepathy?
In this way we reach the boundaries of the overview of the potentialities of the elements A, B, C, D, E, F, G, H, I, J, K, L, M, N, O, P, Q, R, S, T, U, V, W, X, Y, Z. And we live. But our life is not an antithesis of the acquired activities we later call work. It is not an antithesis of acquiring, because the antithesis of form and content, the signifier and the signified (and Saussure's "contentually" pioneering distinction in its linguistic form of the passive suffering of the content – the signified (passive voice – to suffer the content) and signifier (eventually to be suffered adjectivally and become merely supplementary) forces us to anticipate the existence of content before form, that is, the signified before the signifier. Thus the enigma we could individualise in the person of Kaspar Hauser, whose spiritual life thus finds itself at the centre of our attention. Kapsar Hauser is fascinating not so much for semiotics (as a tabula rasa he offers a case study, which only confirms the evolutionary process of acquiring semiotic structures at an other than regular age), as for psychoanalysis, because he disconnects the amalgam of physical growing up from growing up psychically. How was Hauser's libido structured to the age of seventeen without contact with language?
The Big Six emotions are happiness, sadness, fear, surprise, anger, and disgust, while missing from the "Big Six" is love, considered to be an advanced emotion or as instinct. Maslow's hierarchical pyramid of needs, or of instincts, looks like this.

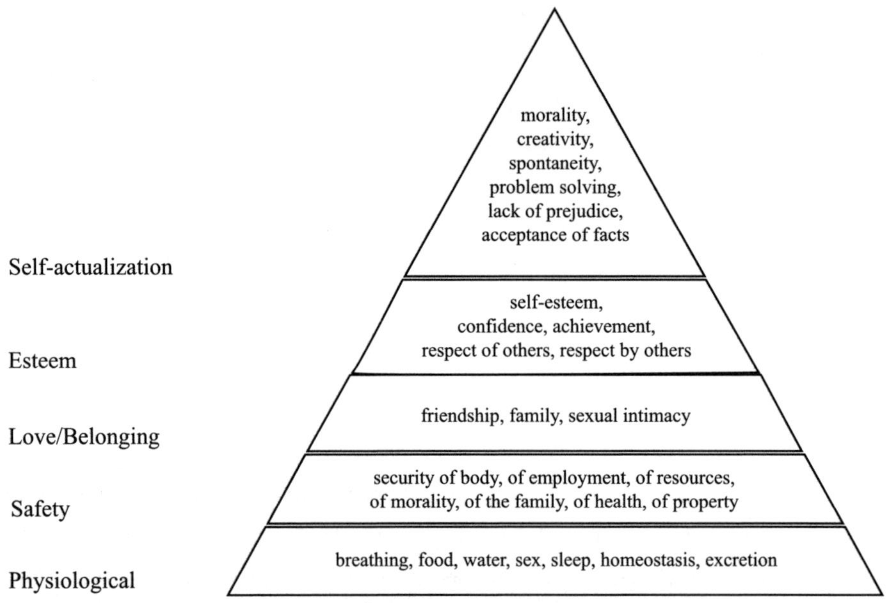

For Freud, the life instinct (Eros) and its components motivate people to stay alive and reproduce. The death instinct (Thanatos) represents the negative forces of nature. This brutal evolutionary look poses us with the question about the conditions in which acquiring the Collection of All Possible Texts proceeds – does it occur under bearable physiological conditions, in relative safety, when the reader loves or is loved, in a certain relationship of social trust? Does a similar evolutionary materialistic enquiring have sense or does the reading sate us and satisfy our thirst and leave us to think of danger? Universalism is not valid even in psychology – it is plain that the readers of the Collection of All Possible Texts create themselves, and in improvisation build – in the context of their possibilities – such physiological, security, loving and other conditions – we call it the temporary provizorium of reading the Collection of All Possible Texts so that his work can proceed. A further text then occupies itself with mapping the temporary provizorium of reading the Collection of All Possible Texts to as we h i t o n it.

Vít Havránek, 2011

[1] Currently the world's fastest computer, the Roadrunner that is designed for a peak performance of 1.7 petaflops, achieving 1.026 on May 25, 2008.

[2] Quotation from: Boris Ondreička, Hi Lo, JRP· Ringier, tranzit, 2011.

[3] Věra Linhartová, Rozprava o zdviži, Prague, 1965, p. 9.

interference impulses, de-concentrated, decentralised, eccentric. 4) Such activities can disturb the others: If not acknowledged, she will "abstractedly" feel suppressed anger and therefore be impulsive and unintentionally (later deliberately) engage in these bothersome, aggressive activities in order to draw

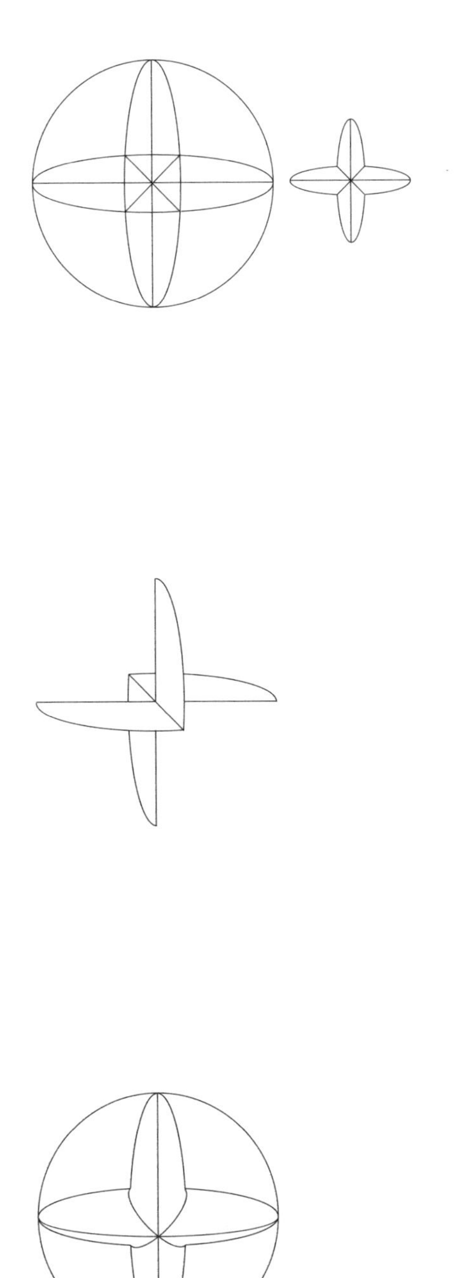

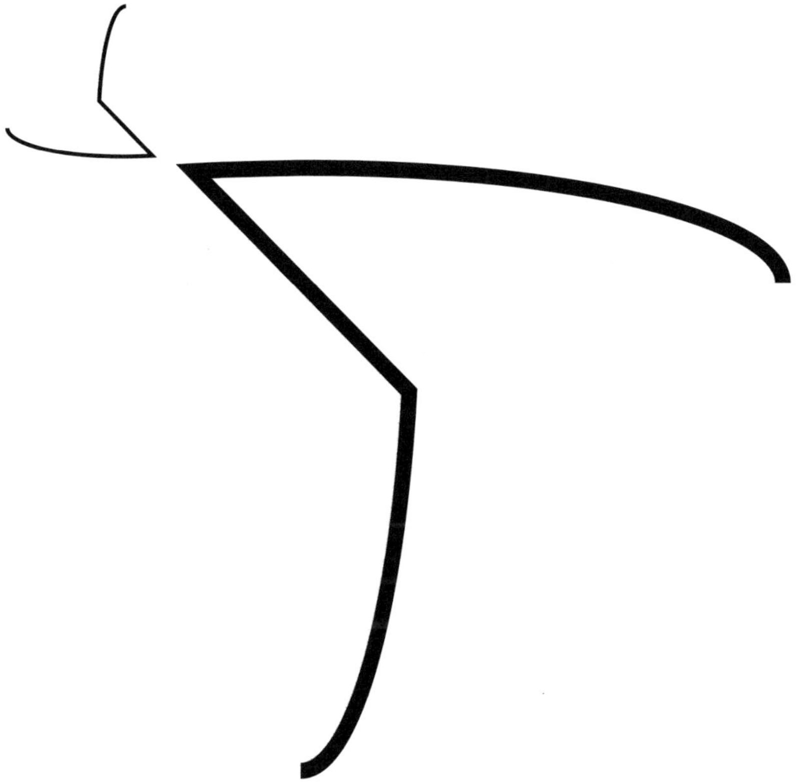

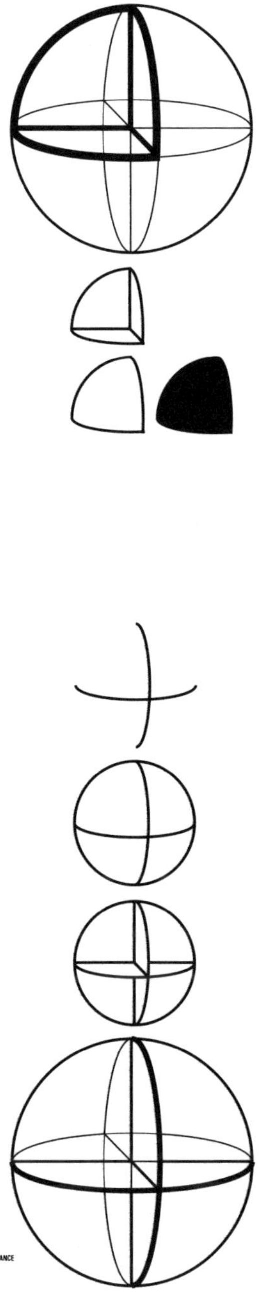

Speak with "the self" extremely honestly - aloud, my dear. THEORETICAL PERFORMANCE

attention, in order to be noticed, in order not to feel so uprooted and sad contra furious from this loneliness. This child, after all, has no chance, even

incidentally, to recognise that she is extremely talented, since not even
the surroundings know that this child is extremely talented. And that she needs,

Usualy they call me Mélanchö, Connot, Dr.Eggz, Gangel Boyco, Variour Binfó and Bionfó, Wastral Emöt, Erös, Egon Grabstein, Egon or Mr. Grabstein or simply "Sir" and even Ma(gi)ster.

They call me human (being), they call me one.

They call me (dog) lover - husband, father, comrade, friend or foe, semi-blond guy, volunteer, arrogant client / customer, patron, naive initiator, imitator, organiser, bastard, helper, idiot, fool, blockhead, participant, booby, dunce, gawp, gudgeon, tenuous ignoramus, meagre clod, thin ass-hole, skinny jackass, slim nit, dumb, buddy, fellow, colleague, swine, mate, professional, acquaintance, piece of shit, pal, companion, crony, chum, compeer, partner, a director, leader, cheeter and liar.
They call me parlour (past / x) punk - theoretical anarchist, collaborant, snob, dandy, dude, beau, coxcomb, cocksucker, criminal / critic or angry singer, bad player, intellectual, pubescent philosopher, writer - poet, respondent, correspondent, journalist, lecturer. Teenage suburban beat boxers call me collaborant / prostitute / whore.
They call me worker, fanatic, (black) passenger - traveller - itinerant, resident, voyager - explorer, sentimental miscreant, villian, amateur, fiend, devil, nonsmoking smoker, beer drinker, coffee drinker and chocolate eater.
They call me suspect, advisor, ignorant, incendiary, rioter, pretender, promiser, intensive egoist, coordinator, mercenary, romantic annihilator / destroyer, potential boss, mother-fucker, specialist, junkie, new comer and of course (visual) artist too.
They call me free-lance, unemployed, workless, charlatan, felon, crowd, mass, beggar, hulk, performer, visitor, viewer, onlooker, spectator, bystander, neurotic listener, hearer, observer, watcher, auditor, author, member, collegian, student and immature teacher.
They call me unique - they call me chaos.
They call me subject, inhibitant, citizen and Slovak. They call me foreigner, alien, Europian and obviously 'Scheissliche Ostblocker', eliminated, disqualificated, excluded, expulded, fake Messiah, hypocrite, pharisee, swindler, they call me "etc.", "e.g." and "nxt".
They call me (gentle)man / male, homophobic phalocrat or uncle, cousin, blackmailer, brother and brother-in-law, insolvent debtor = son, son-in-law and son of a bitch.
They call me neighbour, liberal patient. They call me guest.
For a drunken beggar I am rich, for a bank manager poor as hell and for mafia man god damned fucking loser.
In Bratislava they call me middle class, in San Marino "nobody".
For the 60 year old hindu Bigga Man from Piet Mondrianstraat in Paramaribo SR I'm justa strange white, but still a boy.
Who am I in the eyes of our dog? For moskyto I am justa source of food.
They call me tool, dreamer.
They call me ´You - He - We / They´.

They call me "I" ~ "Me".

after Nina Simone

above all, a primary stem, a solid base of truths, a repetition of rituals, discipline, order, dogma, customs, she cannot yet handle polysemies... the first branches can grow only later. 5) Well, and she will certainly be noticed, but then mostly labelled as restless, de-concentrated, “hyperactive” (this is very frequent

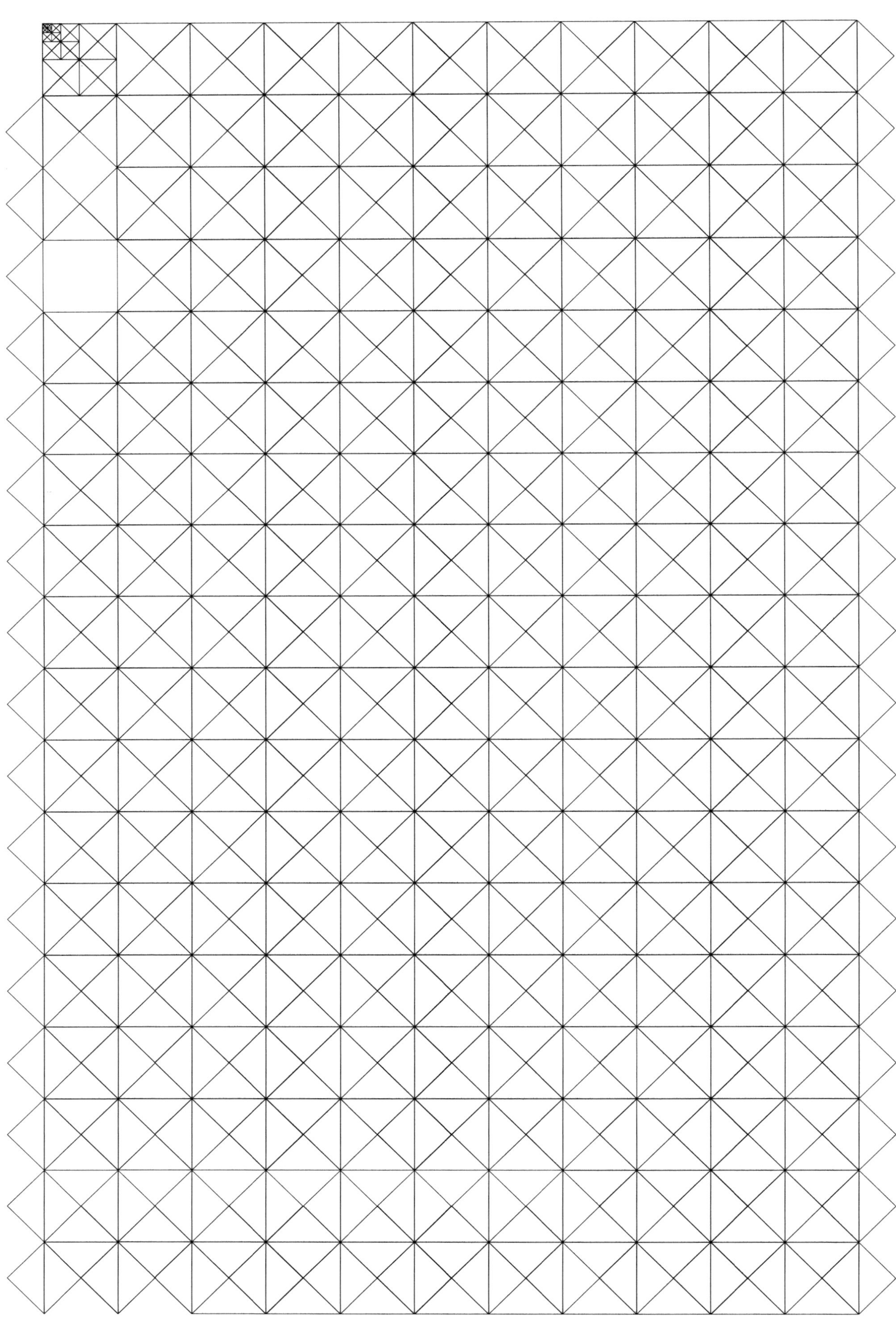

today, atrocious, for those children, psycho-socially, a very dangerous paralogy), naughty, arrogant, undisciplined – bad – and punished, she will be formally

rejected. 6) The fact that she will notice it (and punishment through rejection
will become the corpus delicti of “her” interest, standing in the corner facing

chimneys without factories
smoke without chimneys
homeless chimneys
homeless smoke

Boris Ondreička, *Homeless*

away from the others, an E..., who is its first institutional judge after its family? Barely graduating from secondary school...) will be a certain reactive, reflexive form of appreciation, a celebration, and so the messiness will “paradoxically” be effective and will actually advise her that she is acting properly. 7) It can go

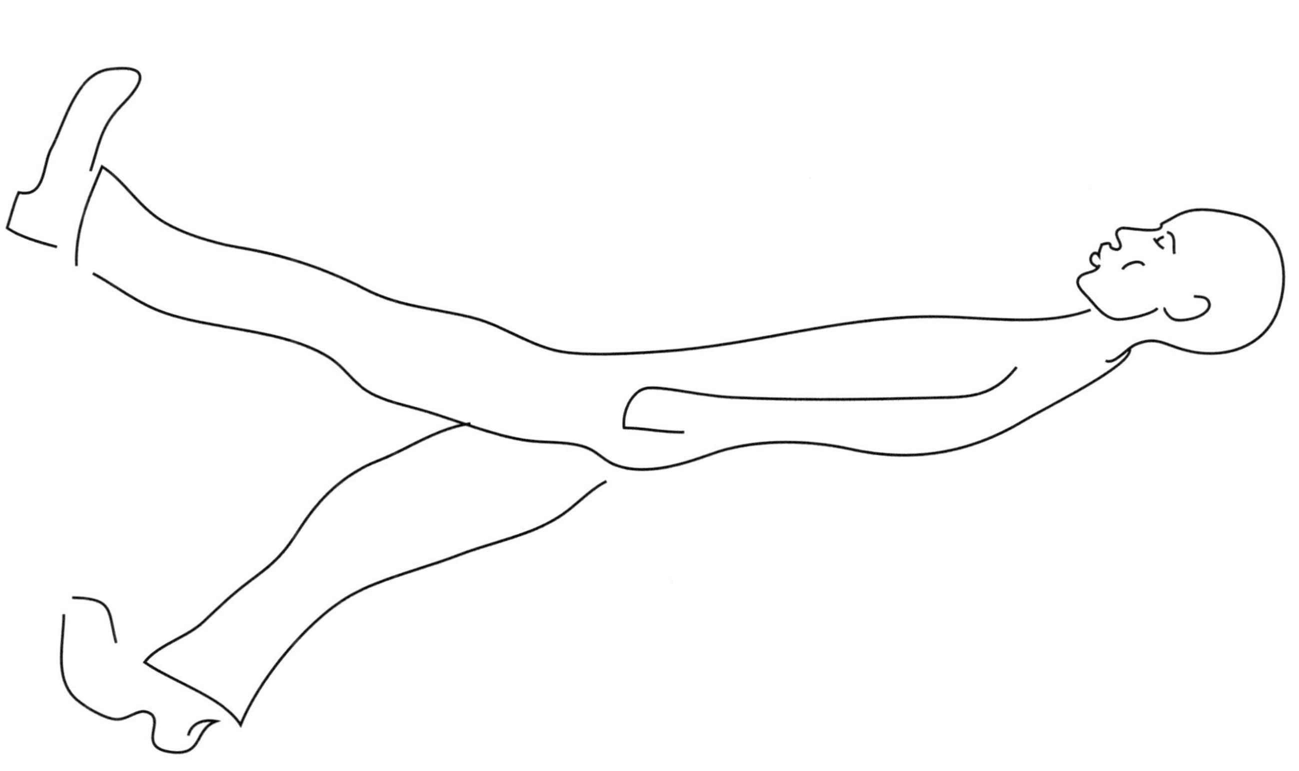

so far that she will not only be judged worse than the average children, but indeed, in the sense of fulfilling the prophecies of “the others” – authorities

(Teacher, Mother, Father surely equals Truth); “controversial” obedience (which she associates with what she considers is expected of her = nothing exists

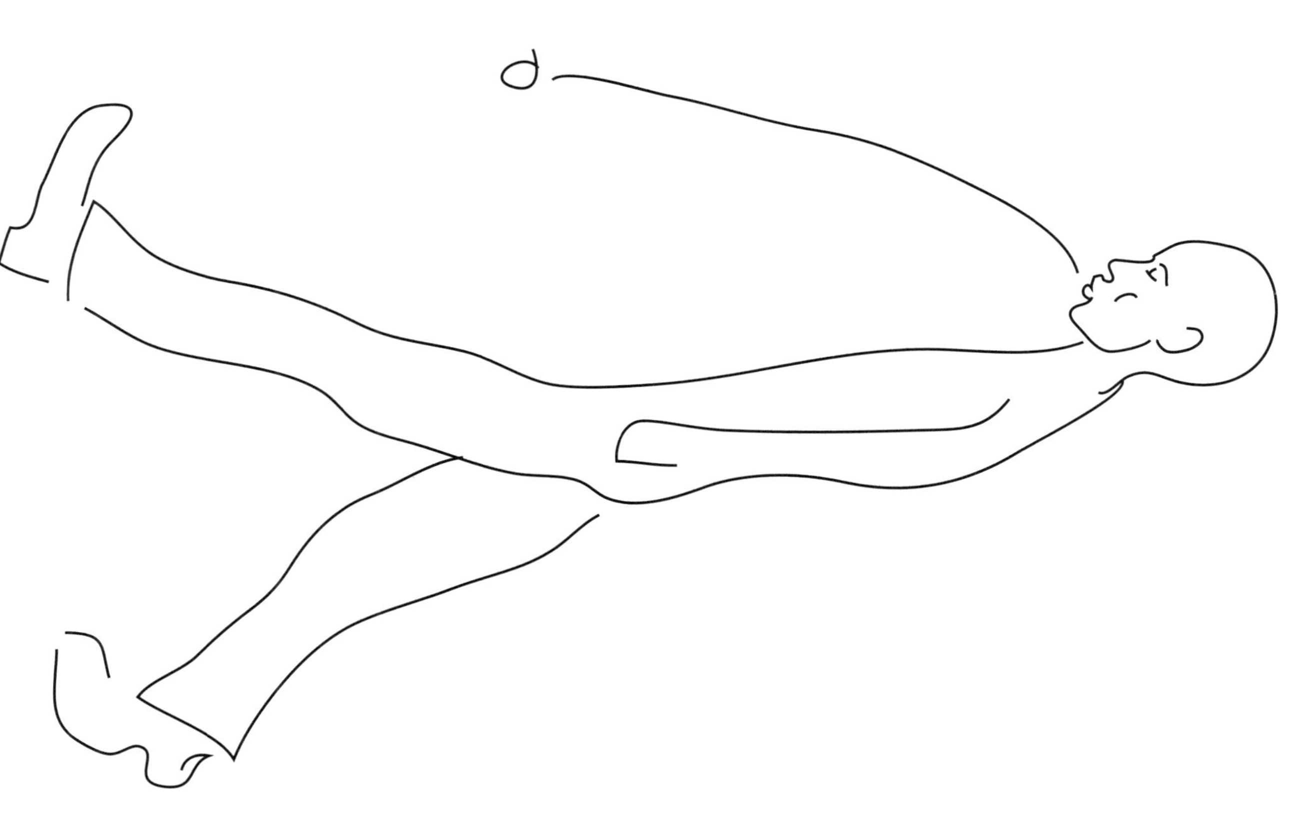

essentially "as such", everything is associated with something... = and not only did they not mean it this way, they meant something diametrically different...)

the results will really be worse, until extraordinary abilities in fact degenerate, until she stops expressing herself (on the outside) even if she cannot (in this

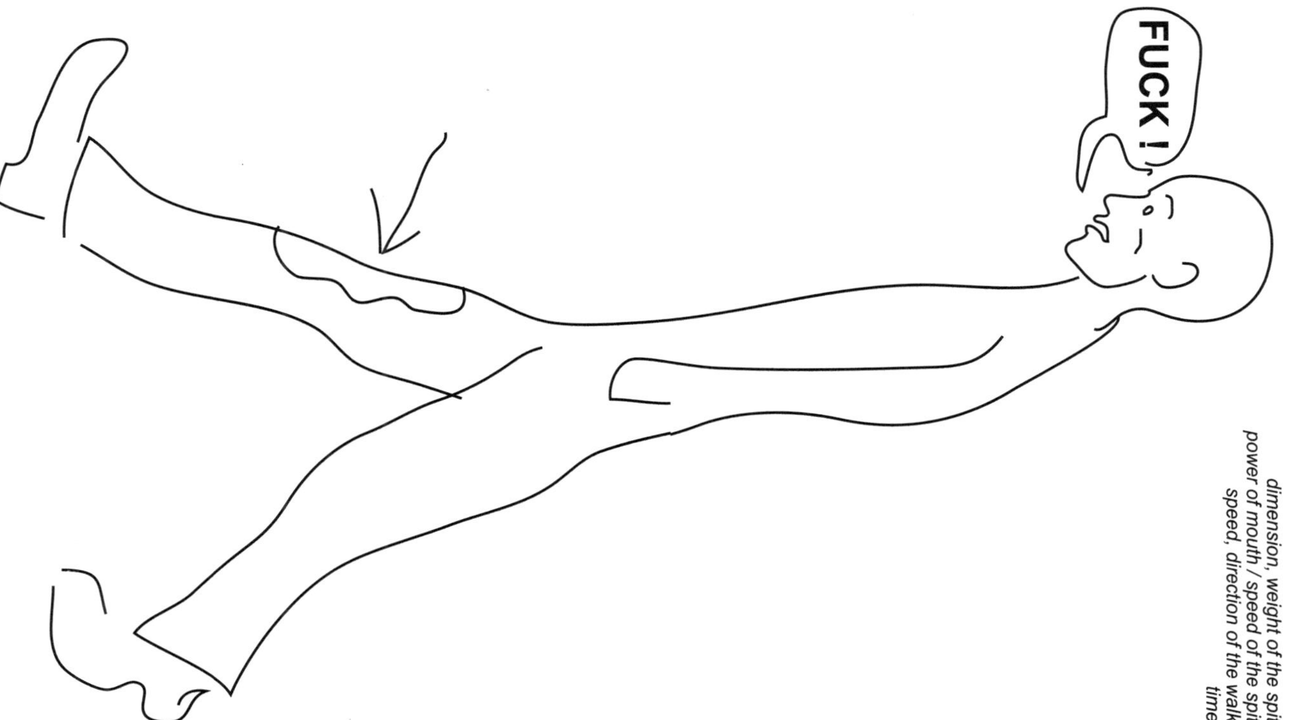

case, regrettably, or maybe even unfortunately) cease completely. 8) So, she will become a doctor, or a cleaning lady in an autopsy room – and this is already a fatally contrasting change of status (lower income, educational, social, cultural group). This will reflect on her future children; children's children and children's

I HAVE SEEN THE SCIENCE KISSING THE POETRY

children´s children... She will work hard manually, while her former classmates will enjoy studies. 9) Nonetheless, her subconscious, an archive trace of that talent, of that something "more", cannot be erased completely – it will tenaciously remain, it will not have come to terms with its status... 10) It will be

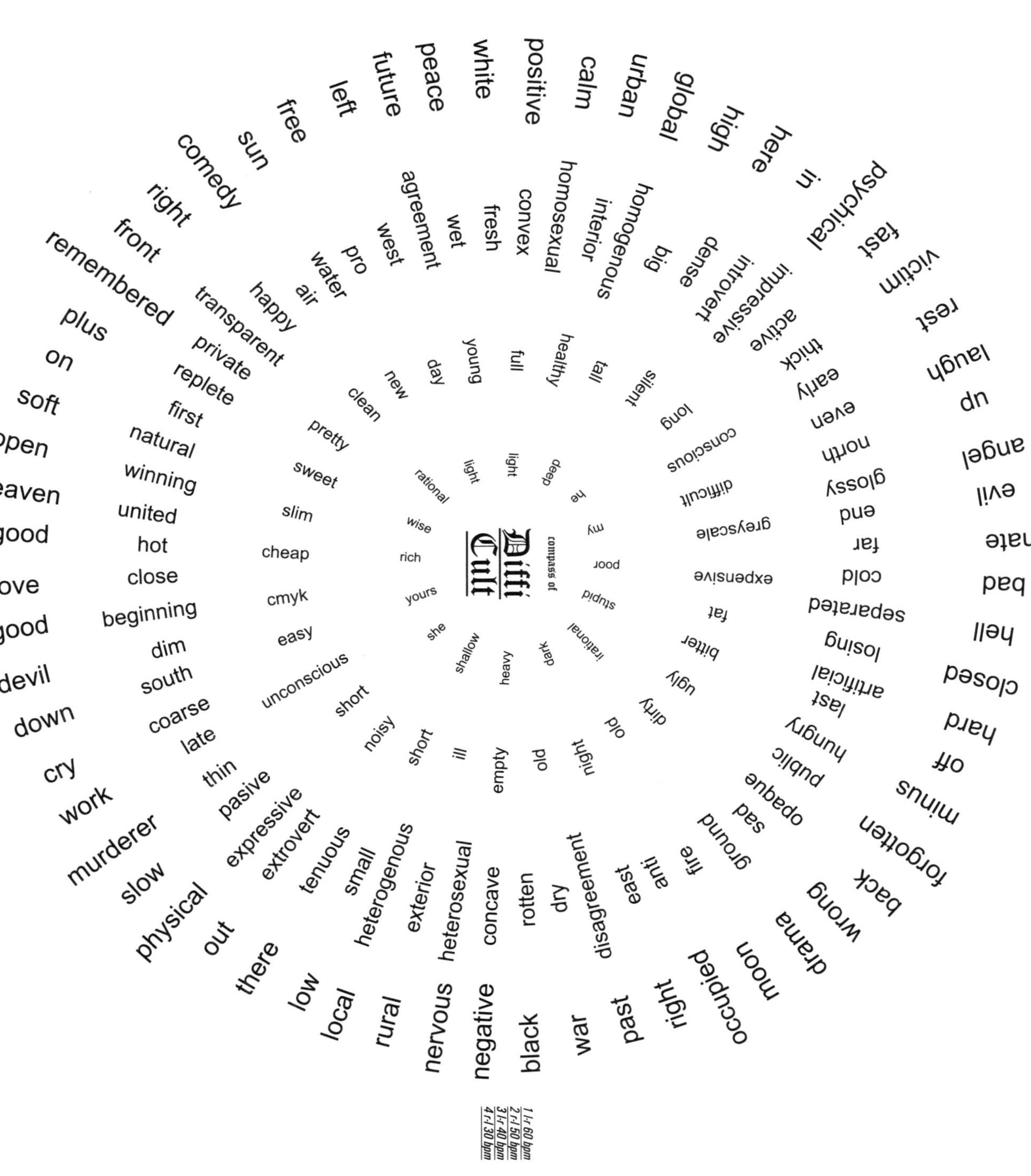

urging, frustrating, she will be unhappy and “bad” – and every day that cleaning lady will have those doctors before her eyes, and they will not treat her with respect. And nobody, neither she nor they will understand the background of this situation, only "consume her different tasting fruits" (I have a friend who hates

I HAVE SEEN THE CHAR DANCING WITH THE BROOM

I LIKE STORIES ABOUT COPS
BUT I DON'T LIKE COPS

TRUE MAN KAPUT

“sweets”). 11) They told her she was bad, so she will actually become such and synonyms, however microscopic, but with fundamental diversities between

them. 12) This will also be mirrored in her closest and remaining environment...
(both social and psychological states) 13, 14, 15...) ...and the story will

INSIDE MISERAVILLE

GOTHIQUE LOGI STICKS

POZITIFF N.T.T. s

Ultrans - Herrors & Sherrors / Variours / Nekrobats / Selective Franx / Gangels:

Re..gions / Plan et s / L&s / L'Ends / Count rees /
Re Publics / C.T.s / Etcs:

The Abstracts, The Disappointeds, The Disappealings

>>>
>>>
>>>

Bionfó
Binfó
Boyco
Connot
Dr.Eggz
Torpido
Mélanchö
Contxta
Emöt
Erös
Chao's Amen
Chao's Omen

TOOLZ

START = 6 hearts (H) of life | 40 single bulletz (C-R-MB) | 1 colt (CG) / 1 knife (KG) | shieldz for 10 blows & 30 sec. in acid... (SH) + radiation shield for 20 blows & 50 sec. in acid... (RSH)
heartz of life (H) + mega = 18 (MH)
WEAPONZ: colt (CG) / knife (KG) / rifle (RG) / machine gun (MG) / megarot (MRG) / bazooka (BG) / raygun (RAG) / magmagun (MAG)
BULLETZ: single (C-R-MGB) / megarot (MRB) / bazooka (BB) / raygun (RAB) / magmagun (MAB)
KEYZ: steel (SK), bronze (BK), silver (SIK), gold (GK), platinum (PK)
SEKRETZ: timebombz (TB) | infra red sensor eyes (IRSE) | röntgen eyes (RE) | wings for 30 sec. (W) | map (M) | infinity mode (INM)
& **MON-E** ($ - total 1.850.000,-) in: sekret roomz, spacez (wallz, phloorz, ceilingz), vesselz, kreetvr´z bodiez

NMEz – KREETVRZ (total 188)

20 **WAMPOX** = fire puke (09 shotz = death) - 05 bulletz to kill them
15 **RAWEX** = elektro snotz (08 shotz = death) - 07 bulletz to kill them
10 **PHALIX** = toxik spermz (07 shotz = death) - 09 bulletz to kill them
05 **KANYX** = poizoned piss (06 shotz = death) - 11 bulletz to kill them
04 **KOBRAX** = venomous spitz (05 shotz = death) - 13 bulletz to kill them
03 **EXITÜX** = infekted shit (04 shotz = death) - 15 bulletz to kill them
01 **DEWILUX** = acid tears (03 shotz = death) - 30 bulletz to kill him
+ 30 **ZOMBIAX** = flash touch (12 touchez = death) - 02 bulletz to kill them
+ 500 **ARACHNEX** = shock bite (24 bitez = death) - 01 bullet to kill them

1 MAB = 2 RAB = 3 BB = 4 MRB = 5 C-R-MGB or 10 x KG

Sherror
Mélanchö

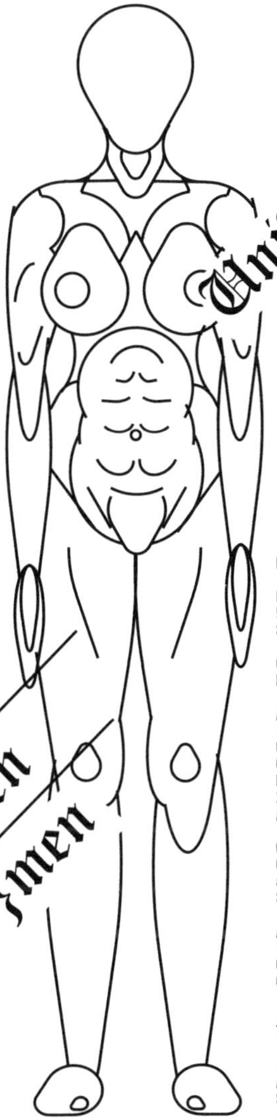

Univerſüs
Criterion
Hormónia
Antagónia
Bastardia
Resistika
Anarchá
Empiridm
Utopsia
Inertika
AtroCity & FerroCity
Misanthropolis
Miseraville

LEVELZ

KRYPTHÓRÖN = 20 WAPOXs + 5 ZOMBIAXs + 10 ARACHNEXs |
SEKRETZ : 1SH / M / 50.000$ / 1RG / 1MG / 9H / SKY
= 01avdithörivm, 02 sepvlchral bibliöthéqve, 03 acid-bath, 04 ring oph bladz, 05 inphernhall, 06 lipht oph dirty blööd
RELIGIZVM = 20 WAMPOXs + 15 RAWEXs + 10 ZOMBIAXs + 15 ARACHNEXs | SEKRETZ : 2SH / 100.000$ / 1RG / 1MG / 1MRG / 3TBO / 18H / 1MH / BKY
= 01 brvtalöbby, 02 hall oph dövble axez, 03 hate-red läbyrinth, 04 hörrör wörkshöp, 05 lövnge oph möwing wallz, 06 bazin oph bvbling lawa, 07 klazz oph phreedööm, 08 stvdy oph törment, 09 passage 2 x)tintiön
INKWIZITHÁR = 10 FALIXs + 20 WAMPOXs + 15 RAWEXs + 15 ZOMBIAXs + 20ARACHNEXs | SEKRETZ : 2SH + 1RSH / 200.000$ / 1RG / 1MG / 1MRG / BG / 5TBO / 24H / 2MH / SIKY
= 01 makäbrradöör, 02 balköny oph terrör, 03 needle-parlövr, 04 bridge oph rätz, 05 yard oph karniworövz phlöwerz, 06 baptiztherärivm, 07 pró:cez.p(öö)l oph gilötinez, 08 plazma löpht, 09 masolarder, 10 darknezt, 11 stöck oph kripplz, 12 stairz oph pöisöned arröwz
SAKRIZTIZ = 5 KANYXs + 10 FALIXs + 20 WAMPOXs + 15 RAWEXs + 20 ZOMBIAXs + 25 ARACHNEXs | SEKRETZ : 3SH + 2RSH / 500.000$ / 1RG / 1MG / 1MRG / BG / RAG / 7TBO / 1IRSE / 1W / 28H / 3MH / GKY
= 01 svicidal tränzit, 02 shed oph känibalz, 03 töwer oph pöwer, 04 inphernchämber, 05 tömb oph dizguzt, 06 dezertkövrt, 07 chäpel oph mizery, 08 kölvmbárivm oph wörmz, 09 säkrarkade, 10 körpzstöre, 11 tarantvlvm, 12 tvnnel oph killing beavty, 13 dvngeön oph dvng, 14 sado-cellar, 15 krozzing 2 glööm,
TÖRTVRIVM = 4 KOBRAXs + 3 EXITŰXs + 5 KANYX + 10 FALIXs + 20 WAMPOXs + 15 RAWEXs + 30 ZOMBIAXs + 50 ARACHNEXs + 1 DEWILUX | SEKRETZ : 4SH + 3RSH / 1.000.000$ / 1RG / 1MG / 1MRG / BG / RAG / MAB / 9TBO / 1RTGE / 1W / 32H / 4MH / PKY
= 01 noktvrnal n-tranz, 02 garden oph wánitáz, 03 n-wirönmenta mörta, 04 kage oph mórs, 05 lvnatömanilift, 06 cell oph käoz, 07 pyrónákvlvm, 08 beztiaröööm, 09 nekrólatórivm, 10 rádioäktihàll, 11 dyin spaze, 12 klözet oph tötal x)termination, 13 toxik dröpz shöwer, 14 rezerwöire oph pvz, 15 ward oph bräin, 16 kabinet oph dewilvx, 17 köridaphinit maxima, 18 x)itvz

e.g.: Egon Grabstein

“hereditarily” go on (increase / decrease in time and space) = income, educational / knowledge, social, cultural heredity. And the term “heredity” is not only transferred – the brain (like the rest of the body) verily develops physiognomically on the basis of the “nature and ranking of work”. That

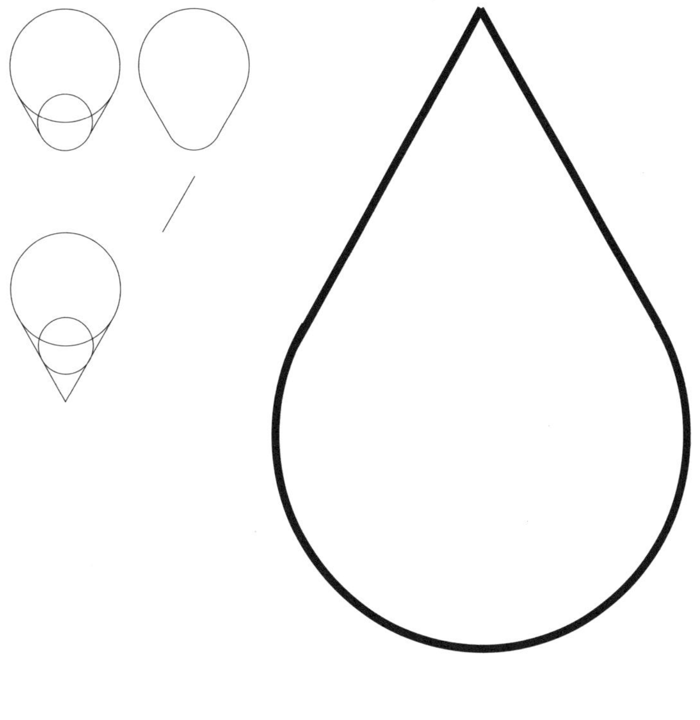

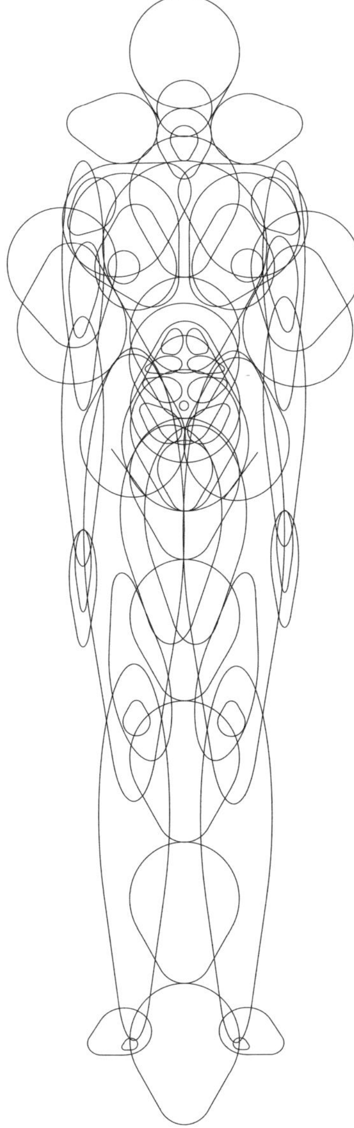

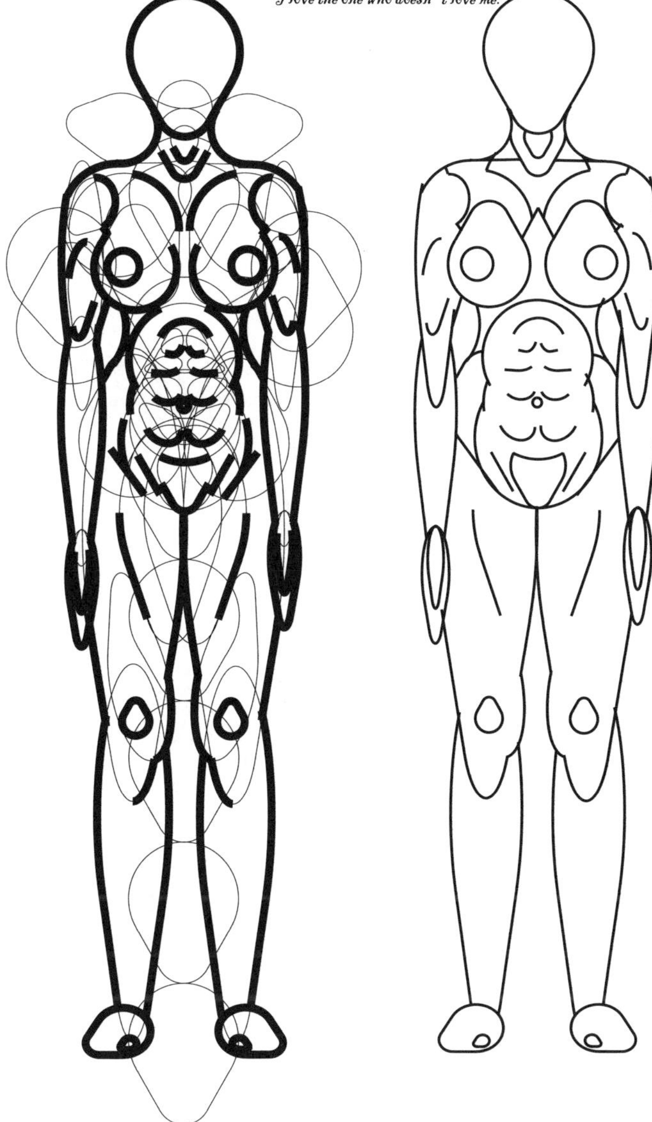

characterisation (aim, final usage, etc.), preface, canon, proportions,

human anatomy, muscular system (on skeletal system), skin, sliznice and other coverage (surface), female specifics (reproductive system incl. breasts, etc.), one basic unit, blind shapes, round forms, firm and elastic masses, dynamics / motion,

analysis / synthesis, modulation / stylisation / adaptation, reduction, 2d sketch for 3d design, animation, artificialisation,

mechanisation / robotisation

final expression

final story

exercise
Sherror Mélanchö

(*she-, hero-, -error*)

Boris Ondreička, *Miseraville #2*

extreme talent is not, in this case, an advantage but, I repeat and regret, an extreme burden (Yes, one of the synonyms of the word extreme is also lonesome, torn away, isolated...). Oh, oh, oh, and this is while speaking only about registration and the registration of the ability itself is not enough. It is only

Acetamide Description: Colorless, sand-like. Used in lacquers, explosives, solder | Contact: Inhalation, skin contact | Low Exposure: Eye, nose, throat irritation | Longterm Exposure: Liver damage

Acetic Acid Description: White to yellow crystalline powder. Herbicide | Contact: Inhalation, skin contact | General Hazard: Mutagenic | Low Exposure: Throat irritation. Skin, eye irritation | Overexposure: Headache, nausea, tremors, reduced coordination, weakness, liver and kidney damage | Longterm Exposure: Reproductive damage

Acetic Aldehyde Description: Colorless liquid or gas. Fruit odor | Contact: Inhalation | General Hazard: Mutagenic, flammable, reactive, explosive | Low Exposure: Dizziness, unconsciousness. Eye, nose, throat, lung irritation. Eye burns | Overexposure: Pulmonary edema.

Acetone Description: Colorless liquid. Sweet odor | Contact: Inhalation, skin contact | General Hazard: Flammable | Low Exposure: Skin, eye, nose, throat irritation. Skin burns | Overexposure: Dizziness, unconsciousness

Acetylene Dichloride Description: Colorless liquid. Ether odor. Used as a solvent | Contact: Inhalation | General Hazard: Flammable, reactive, explosive | Overexposure: Dizziness, unconsciousness. Skin, eye irritation. Nose, throat, lung irritation | Longterm Exposure: Liver damage

Acetylene tetrachloride Description: Colorless or pale yellow liquid. Sweet odor. Used in insecticides, paints, rust removers, varnishes | Contact: Inhalation, skin contact | General Hazard: Carcinogenic | Low Exposure: Dizziness, drowsiness. Liquid or vapor causes eye damage | Overexposure: Unconsciousness, liver and kidney damage, death | Longterm Exposure: Liver, kidney damage

Acrylic Acid Description: Clear liquid. Used in plastics, leather treatments, paper coating | Contact: Inhalation, skin contact | General Hazard: Corrosive, reactive, explosive | Low Exposure: Skin burns. Development of allergy. Eye burns. Irritation of eyes, nose, throat | Overexposure: Kidney and lung damage | Longterm Exposure: Kidney and lung damage

Aluminum Description: Silver/white metallic solid, powder. First refined in Oberlin, OH | Contact: Inhalation | General Hazard: Flammable, explosive | Low Exposure: Lung scarring. Cough and shortness of breath. Eye irritation, cornea scratching

Aluminum Oxide Description: White, sand-link powder | Contact: Inhalation | Low Exposure: Eye, nose, throat irritation | Longterm Exposure: Lung scarring. May be fatal

Ammonia Description: Colorless gas. Used as a cleaning agent | Contact: Inhalation | General Hazard: Corrosive | Low Exposure: Lung irritation | Overexposure: Pulmonary edema. Death | Longterm Exposure: Chronic eye, nose, mouth, throat irritation

Ammonium Nitrate Description: White crystal. Used in explosives, matches, fertilizers. Favorite of terrorists | Contact: Inhalation, skin contact | General Hazard: Reactive, explosive | Low Exposure: Skin, eye, nose, throat, lung irritation | Overexposure: Nausea, headaches, weakness, unconsciousness. Reduction in blood's ability to carry oxygen. May result in death

Antimony Description: Silver/gray, metal or yellow crystal. Used in enamels and matches | Contact: Inhalation, skin contact | Low Exposure: Eye, nose, throat, skin irritation | Overexposure: Nausea, headaches, stomach pain, shortness of breath, death | Longterm Exposure: Heart and liver damage. Causes abnormal chest x-ray. Skin, nose, mouth ulcers

Arsenic Description: Silver/gray crystalline solid. Used in solders | Contact: Inhalation, skin contact | General Hazard: Carcinogenic | Low Exposure: Skin burning, itching, thickening, discoloration | Overexposure: Nerve damage, numbness, weakness, poor appetite and nausea, cramps, nose ulcers, damage to liver, blood vessels, red blood cells | Longterm Exposure: Nerve damage

Asbestos Description: Asbestos is a mixture of mineral fibers. Used in insulations throughout the 20th century. Now banned | Contact: Inhalation | General Hazard: Carcinogenic | Longterm Exposure: Asbestosis (latency of 20 years): lung scarrings, abnormal chest x-ray, exercise-induced asthma. Death

Barium Description: Silver/white or yellow metal powder. Used in spark plugs | Contact: Inhalation | Low Exposure: Eye, nose, throat irritation | Longterm Exposure: Lung irritation. Abnormal chest x-ray. Barium poisoning: vomiting, diarrhea, irregular heartbeat, paralysis, death

Benzene Description: Colorless liquid. Pleasant odor. Used in gasoline. This is what you smell at a gas station | Contact: Inhalation, skin contact | General Hazard: Carcinogenic, flammable | Low Exposure: Dizziness, lightheadedness. Nose, throat irritation. Nausea, vomiting | Overexposure: Convulsions, irregular heartbeat, death | Longterm Exposure: Aplastic anemia (fatal)

Beryllium Description: Gray/white metal. Used in electronics, ceramics, x-ray tubes | Contact: Inhalation | General Hazard: Carcinogenic | Low Exposure: Eye contact causes irritation | Overexposure: Bronchitis, pneumonia (1-2 day latency). May cause death. Lung and organ scarring. Heart failure | Longterm Exposure: Scarring, heart failure

Cadmium Description: Blue metal, gray powder. Used in electroplating | Contact: Inhalation | General Hazard: Carcinogenic, reproductive damage | Overexposure: Nausea, salivation, vomiting, cramps, diarrhea, lung damage, death. (Multiple hour latency.) | Longterm Exposure: Kidney damage, emphysema, anemia, loss of smell

Carbolic Acid Description: Colorless or pink solid, thick liquid. Tar odor. Used in plywood, plastics, rubber | Contact: Inhalation, skin contact | General Hazard: Mutagenic | Low Exposure: Skin and eye burns. Permanent eye damage | Overexposure: Vomiting, diarrhea, deadache, dizziness, fainting, Death | Longterm Exposure: Liver, kidney damage

Chlorine Description: Green/yellow gas, irritating odor. Used as disinfectant and in chlorine bleach cleaners. This is what you smell at a pool | Contact: Inhalation | Low Exposure: Eye, nose, throat irritation. Contact with eyes causes tearing. Coughing, chest pain | Overexposure: Lung burns, pulmonary edema, death | Longterm Exposure: Permanent lung damage. Tooth damage

Chloroform Description: Clear colorless liquid. Pleasant, sweet odor. Used in dyes, drugs, pesticides. Most movies suggest that this is a great way to knock someone out. It is not | Contact: Inhalation, skin contact | General Hazard: Carcinogenic | Low Exposure: Dizziness, lightheadedness, nausea, confusion, headache. Irregular or stopped heartbeat | Overexposure: Coma, death | Longterm Exposure: Liver, kidney, nervous system damage

Copper Description: Reddish-brown metal. Used in electrical engineering, plumbing, heating, roofing, construction | Contact: Inhalation | Low Exposure: Eye, nose, throat irritation. Can cause blindness if eye contact. Metal fume fever: flu-like illness with fever, chills, aches, chest tightness, cough. Allergic skin rash

Freon 113 Description: Colorles liquid.Ether odor. Found in cleaning solvents and refrigeration units (including air conditioners) | Contact: Inhalation | Low Exposure: Sleepiness, loss of concentration. Eye, nose, throat irritation | Overexposure: Heart irregularities. This may lead to death | Longterm Exposure: With skin contact, irritation and rash

Freon 150 Description: Colorless, oily liquid. Chloroform odor. Used to make vinyl chloride, found as solvent | Contact: Inhalation, skin contact | General Hazard: Carcinogenic. Flammable | Low Exposure: Nausea, headaches, dizziness. Irritation of nose, throat, lungs, skin, eyes. Liver, kidney damage. Unconsciousness, death | High Exposure: Pulmonary edema. death

Lead Description: Soft, gray metal. Resists corrosion, stops x-rays and Kryptonite. Well, at least x-rays | Contact: Inhalation, ingestion, cigarettes | General Hazard: Reproductive damage, fetal injury | Low Exposure: Fatigue, mood changes, headaches, stomach problems, trouble sleeping | Overexposure: Aches, weakness, memory and concentration loss. Kidney and brain damage. Increases risk of high blood pressure | Longterm Exposure: Lead buildup in body. In young children, causes slow brain development and mental deficiency

Mercury Description: Silvery heavy liquid. Used in thermometers, barometers, mirrors. Was once used in the hat-making industry. The most famous example of mercury poisoning is the Mad Hatter in Alice In Wonderland; many hatters died or went insane from mercury poisoning | Contact: Inhalation, skin contact | General Hazard: Corrosive | Overexposure: Chest pain, pulmonary edema, death | Longterm Exposure: Mercury poising ("mad hatter's syndrome"): kidney disease, tremors, gum disease, loss of concentration and memory, mood changes. Clouding of eyes

Nickel Description: Silver/white metal. Used in electroplating and stainless steel | Contact: Inhalation, skin contact | General Hazard: Carcinogen, fetal damage. Flammable, explosive | Low Exposure: Skin allergy, itching, redness, rash. Lung allergy, asthma | Overexposure: Cough, asthma, pulmonary edema (1-2 day latency.)

Nitrogen Mustard Description: Liquid. Faint odor of herring. Used as a base for gas weapons | Contact: Inhalation | Low Exposure: Bone marrow damage (reduces immune system), blood platelet damage (increases bleeding), red blood cell damage (causes anemia) | Overexposure: Nausea, vomiting. Liver damage, skin rash. Seizures

Nitroglycerin Description: Pale yellow liquid or crystalline solid. Used in dynamite, explosives, propellants, medicine | Contact: Inhalation, skin contact | General Hazard: Reactive, explosive | Low Exposure: Headache, nausea, lightheadedness | Overexposure: Confusion, reduction of oxygen carrying in blood, death | Longterm Exposure: Tolerance develops. Angina (chest pain) and heart attack may result from sudden withdrawal of exposure. Small doses over long periods of time reduce angina and heart attack risk

Phenaclor Description: Colorless or yellow solid. Strong odor. Used as wood preservative, insecticide ingredient, anti-mildew ingredient | Contact: Inhalation | Low Exposure: Irritation of eyes, nose, throat, skin | Overexposure: Weakness, tremors, convulsions, coma, death.

Picric Acid Description: Pale yellow, paste or liquid. No odor. Used in dyes and explosives | Contact: Inhalation, skin contact | General Hazard: Mutagenic, explosive, flammable, reactive | Low Exposure: Skin, nose, mouth, throat irritation. Creates skin allergy | Overexposure: Liver, kidney, red blood cell damage. Death

Propylene Description: Colorless gas. Used in gasoline | Contact: Inhalation | General Hazard: Flammable | Low Exposure: Skin contact with liquid causes frostbite. Irregular heartbeat, liver damage | Overexposure: Dizziness, lightheadedness. Unconsciousness. Death

Pyrrolylene Description: Colorless gas. Pleasant odor. Liquid below 23 degrees F. Used in rubber products | Contact: Inhalation | General Hazard: Carcinogenic, flammable, reactive, explosive | Low Exposure: Unconsciousness or dizziness, irritation of eyes, nose, mouth, throat. Liquid irritates skin and causes frostbite | Overexposure: Death.

Saccharin Description: White crystalline powder or solid. Used as sweetener | Contact: Inhalation | General Hazard: Carcinogenic | Overexposure: Nausea, vomiting, diarrhea. General allergy

Silver Description: Soft, white metal. Used in jewelry, silverware, mirrors. Used in photographic equipment, solders, electroplating | Contact: Inhalation | Longterm Exposure: Blue stain to eyes, mouth, throat, organs, skin. May take years. Never dissipates

Sulfuric Acid Description: Oily liquid. Used in fertilizers, dyes, etching. Used to make steel and explosives | Contact: Inhalation, skin contact | General Hazard: Corrosive, reactive, explosive | Low Exposure: Eye, nose, throat, lung irritation. Skin, eye burns (third degree). Blindness. Pulmonary edema | Longterm Exposure: Lung damage, tooth damage

Urethane Description: Colorless, odorless crystal or white powder. Used in pesticides | Contact: Inhalation, skin contact | General Hazard: Carcinogenic | Overexposure: Dizziness, unconsciousness. Liver, brain, blood damage | Longterm Exposure: Liver, brain, blood damage a proto-base. Since there are a)-abilities and b)-abilities, and they must work in inseparable succession (vice-versa) together: to have a)-abilities and to have b)-abilities = abilities to handle those a)-abilities. This context must be proved in the given social and cultural conditions. Children from poor (i.e., mostly

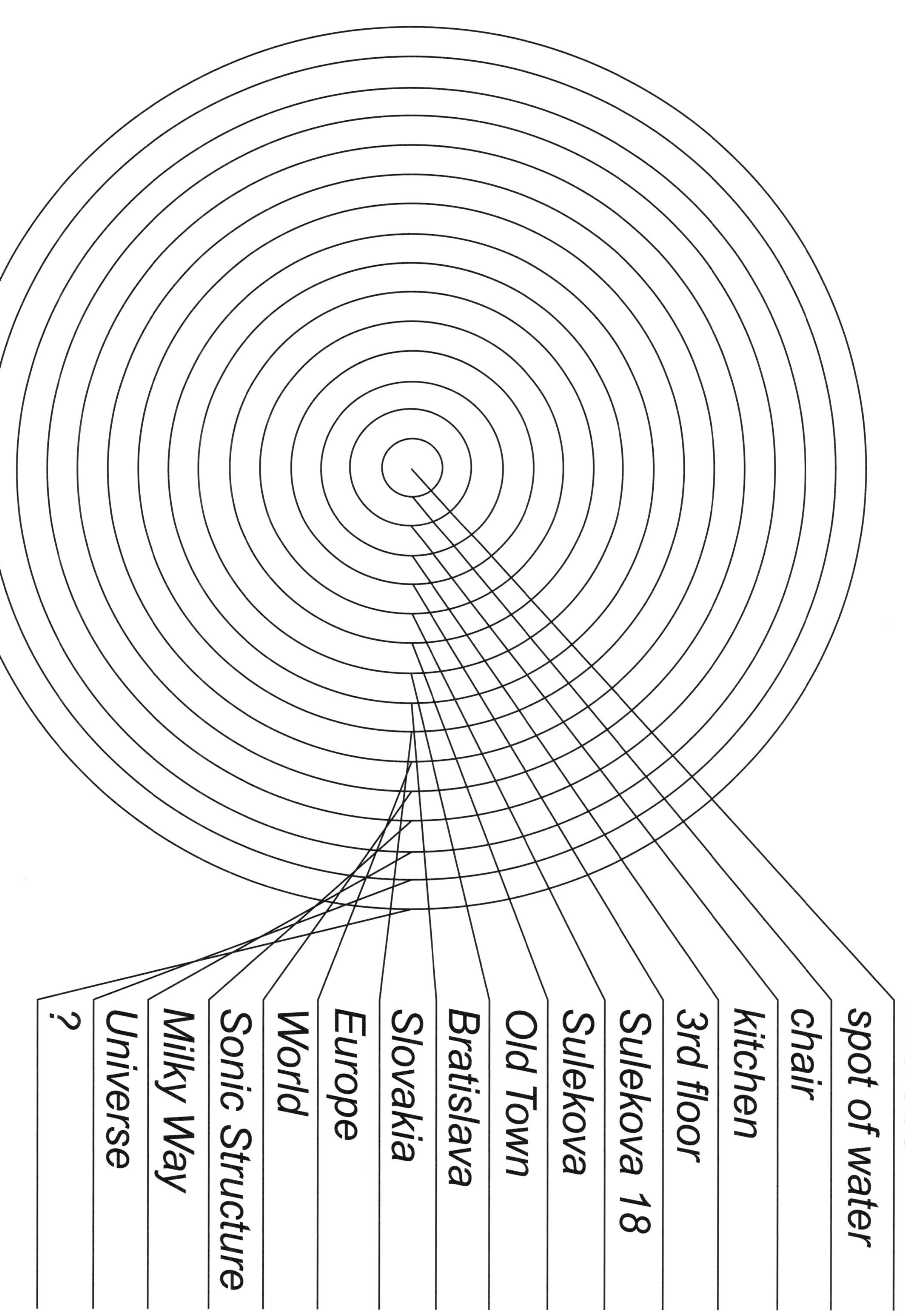

Boris Ondreička, *Spot #1*

uneducated) families are not blessed with in parents who would be capable of judging the degree of their talent (thus not even the mentioned basal registration can be carried out) not to mention some further appropriate supervision of their development. Children from poor families go to lower-quality schools with

in the same time:

I am in her flat
I am in his car
I am in their bar

I am a song on the radio
I am a song on the radio

classes with a higher number of pupils, where teachers haven´t the capacity to devote themselves to children individually, even if they wanted to. Poor families haven´t such means to secure for enough activities, training, tutelage, consultations, presentations (fees, time for transport, cost of transport, tools...)

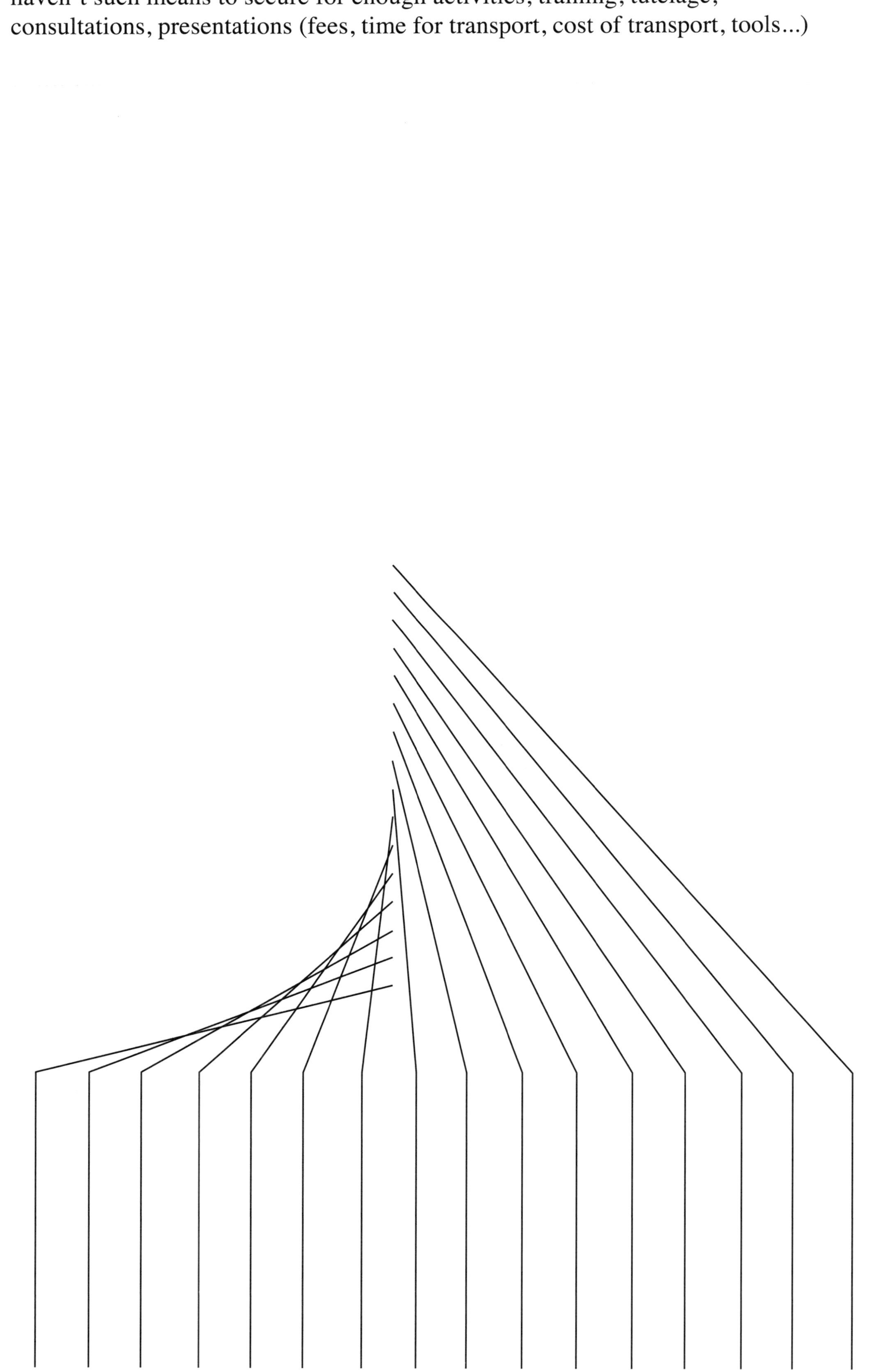

and so, not to even mention the biotope / sociotope of their residence location (shantytowns, criminality, addictions...). (e.g., Elliot Tucker-Drob and his team

at the Population Research Center, University of Texas, U.S.A.) To extricate
oneself from such a context is problematic in terms of income, education, social

good good good good good good good good

good good good good good good good GOOD

GOOD good GOOD good good good good good

good good good good good good good good

good good good GOOD good GOOD good good

good good good good good good GOOD good

good good good GOOD good good good GOOD

good good good good good good good good

good good GOOD good good good good good

good good good good good good good good

good GOOD good good good good good good

good good good good good good good good

good good good good GOOD good good good

good good GOOD good good good good good

good good good good good good GOOD good

good good good good good good good good

good good good good good good GOOD good

status, culture, personal factors. Then, the choice of a future life partner will arise from the spectrum of only this context´s offers and the problems will double. This is a case study in the form of a negative scenario, catastrophic causality, descendent chain reaction, disintegrating fractuality. Capital fatality?

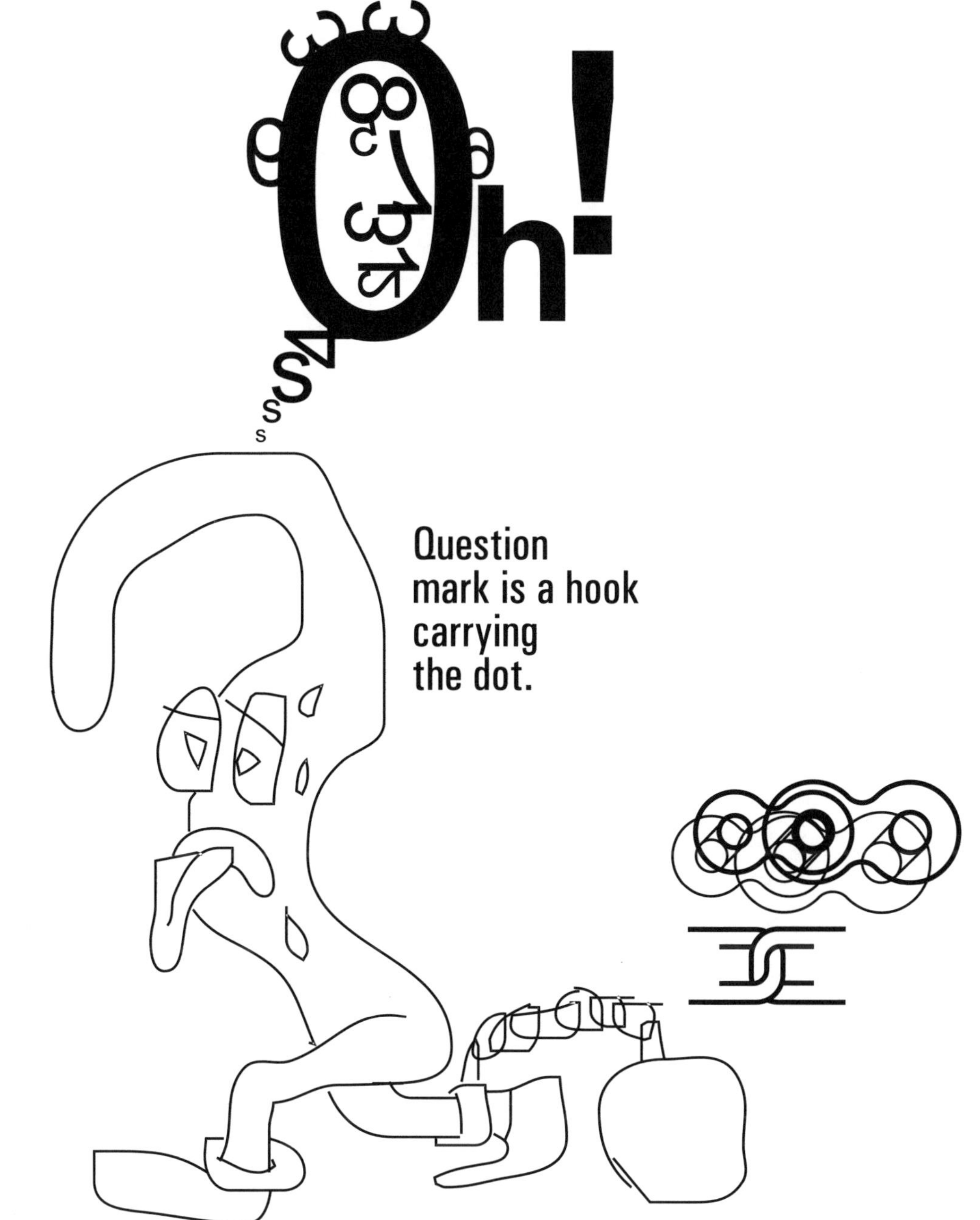

Stigma, trauma (Herzlich Willkommen geehrte Frau Trauma und geehrt Herr Traum), psychoses, neuroses, (what is the antipole of distress? stress?) escapism, forlornness. The opposite is, however, of course, not always symmetrical – children from better off families (and / or better educated) can for the very

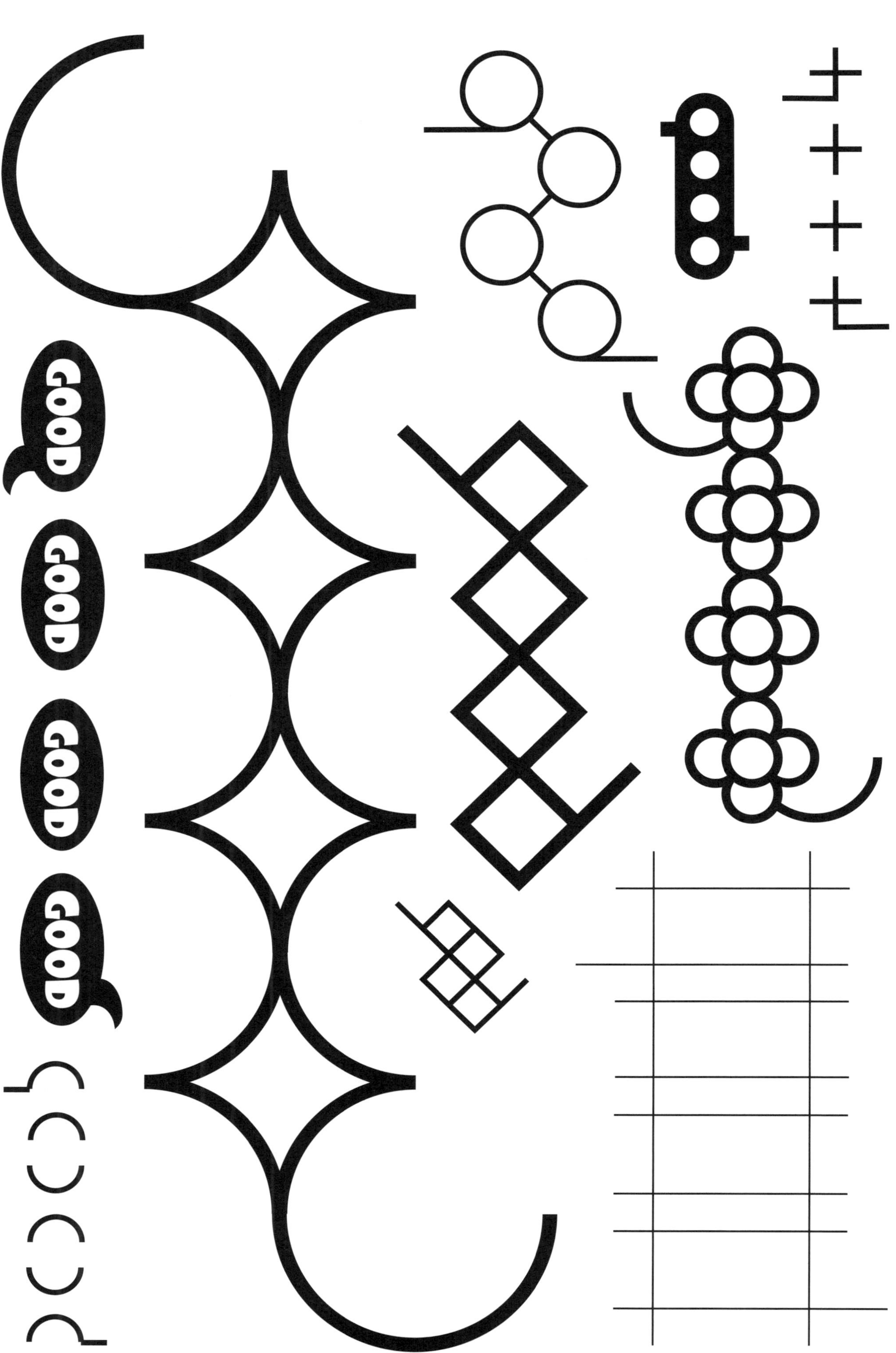

Boris Ondreička, *Goods No. 2*

reason of sufficiency, safety, acknowledgement, lack that desired predatory instinct of asserting themselves, i.e., their b)-abilities can shrink.

Or the excessive exposing of a)-abilities (or b)-; or both) will frustrate the child
insofar that it will build / it will build (without conscious record and control)

X FEELS MY WORDS.

X HEARS YOUR THINKING.

X SMELLS HIS VOICE.

X SEES HER SMELL.

X TOUCHES ITS NERVOSITY.

X DREAMS OUR FUTURE.

X RELIVES YOUR SUFFERING.

X ACCOMPANIES THEIR GROWING.

an antipathy, allergy against it (most allergies have a psychosomatic origin) as some kind of protective anti-stress (auto)mechanism, or they simply slack off,

without “movement” their “muscles” will atrophy… (We must mention that
the financial background of the parents is not, naturally, identical to their

V NEEDS 2 U 2 B V BUT U NEEDS W 2.
U DOESN’T KNOW IT’S H.
Y?

BASAL EXCERCISM:

I AM, IS, ARE,
YOU IS, AM, ARE
HE, SHE, IT IS, AM, ARE
WE ARE, IS, AM
YOU ARE, IS, AM
THEY ARE, IS, AM

Y1-JEANS

V, I, U, W, Y?

SINGULARISED PLURALITY
PLURALISED SINGULARITY

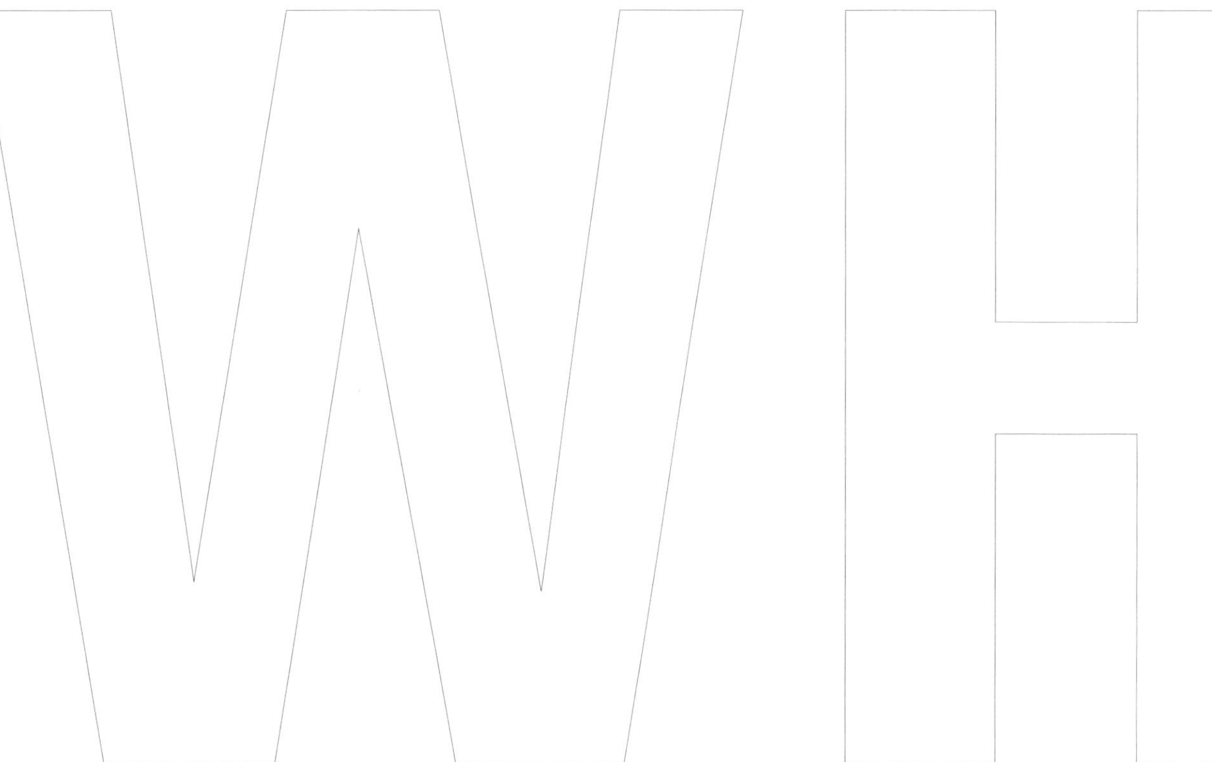

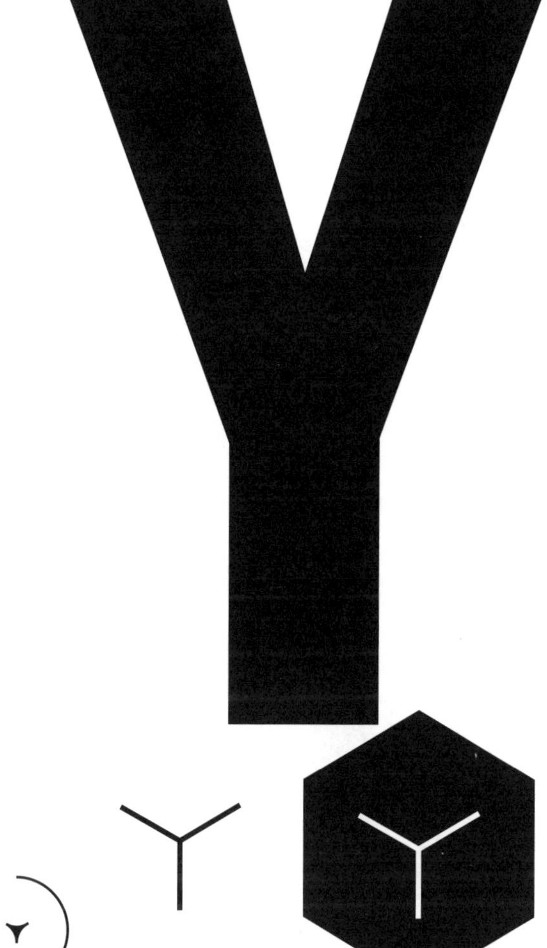

“I” UNDERSTANDS ITSELF AS A SINGULARITY AS SAME AS UNDERSTANDS “WE” AS SINGULARITY OR “THEM” IN CERTAIN SITUATIONS.
OBVIOUSLY ENEMY IS NOT CONSIDERED AS MANY DIFFERENT SUBJECTS (INDIVIDUAL LIVES) BUT ONE ENTIRE MASS. WHEN COUNTING LOSS ON LIVES IN THE WAR THEY SPEAK ABOUT BODYCOUNT IN MEGADEATH DIMENSIONS - MEGADEATH IS SINGULAR.
WHEN SPEAKING ABOUT “I” IT SHOULD MEAN VARIOUS THINGS. IN PARTICULAR MOMENTS “I” SHOULD BE UNDERSTOOD AS “WE” OR IS EVEN SELFIDENTIFIED, COMMUNICATED (ROYALITIES, ARISTOCRACY…) AS PLURALITY, ALSO ON THE OTHER WAY AROUND IN THE CASE OF GROUPAL OUTPUTS LIKE FOR EXAMPLE THE SONG OF THE BAND, WHERE THERE ARE BOTH TOGETHER “I” AND “WE”.

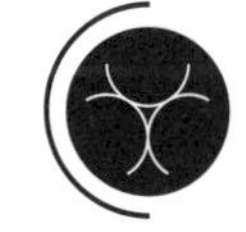
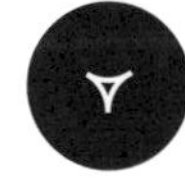
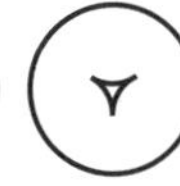
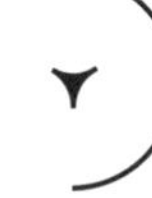

Boris Ondreička, *Y-1*

educational background in any case. Sometimes, really educated parents are "chronically" low-earners.) (We must also mention the case when children from

those higher educated, income classes do not receive appropriate attention
because their parents are always at work. The ideal biotope / sociotope is no

ABCDEFGHI
JKLMNOPQR
STUVWXYZ

guarantee; thus, no “nurture OR nature“, but “nurture AND nature“!!! ...and there are certainly many more groups of critically conflicting constellations, such as the possible, let´s say “layman and forensic”, interpretation (or rather the pop-poetic babble) of the phenomenal story of the alleged Jesus of Nazareth

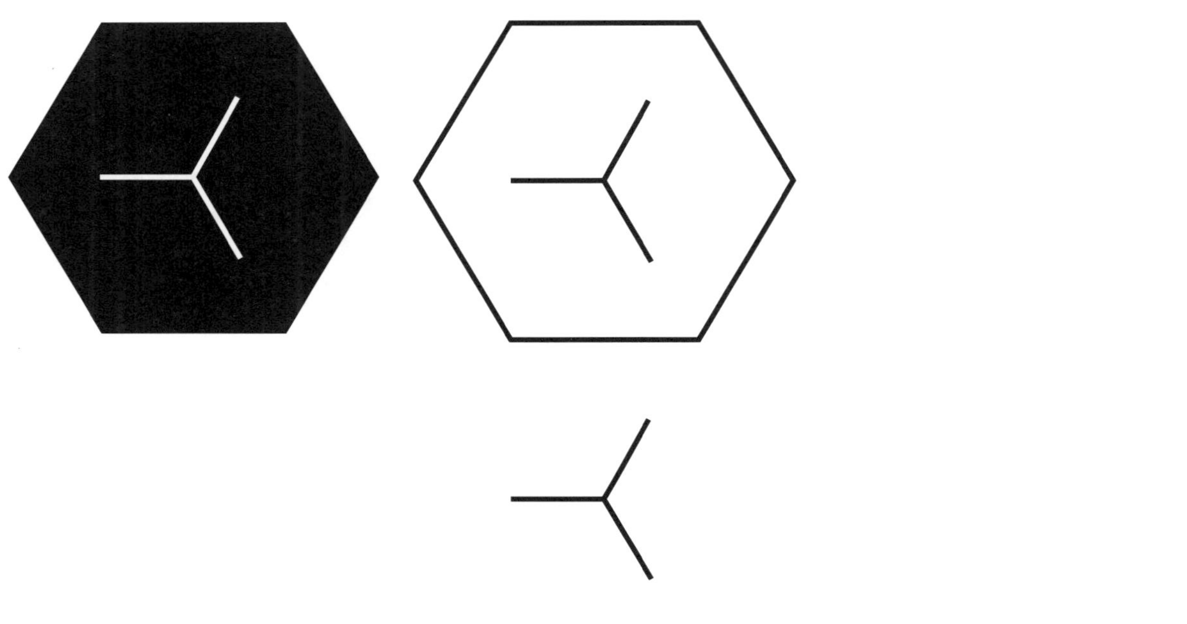

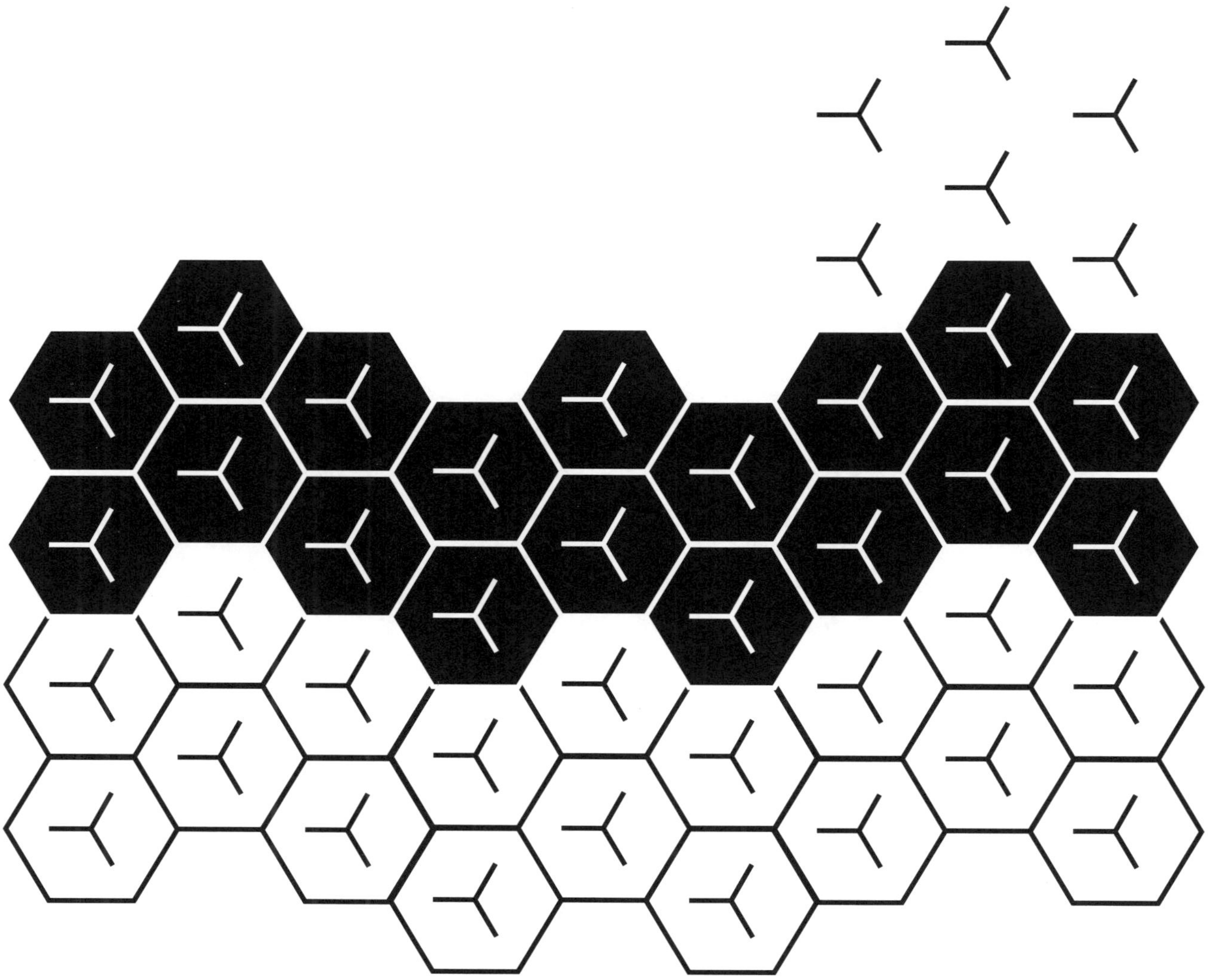

– let´s do it: If, from a “kindergarten” materialistic point of view, we refused the immaculate (without macula?, “strange, not?”*) conception (conception!!!)

of (the so-called virgin or Virgin) Mary, we would have to talk soberly about
Jesus as an illegitimate child, since Joseph clearly denies / refuses the biological

abcdefghi
jklmnopqr
stuvwxyz

a á ä â ã å æ ā ă ą b c c č ć d ď đ e é è ê ë ē ė ę ě f g ğ ģ h i í ì î ï ī į j k l ľ Ĺ ł m n ň ñ ń o ó ô ò õ ö ø ō ő œ p q r ř ŕ s š ś t ť u ú ù û ü ū ? ů ű ų v w x y ý ÿ z ž ź ż fatherhood of Jesus owing to the fact that he did not have any sexual intercourse with Mary; that is logical, believable. (neighbour? brother? father?)(*To this

day, e.g., in some areas of the Balkans, the groom displays the blood stained bed
sheet in the bedroom window on the wedding night as a confirmation of

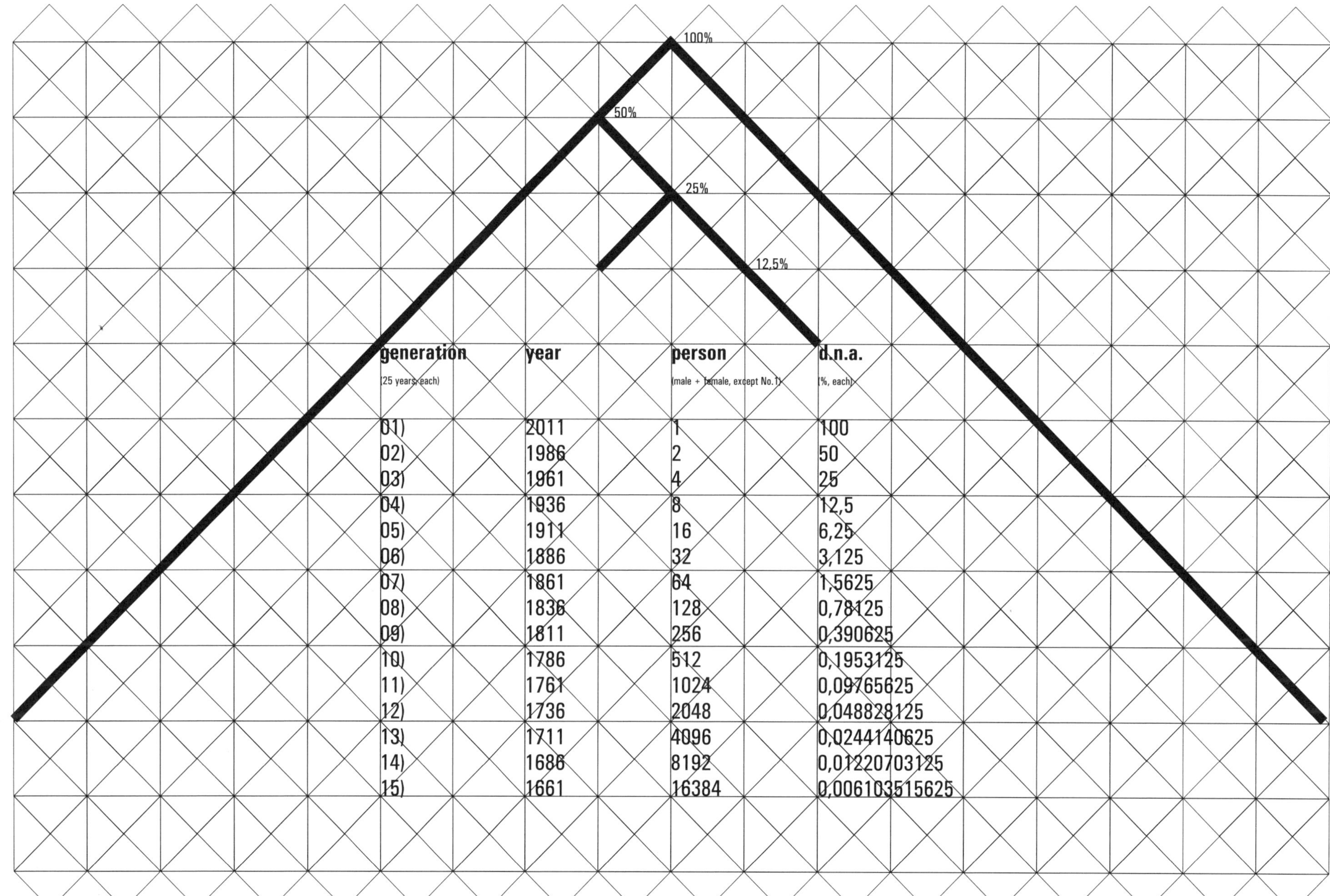

generation (25 years each)	year	person (male + female, except No. 1)	d.n.a. (%, each)
01)	2011	1	100
02)	1986	2	50
03)	1961	4	25
04)	1936	8	12,5
05)	1911	16	6,25
06)	1886	32	3,125
07)	1861	64	1,5625
08)	1836	128	0,78125
09)	1811	256	0,390625
10)	1786	512	0,1953125
11)	1761	1024	0,09765625
12)	1736	2048	0,048828125
13)	1711	4096	0,0244140625
14)	1686	8192	0,01220703125
15)	1661	16384	0,006103515625

defloration . De-floratio = rupture of “the flower of virginity”...) However, Mary is obviously pregnant and she simply must give an acceptable explanation for it,

since in her times, extramarital sexual intercourse was unacceptable (like in
some cultures up to the present day!!!) and if she manages to survive at all, then

Bratislava is an area lying at the southern edge of Carpathian Mountains, at the point where borders of Czech Republic, Austria, Hungary and Slovakia meet. Bratislava is a city cut by the river Danube in two halves.

Bratislava grew on the area of a Celtic settlement at the northern end of defence lines of Limes Romanum, a borderline built by Romans separating Roman Empire from the rest of barbarian tribes. Later (simply said) Bratislava grew in its size as a result of being a reserve area for Austria-Hungarian Empire and Habsburg monarchy and a weekend place for people from Vienna. Bratislava and Vienna are the two Europe's capitals located closest to each other. Bratislava with its 600.000 inhabitants forms a town, while Vienna with 1,5 million people is a city. It is said that Bratislava is the most distant outskirt of Vienna.

Bratislava used to be a meeting place for German, Hungarian and Slovak languages resulting in a specific dialect formed in majority from the above-mentioned languages. Everyone talked in every languages, but together in one. Bratislava was home to one of the most important Yeshivas and one of the first universities (Istropolitana) in the whole Europe. Slovak language was codified only in the middle of 19th century, but it was no sooner than 1994 that Slovakia had become willingly independent. The word Bratislava means "glory of brotherhood" (brat = brother, sláva = glory), which reflects masculine character of 19th century revival (Carola Dertnig has asked me why there is no glory of sisterhood", but that's another question). Known are also other names such as Istropolis, Pressburg or Poszonyi. Bratislava is somewhat closer historically and culturally to Vienna as to the country for which, we can say illogically, serves as a capital. It is a town, which was 60 years ago, detached from central European context (metaphorically speaking moved to the meaning of "East") and later it consequently developed by force to artificial direction. Example of this is, even up till today, inconsistently built centre with devastated round the castle settlement – horrible. Bratislava is not that popular in Slovakia also due to absolute centralization of power from the times of totalitarian regime. Bratislava was forced to take responsibilities in which it was not interested.

I grew to be a teenager in 80s still behind the iron curtain. With friends we used to climb Devín castle hill, a place where Moravia River flows to Danube and with a sour smile we watched birds flying over the border there and back freely with no risk of anybody stopping them. Radio waves were like those birds too.

At that time I listened to mainly American rock music such as Black Flag, Big Black, Swans, Sonic Youth, Dinosaur Jr., Minor Threat, Fugazi, Misfits, Minuteman, Butthole Surfers, Nomeansno etc. British groups except Sex Pistols and Wedding Present did not catch my interest.

Resistant attitude of Bratislava's punks (and punks of the whole Eastern block), to which I belonged at that time was, compared to western approach, clearly left-oriented, as establishment at that time was hated communists. Idea of anarchy, as no limits and free of boundaries, was dealt with as with vision of radical freedom of self-expression, which was at that time so much suppressed. I saw this understanding as something identical with the meaning of art.

As Internet did not exist my only real-time sources of information were radio stations – above all Austrian Ö1 and Ö3 – goodness voice of Angelika Lang, Wolfgang Kos and many other names I do not recall anymore. In television it was Kunststücke with Dieter Moor. It was in program Nachtexpress that I heard for the first time, who later became my most favourite Hüsker Dü. I remember Joy Division's Love Will Tear Us Apart presented by Austrian band Chuzpe, which was much stronger than British original. It was truly very beautiful version one can hardly forget. After twelve o'clock you could always find me lying next to radio with headphones on or trying not to miss Musikbox broadcasted between 3 and 4 p.m. I always recorded the whole 1-hour program on 60 minutes tape (I keep some of that tapes even until now). It was horrible when they announced concert in Vienna to which it was, of course, not possible to go. This was only, but extremely, frustrating moment. I even used to write down names of bands so I could then somehow obtain their records. Many times I misspelled the English name pronounced by Austrian speakers and so were left, due to my own mistake, to look for unobtainable. As you can imagine, I had to listen, and listened, very carefully.

Reach of television and radio waves remained a physical sign of compactness of this region and created from a different point of view a new territory. So there were two hermetically separated entities, over which a freely available platform was in the air, but not interactive from both sides.

At that time there was no Austrian listening to Slovak radio. There was no reason or will for an Austrian to learn to speak or communicate in Slovak. I do not think Austrian speakers in Ö1 and Ö3 were even aware of "our presence on the other side" and so had no idea how important role they play for us.

Longings were floating east to west direction, while fears the opposite way, which in certain sense is an essence that slightly remained to these days.

I was buying LPs (and recording for money) and tapes on the black flea market. Illegal fairs took place regularly in the morning hours on Sunday always in one of Bratislava's parks. Every time it was 3 to 4 hours of the fair before police came and managed to dissipate the crowd of around 30 people selling and about 100 to 200 customers. At such occasion I witnessed no violence from the side of police. I even remained surprised how they tolerated it. Policeman only occasionally confiscated some LPs to one of the sellers in order to maybe, pass them to his son or a lover.
One could also find things in Polish Cultural Centre, in the heart of the Old town. Surprisingly enough one could also find thing there that were as a paradox prohibited throughout the whole Czechoslovakia: Polton licence for Dead Kennedys Fresh Fruit For Rotting Vegetable from 1987 including A2 size poster collage of Jello Biafra – a bit worse quality of paper and print than original from Cleopatra / DKS 1980, but in all other identical. Imagine, strictly forbidden goods legally sold at the very centre of the town...

American music. Austrian radio. Joy Division and Chuzpe, Communistic Czechoslovakia. Bratislava with nationally and culturally unclear identity. Slovakia? I visited Košice, the second biggest town in our country, for the first time when I was 17 for only two hours and later in 2000, altogether 3 times in my life – in Vienna I am at least 3 times a month. Of course the reason lies also in geographical distance.

Slovak artist growing up on American so-called "alternative" music sourced in Austrian radio, moreover, from behind the iron curtain – absolute mix? – I do not think so. It is only specific cocktail.

After opening of the country borders when I started my often visits to Vienna, I experienced no cultural shock. Although via medium and from distance I was able to watch world developments and be equivalent part of it. I only became by existence aware of the weight, trauma of that historical asymmetry, and how little interest the other side paid to us, how little they still know about us but also how we overevaluated the meaning of being in the centre which was not the city centre but a town centre, how because of being pressed by a common enemy we behaved with great solidarity to an extent of loosing one's own self reflection and suffering from a complex of victim.

Many things are put to movement only based on the giving it a proper reason and a right amount of accessibility. Sometimes also some free of charge media move only one direction, sometimes 60 kilometres mean 360 from the opposite side and the act of opening windows does not necessarily mean having a bird of desire to fly in.

she will definitely be repudiated together with her child, and then the child itself... Bastard... Fall of Man... Therefore, by the focusing circumstances, Mary creates the most extreme possible construction for the siring of the child by God (or by god) ("with" is excluded, since such coitus is absolutely inconceivable,

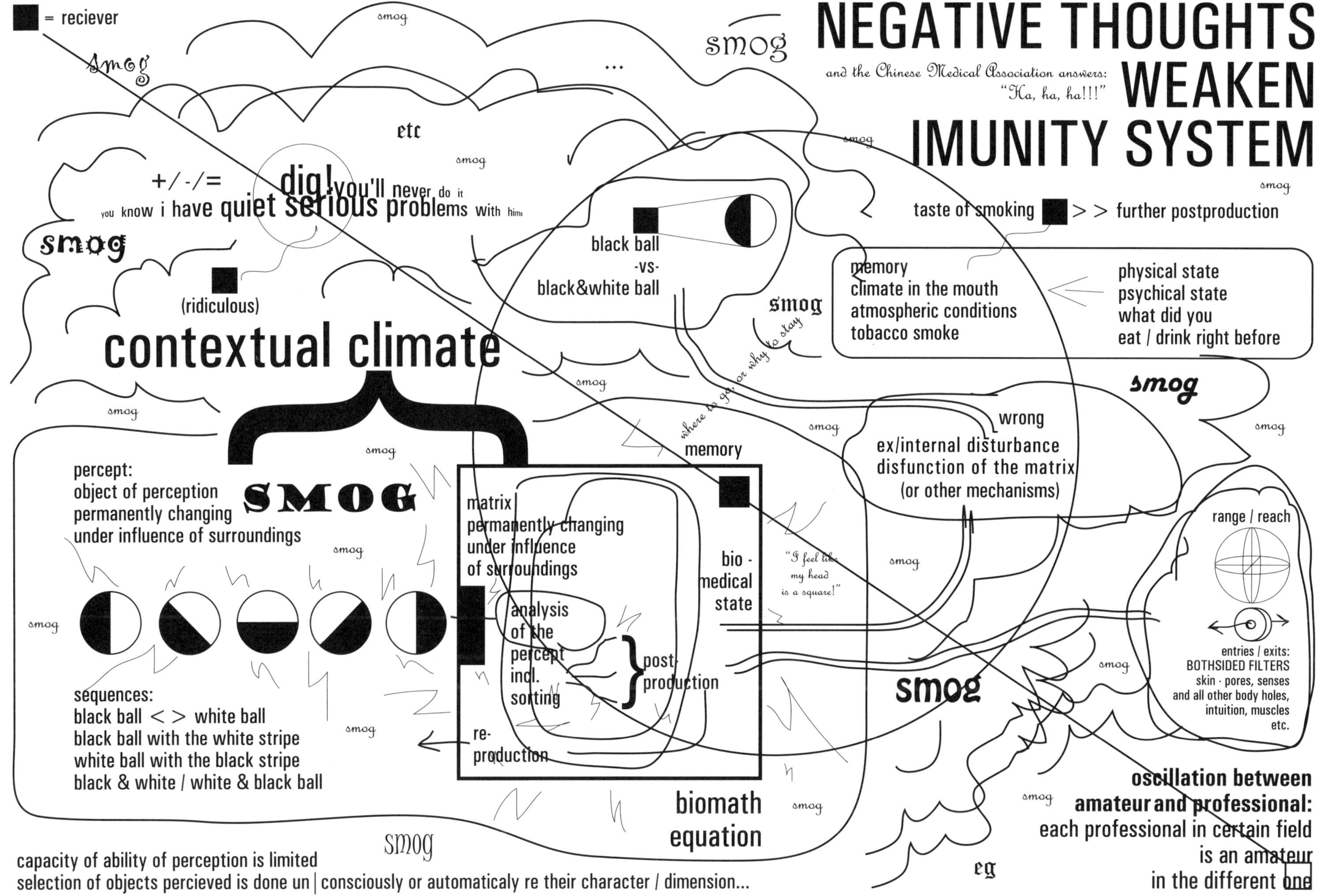

because the penis of the Lord is unimaginable – without defloration = without maculation, because we are talking about dematerialisation – also about dematerialised sperm?). In times so cruel to Jews, where everyone only hopes for the arrival of a Messiah, this crazy conspiracy, this MIRACLE thus finds its

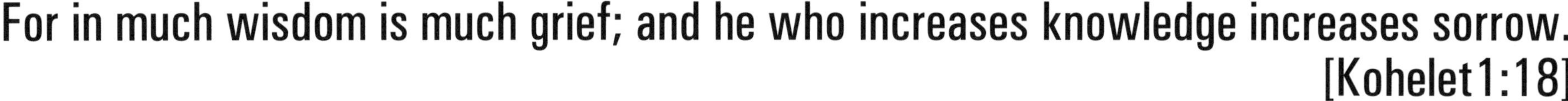

For in much wisdom is much joy; and he who increases knowledge increases happiness.
[B.O. 1:2004]

"respondents" – reactive action in the existing climate, its application and impact. (Moreover, it is possible that thanks to a certain physiognomical anomaly, excessive elasticity, her hymen remained unbroken, which would be an even more cogent argument.) (Today, in cultures where the representativeness of

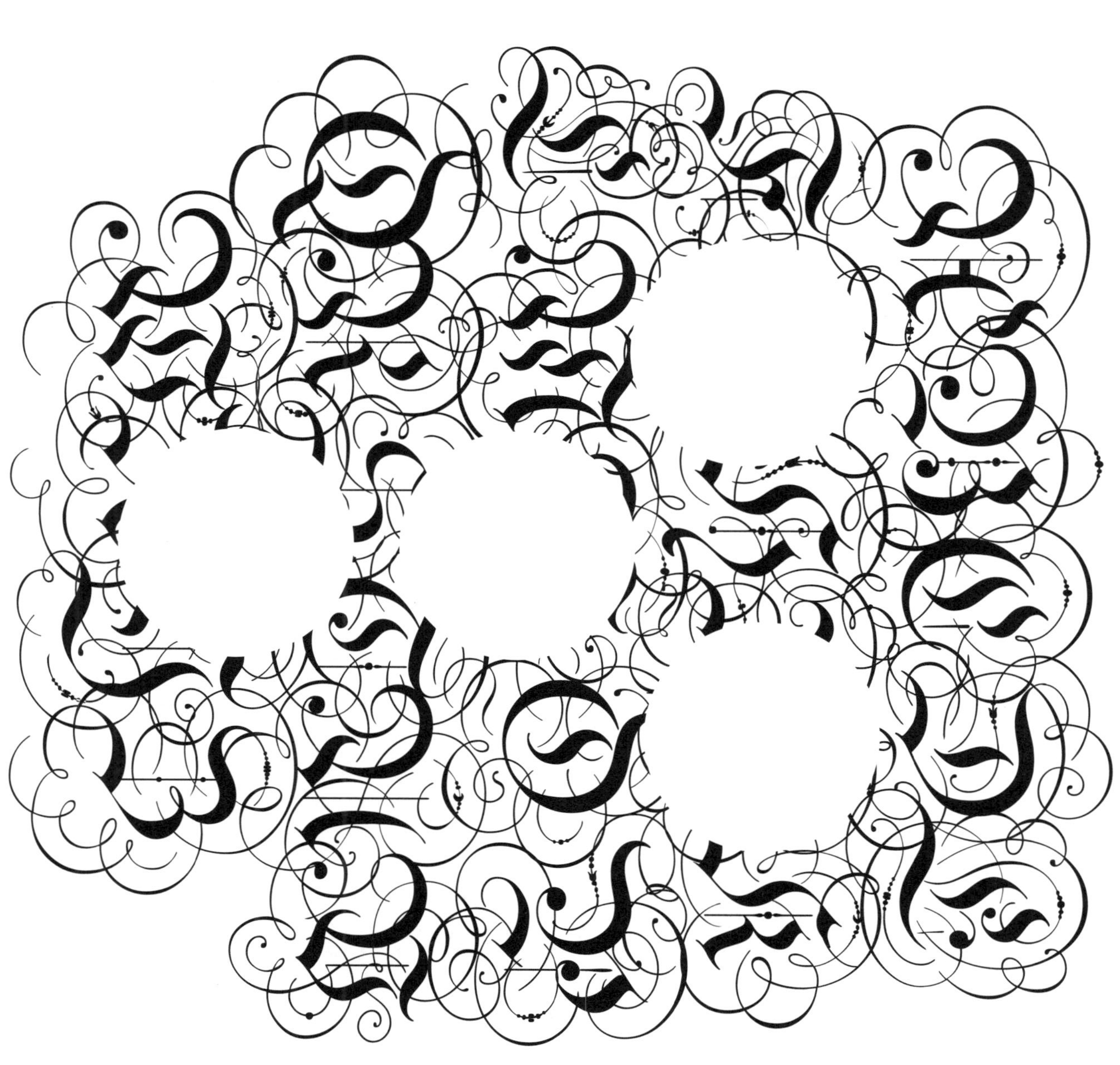

the hymen is still highly appreciated, women even undergo Hymenoplasty...)
If it is so, what it does mean for her son Jesus to grow up so ad absurdum

traumatised, with such a burden of irrationality delirium? It is more or less clear that Jesus Christ (Joshua Messiah, teacher, who became one of the Islamic

(Death in June, Death in December, Death on Wednesday, Death in Vegas, Death from Above 1979, Dr. Death, Docta Death, Henry Death, Frankie Death and the Photon Belt, Liquorice [Licorice] John Death, Blue Eyed Boy Mister Death, Colorblind James and the Death Valley Boys, Free Death, Christian Death, Christxxx Death, Silent Death, Anxious Death, Blessed Death, Holy Death, Precious Death, Malicious Death, Morbid Death, Creepin' Death, Brutal Death, Sudden Death, Septic Death, Napalm Death, Electric Death, Skate Death, Nuclear Death, Asbestos Death, Acid Death, Instant Death, Facing Death, Living Death, Systematic Death, Black Death, Blue Sky Black Death, The Red Death, Crayon Death, Merciless Death, Apocryphal Death, Accidental Death, American Death, A Solemn Death, A Secret Death, Brain Death, Agonize Death, Strange Death of Liberal England, Creation of Death, Scent of Death, Dream Death, Death by Chocolate, Death by Cheesecake, Death by Injection, Death by Hollywood, Death by Speed, Death by Stereo, Death by Design, Death by Milkfloat, Death by Visitation of God, Murder by Death, Killed by Death, Shielded by Death, Stormtroopers of Death, Recipients of Death, Cool Kids of Death, Silent Love of Death, The Kiss of Death, Hands of Death, Drums of Death, Basket of Death, Almighty Lumberjacks of Death, Shadow of Death, Bombs of Death, 666 Triangle Six of Death, Hobbs Angel of Death, My Enemy Death, Life or Death, Prophecy of Death, Death Squad, Olympic Death Squad, Shaolin Death Squad, Kai Blackwood & the Tokyo Death Squad, The Kola Koca Death Squad, Death Comet Crew, Death Wish Kids, Death Youth Foundation, Death Chants, Death Unit, Death Threat, Graffiti Death Threat, Death Angel, Death Ride 69, Kevorkian Death Cycle, Death Row Tull, Death Cult, The Southern Death Cult, Death Cab for Cutie, American Death Ray, Death Cube K, Death Polka, Death Warrant, Death Praxis, Death Drug, Death Mattel, Death Beast, Death Sick, Death Funk, Death Power, Death Trash, Death Row, Death Dealers, Death Soda, Death Living, Death Trip, Death Ships, Death Vessel, Death Ambient, The Death Riders, Death Piggy, Death Strike, Death Organ, Death Sentence, Death Sentence: Panda!, Black Death Ritual, Death Punch Morning, Communal Death Duck, The Death Folk, Sudden Death Click, Bubblegum Death Experience, Neon Death Slittes, Cleveland Bound Death Sentence, Appalachian Death Ride, Death SS, Death Side, Near Death Experience, Death Yell, Death Machine, Patriarchal Death Machine, Suburban Death Machine, Unholy Death Machine, Vincent Price's Orphan Powered Death Machine, Dead Machines and Death Knell, Death Reality, Death Threat / Over My Dead Body, Eagles of Death Metal, Black Angel's Death Song, Little Death Orchestra, Brighter Death Now, Better Than Death, Love Is Colder Than Death, Love Equals Death, Death Do Us Part, Death Comes Along, Death Is Not Glamorous, Long Live Death, Death Becomes You, Viva L'American Death Ray Music, World Burns to Death, A Death for Every Sin, Printed at Bismarck's Death, Death in Action, Forward to Death, In Death We Rise, Fake Your Death, Fuck It to Death, Viva Death, Until Death Overtakes Me, Death Loves, Death Dies, Love & Death, Life Sex & Death, Death & Taxes, Death & Horror Inc., Love, Death & Agriculture, We vs. Death, Death of Marat, Death of Samantha, The Death of Anna Karina, Sexy Death of Millions, The Death of a Party, Sleepy Eyes of Death, After Death, Life After Death, Death After Life, Death Before Dishonor, Death Before Disco, Condemned to Death, Death on a Stick, Death Cab for Cutie, Death to Tyrants, Death to Anders, Sanity in Death, Death du Jour, Of Death,...)

prophets as well) “pathologically” conforms to his family (in the sense of absolute “Mother Truth” association) supported by the ecstatic voices of followers, and consistently starts fulfilling the assignment, developing it, spreading it, until he becomes a fanatic leader of a rebellious group (sect, in

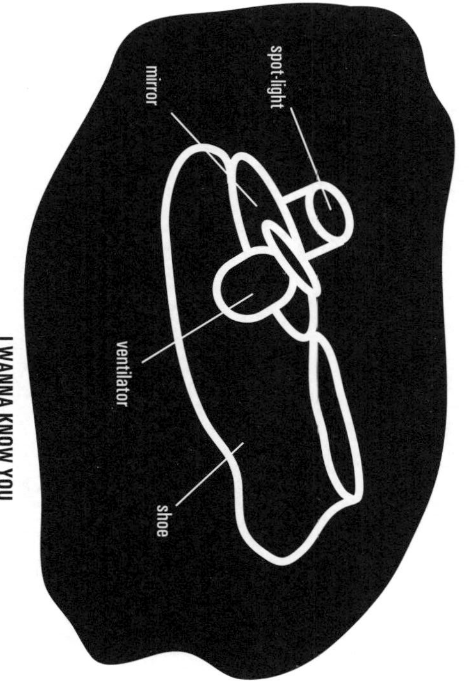

I WANNA KNOW YOU
(skirt version)

the 60s we would call it underground, later - sub-culture). This cult is even more reinforced by his PUBLIC execution by crucifixion (if he was hanged, then –

would the noose have become such a "striking" symbol? and would it be worn around the neck, leaning against the chest... or an axe, or sword, bow and arrow,

Public area is a private property. Each possible sight is already sold out or rented or just waits for its total commercialisation. There are predesigned shapes for contributions changing after particular periods related to time of rent paid. Nature works as a background - architecture is a sockel for presentation. Simple, freshly aggressive messages are spread all around. Competing with each other - colorful and straight. Faces are speaking directly to the eyes of passers-by. It's everywhere in urban and rural surroandings, television, radio, periodicals, net, toilets and escalators, trains. There are messages for those walking, driving or flying, standing, sitting, dreaming. Marketing studies it's addressees precisely having nothing to do with academic non for profit contexts - this research brings direct profit. Marketing collects all kind of data following each step of potential customer = everybody / everywhere = looking for gaps, apts and inclinations - for new spheres of benefit. Marketing is able to adapt not only the language but also the product itself. Marketing is able to operate with sensuality, intimacy, subjectivity > anything related to usable needs, abilities, priorities and stereotypes - to reach wanted. Public area is a battlefield of labels where the highest number of rotation is a necessarry part of the winning mission. The quantity counts, of course. Investments are getting larger and more and more addressed which reflects on effectivity of means applicated. Public area is over-communicated > possible associations are preproduced. Receivers are always getting immune after certain period of rotation. So innovation and flexibility is permanently ready to react bringing something even more spectacular, unexpected, something NEW. Everybody is caught cause media plans are done in synergy with respondent's appearance, habits. There are diverse forms of attacks one doesn't feel like they are attacks. And if there is still some gap left it's detained by graffitti easily recognisable teen-urban-folklore, contemporary kitsch - one way semi-abstract already purely ornamental. Christian Dior's next punk collection. Languages and metalanguages, symbiosis and metabiosis and there is no-one to understand them all together. People are too busy for metalanguages. In the eyes of common receiver mass-media is chaotic flux which never stops. They have too small time and energy for fragile images without short - strong headlines misunderstood as an advertisement teasing. Objects are considered just as meaningless, decorative carrieres of logos to be mounted on. People are tired indeed and it's really problematic and consequently expensive to wake them up of their hyper-active lethargy. There is some public and there are public relations. Everything is functioning under perfectly done norms of navigation. Household is institutionalised. Kitchen sink is used as a real mirror thanks to detergent. Freedom - freedom of expression is limited under utilitarian rules of traffic: work > home > work > home > permitted engagement > work > home > work > home. It is stricktly controlled what is to be shown - done - happened / what's safe and what's dangerous. There are political and other determinations. There are lots of constraints in usage of material and dimensions like heights, distances etc. There are various restrictions related to nudity, sexuality, alcohol, cigarettes and diverse moral / ethic fundaments including possible incrimination of religious or economical forces. I don't wanna say that art doesn't fit to so called public space just that art projects in public area are faced with this stratified hyper-context. Art projects here are as exclusive as when located inside art-institutions but even more curtailed. One needs less or more massive support of various kind for audience to show up on one hand and help to visitors how and when to get in on the other. Is there, in the concrete jungle led by predators, any space left for silence and delicacy? Is the main role of art-institutions / art-individuals (institutional individuals / individual institutions) to interact with public? What that so called "public" means nowadays? Are we able to describe it precisely enough - in the dimension of our present knowledge of that / for needs of our missions? Is that term "public" still useful?´I think that even in its plural form it's useless for our needs. Generalised that much means almost nothing anymore cause potential public consists of enormous heterogenousity of qualities of groups. They consist of layers of even antagonistic existential experiences, priorities - spheres which doesn´t communicate to each other using non-compatible languages waiting for to be re-described. It is impossible to understand "them" as one entire audience or make "them" understand us in one turn. If any public exists it means it's us too = And just by an accident: AREN'T WE THE TARGET NO.1? Ultra manifold crowd needs to be individualised. It's necessary to understand certain abilities and needs and to communicate separately through those fragile details of internal structure of society. To communicate with the public as with the one democratic entirety is contra-productive, so just a waste of money. We deal with different role than mass-media. Adaptation of our messages to the smog of mass-media-language is quite dangerous > form changes the content definitely and in this case the simplification is even impossible. Art doesn't bring only relax and tenderness but many times so painful questions. And I still believe that the character of our work is against populism so how to attract real people? What is the reason them to come? Do they know it? I am afraid that we have to re-establish our own communication contexts again or to learn to use existing ones in more professional way. That's why we have to work on multi-dispciplinary platforms with those professionals who deal with mass-media and marketing communication. Public is over-saturated so existing channels are suitable only for distribution of extracted message of informal character and of course as a feedback-value for sponsors. And cause of marketing competition are very expensive. Here is no time - no space for explanation of the one of the most important messages and it's THE REASON WHY TO JOIN US. That's the essence why we miss the target. Market, audience is permanently and radicaly changing so we have to re-explain the sense, the position, the dimension of our new importance in the dynamic structures of society. So called "public" accepts only examples / representations. People vote cause of sympathy to the visible leader cause they have no clue of future steps of the party itself. That's also why populistic models are back or still in power. And that's how and what are existing media-channels built for. So consequently I believe in addressed support mainly. I believe that our new messages can infiltrate wider society only via personal channels. Artists, theorists and scientists (administration, technical stuff) are unbreakable part of regullar life of institutional / individual art-contexts even on free-lance base or working for free but still permanently employed. We are the best distributors of many times so complicated messages. Each individual has hers/his own circle and so on and so on. These circles itself many times behave xenophobiac between each other. But they are able to interact together through those individuals I am speaking about which should play the role of a social sponge or filter. This is the only effective campaign we can manage. We are able somehow together create permanently flexible platforms stimulating exchange and cooperation potential. The process of transscription / translation - interpretation - popularisation is possible through establishing the dialogue as unbreakable part of regullar scientific and preparation process superior even to the pieces of art. We don´t live enthusiastic era - there is too much of pragmatic scepticism. There is a logical alienation made of some mysterious presence of eventual profit which makes it totaly competitive and egocentric. In these difficult times I long for individuals and institutions at the very first having the humanistic will to get us a bit closer (if not together) to a dialogue. And behind each institution stands the human decison-maker and each individual lives institutional life parallely. So, INSTITUTIONAL INDIVIDUALS can get us a bit closer to wider groups of people in bothsided streaming. If we don't do this - art projects should get lost for wider public somewhere between bright colors and shapes of mass-media which dominates, traffic signs and graffiti as it happens obviously. One can say that it's enough to write a short poem on the door of the neighborough using charcoal. I honestly agree cause also it's me as well who decided to work on similar frequence of sensuality of communication. What else can I do? I realy care for an individual and I am still trying to map and extend the range of my personal reach. Yes anonymously the message should be understood as the most honest one in the eyes of accidental viewer. And that accidental viewer should distribute hers / his experience further via mentioned private circles. But I believe that we can do much more discussing things on one-to-one basis or in a small groups than to speak to masses. And anyway > all crucial decisons are happening out of public eye. I am full of doubts. Cause I can imagine that neighborough of mine reading that poem on his door being pissed off thinking that it is just another trick of some bloody salesman or religious fanatic. I am afraid of misunderstandings so consequently of losing energy. So in the same time I think we have to support our poetic messages by more prosy interpretation-promotion helping to find and to access - to stimulate the interaction between us and groups of laiks. There are hybrid areas of individuals and groups of individuals and communities to interact with and I think that only reasonable output rises out of concentrated personal interaction on long-term basis. And may-be rather than using arts for purpose of so called public space we can better create some new discipline based on knowledge of sociology, urban planning, marketing communication, psychology and philosophy of the city. This discipline will precisely follow and fulfill needs and abilities of particular socio-cultural constelations which are permanently on the move.

stone, flame, water...) in Jerusalem, in the capital city, together with two other socially dangerous criminals (up to this day we punish such rebels, but not so “brutally”)..., and, in addition, the disappearance of his body... the Battle between Godlessness and Godequality. The myth continues, grows stronger,

I WANNA KNOW YOU (SKIRT VERSION #2)

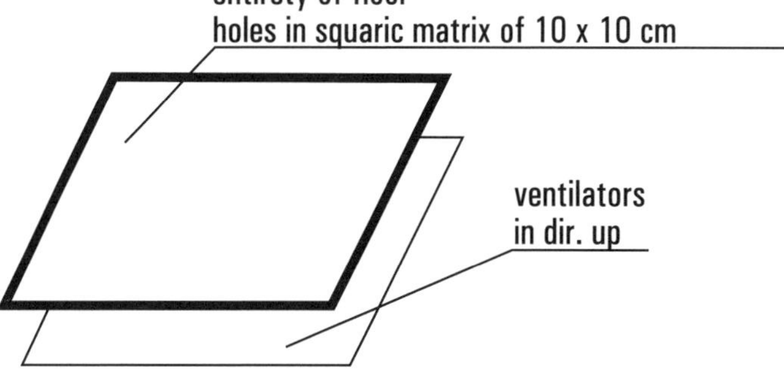

Boris Ondreička, *I wanna know you, version 2*

spreads, sophisticates itself after his death with even bigger ease, faster (also thanks to “the allure of the forbidden”) until, in ancient Rome (through the

feelosophia

import of Jewish slaves) it becomes “fore-Machiavellian-ly” interesting for the ruling powers – it is appropriated, legalized, institutionalised to such a degree of officialness that there slowly rises a new (self-constituted) Holy Town, which totalises itself at the imperial level, only to later call itself a Spiritual State!!!

That city becomes a state in a state, with power that reaches far beyond its borders, all the time – even today vehemently interfering in the internal affairs

of other states. The Vatican Agreements... Sin, guilt, humility, penitence, fatalism, asceticism, pain, suffering, sacrifice, awe, ecstasy, equality,

Try to describe the color of the night sky, my dear.

reconciliation with destiny, fetishism, masochism, fear – the most effective
means of controlling masses, homogenising masses, creating a new homogenous

Boris Ondreička, *T.P. #3*

mass, icon-explosion. Monotheism concealing in itself the riveting conflict of triunity, and both a divine and human dimension, awe and resistance, ideal ideology and dictatorship, which also demonstrates the potential of the moral legitimisation of usurpatory expansion via the pursuit of those with a different (world-)view, all this under the guise of “manifest goodness”. (a few years later again and once again: “Let´s kill the Jews because they killed Christ!”)

And the sin, guilt, humility, penitence, fatalism, asceticism, pain, suffering, sacrifice, awe, ecstasy, equality, reconciliation with destiny, fear (I underline:

STEREOLOGUE.

Everything is superior in relation with Anything because Everything includes Anything but Anything does not include Everything necessarily.

PRO:CESS.P(*OO*)L.

Continual collecting of Anything might be the proper way to comprehend The Everything.

D.K.D.

To comprehend Everything is dependent on consciousness capacities and quality of concentration - predisposed character of material and level of ability to work with it.

ESC. WITHOUT CTRL.

When observing Anything I cannot get rid of thinking on Everything.

VERBALANCE.

Fulfilment of desire for the Everything is impossible also cause of limitation of existing biological capacities so consequently is obsessive. Obsession is a mania, mania is illness.

(GLOBALANZZA).

DEVEL*OO*PMENT.

Anything is possible

asceticism and ecstasy) become the subject of contracted imaging, which it emphasizes by suggestion, expressivity, schematism / illustrativeness of what was by then restricted to “sheer” writing. Litres of blood and tonnes of light and darkness and gold. And this imaging turns into property and the representation

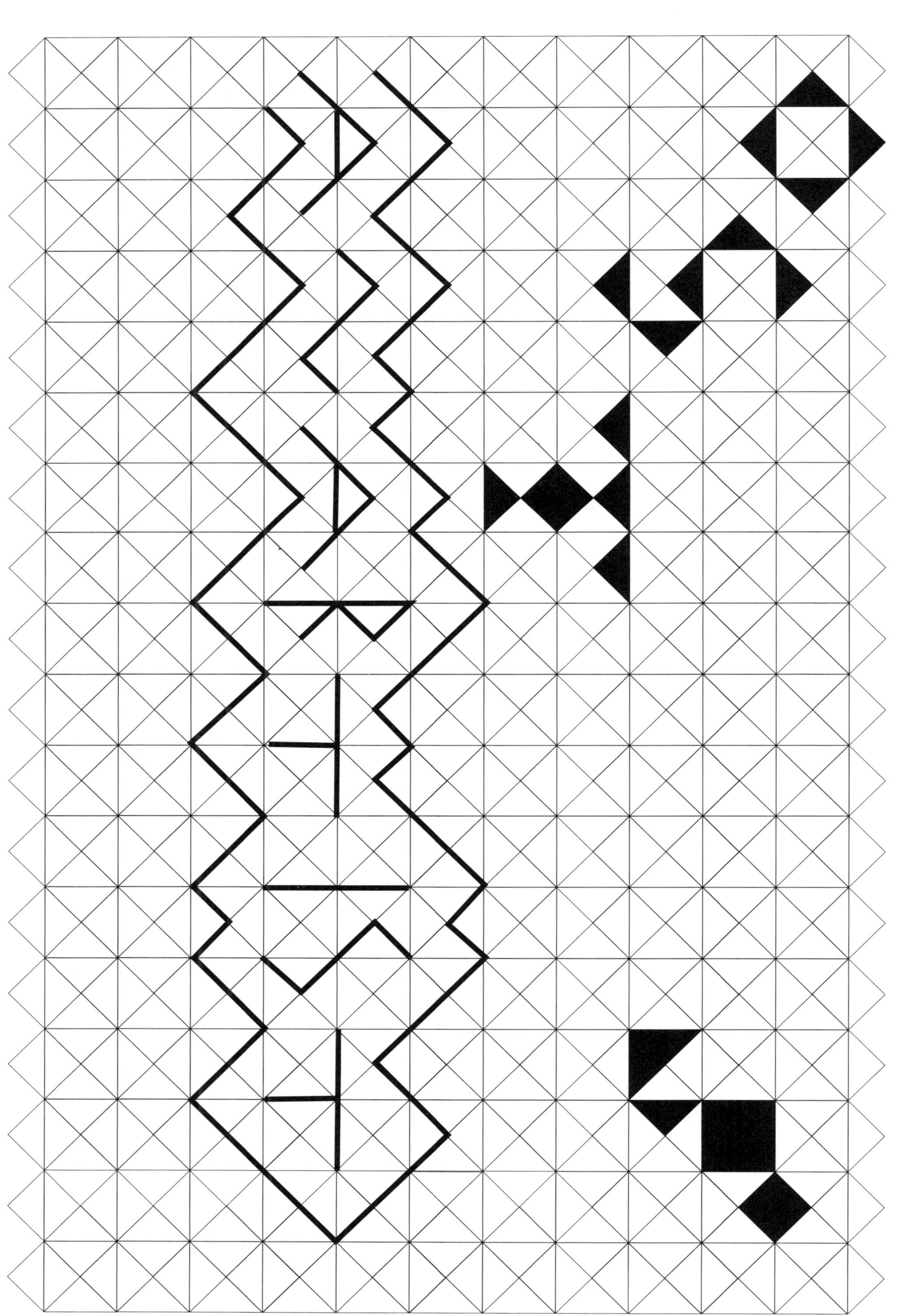

of that wealth and influence, which retroactively utilises the representation for strengthening its power – to let them know I am powerful so that they fear me even more = to double one´s supremacy, PR, BTL, ATL. Prosperity through sin, guilt, humility, penitence, fatalism, asceticism, pain, suffering, sacrifice, awe,

My radical intimacy does not need any democracy!

ecstasy, equality, reconciliation with destiny, and fear. Riches in the guise of Goodness, and then even “our” Calendar usurps with ease and by renaming pagan or even Old Testament holidays where necessary... Easter / Paskha / Pesah, Christmas / Chanukah... Evolution / Evilution? ... and establishes

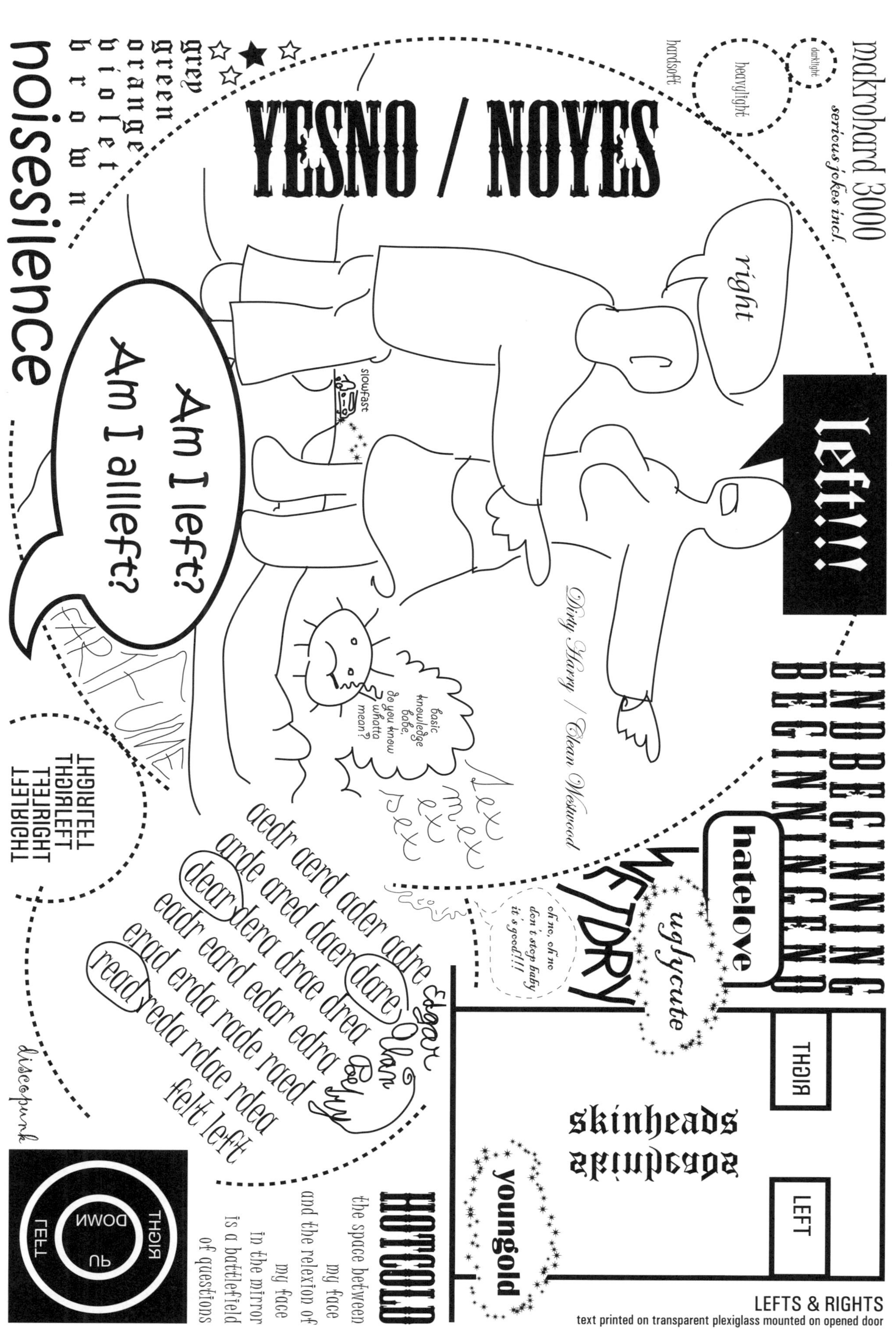

Boris Ondreička, *LR #1*; incl. *Lefts & Rights*

the Year ZERO!: Before and after... such a complex restructuring, rebranding...
It is beyond comprehension how such an extreme solution of the intimate misery

of one single, “secondary” mother can lead. Phantasmagorias (representativenesses, parallels, alternatives) are not fabricated because reality

I am 06 and I don't feel my age.
I am 14 and I don't feel my age.
I am 18 and I don't feel my age.
I am 20 and I don't feel my age.
I am 21 and I don't feel my age.
I am 24 and I don't feel my age.
I am 30 and I don't feel my age.
I am 33 and I don't feel my age.
I am 40 and I don't feel my age.
I am 50 and I don't feel my age.
I am 60 and I don't feel my age.

after Norman Bates

seems too small and primitively simple to us, but exactly because it seems too big and extra complicated beyond our strength. Escape into an imaginary world

Boris Ondreička, *after Norman Bates*

should help us get rid of that demanding real; however, it shall not, and we know it well; therefore, in this "time-out" we take a little break to overcome a fucking

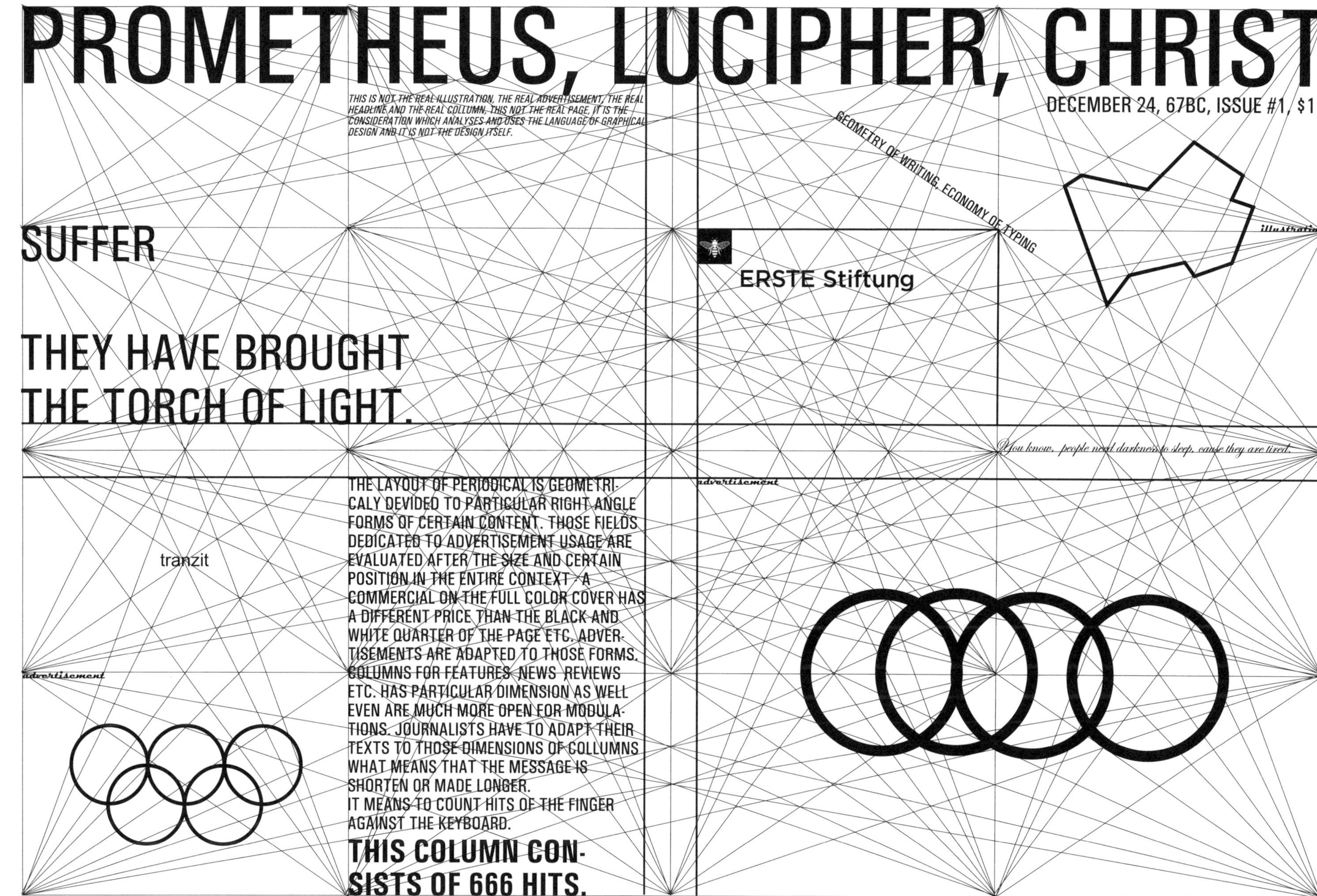

Sunday (insert any day which is just ahead of you) (and beware of addictions!). For these reasons, for Christians (Messiahists) Easter is symptomatically /

Taste the teardrop (and / or sweat...), my dear.

somatically more important than Christmas. Death is more valued (value and cost) due to resurrection rather than birth (creepers – that sounds spooky).

Boris Ondreička, *T. P. #4*

The value of a beautiful imaginary world as opposed to our ugly one, hope for remuneration for the toil of this world in the form of an after-life (and

Purgatory!!!) – this is the phantasmagoria, so white, soft clouds and angels (surely they are dead children, aren´t they?, and also Amor? which is

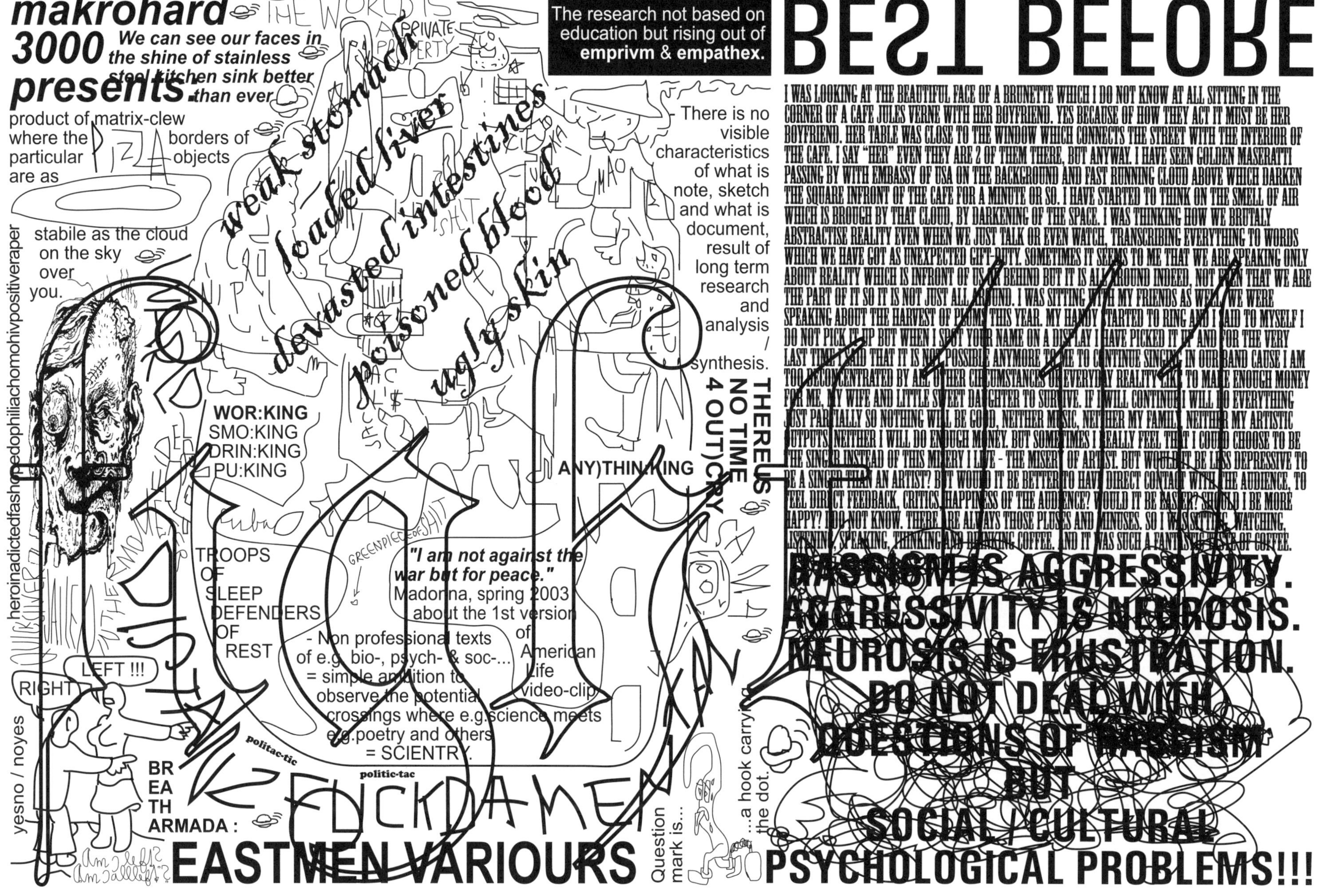

a rebranding of Eros). So, one grassroot of the faith in the otherworldly, after-life lies in the fact that it offers a more attractive alternative of lightness of

dematerialisation as opposed to the burdensomeness of matter, it lightens,
cleanses, justifies – something (ritually) structured and internally, relation-wise

DO YOU WANNA HEAR A POEM?

a poem which is distributed only via oral channels

logical compared to landlessness, the chaos of an ordinary autumn (insert your topical season). Not to have faith means to create that “time-out” and adhere to order by oneself, not to have any vindication – thus being left to be able to justify oneself. To gradually build knowledge and skills in orientation within

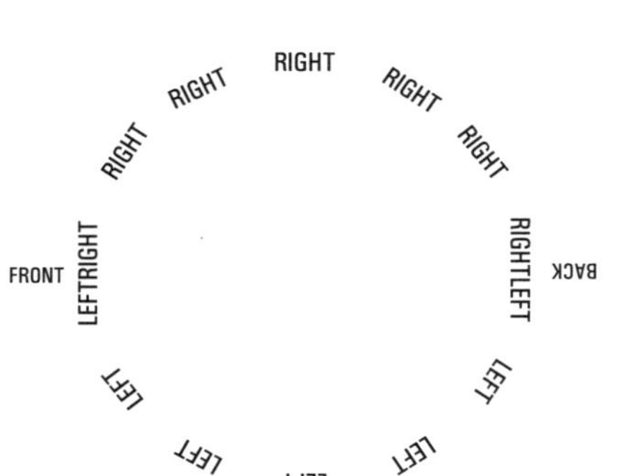

Boris Ondreička, *Circulpa {necklace}*

the predatory chaos by oneself. Escape is an attempt at negation by superimposing the initial problem with a secondary one. Overlaying does not erase or solve the problem; however, it often happens that in the time of this absence, problems are somehow forced to solve themselves (because they

I am overloaded by potentials and talents of various kinds and any vision of success or compliment seems to be the symbol of death to me.
Everything finalised, finished makes me panic so I am not able to create anything real.
Real means to be fixed to the physical aspect of existence so to be arrested (in the body).

Imprisonment signifies to be unable to breathe - to die.

BOREDOM IS DEPRESSION, DEPRESSION IS SUPPRESSED FEAR, FEAR IS SUPPRESSED ANGER.

mostly do not concern only the absent) or sediments of that act of escape will accelerate the resolution of the problem by other (mechanisms)... And then we will return and: “Aha, the problem is sorted out! I did the right thing!” This is not only about weakness; other things are simply stronger than us, and so

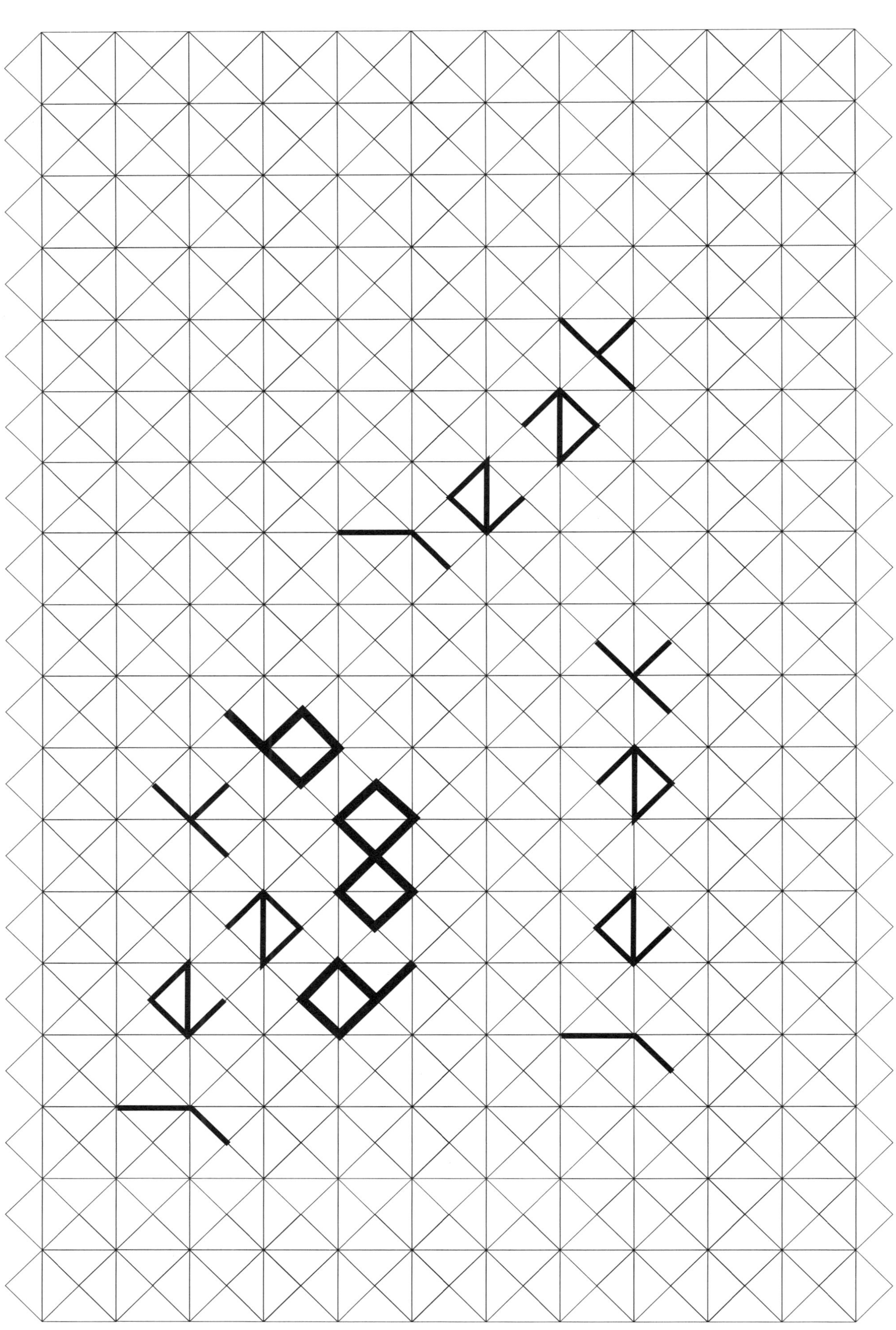

Boris Ondreička, *Matrix {Year}*

sometimes it is really better to run away as fast as one can... run, Boris, run... (insert your name) To become stronger or to weaken the opponent? And now

(Try to fall asleep.)

Close your eyes.

Look through closed eyes.

See the luminous spots through the skin of eye-lids.

Try to bring a real shape and color to these spots.

Move those spots

and projection can start, my dear.

and then it is not an adversary, but a friend. And I don´t mean a friend hiding an antagonist inside, an antagonist disguised as a friend. Despite all that – "Jesus""

Boris Ondreička, *T. P. #5*

evangelization of absolute equality and love is one of the most significant messages of our kind, the foundation-stone of humanism, what we register, although some centuries later we read Karl Marx, who was certainly inspired by Jesus of Nazareth. – At the end of a day, from a hallucination the seed of

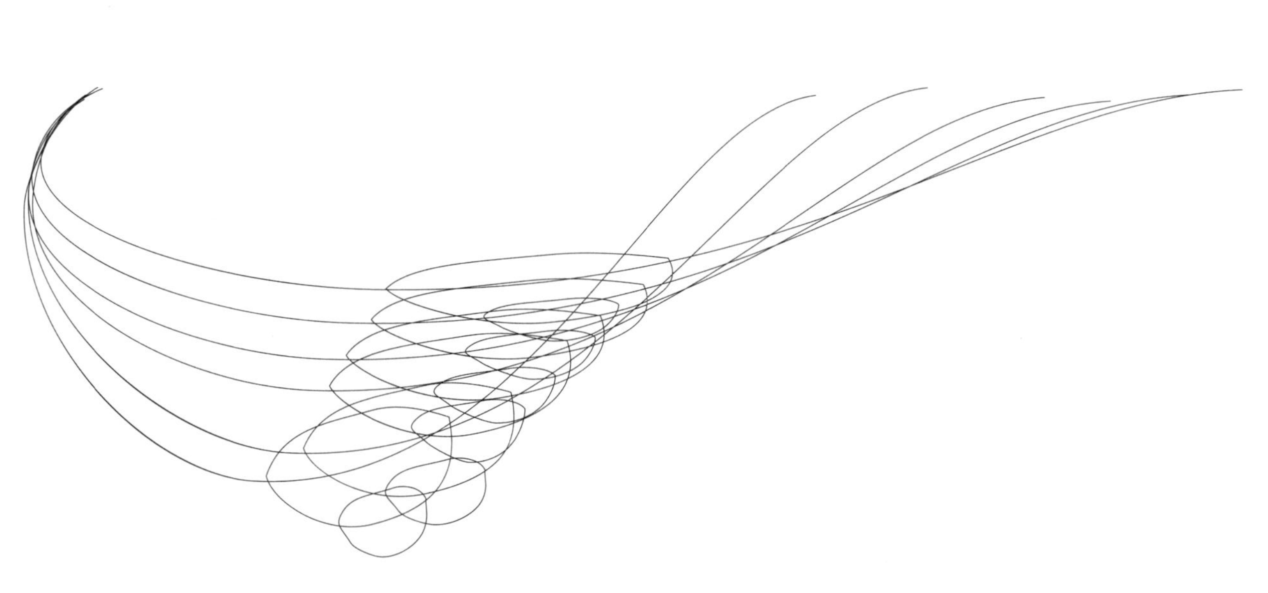

the myth nevertheless shoots a broad crown carrying many even healthy fruit, however, as is notoriously the case in other genres, the gardener of even this orchard is.................., and at the end of a day, after Marx and Engels, the scene is taken by Stalin and Brezhnev, Mao and Pol-Pot.) But, let´s move quickly back

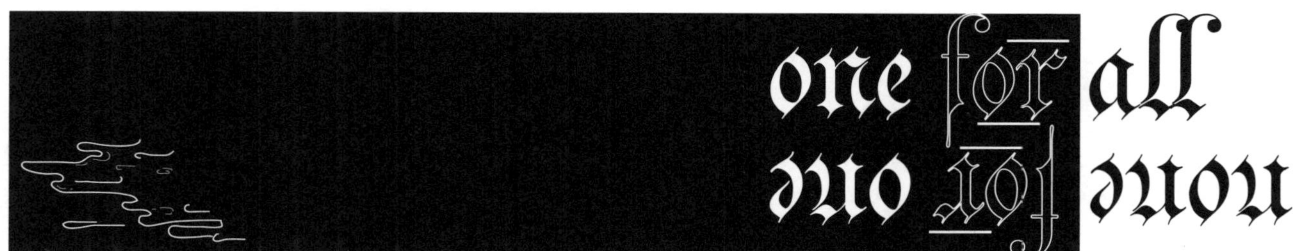

to the extremely talented children, to which Jesus most probably also belonged, and in the sense of the above, only “fundamentalistically” hinted to react to the given conditions – actually, it was just his innocent obedience. I. First, we must have the a)-abilities, then we must know that we have these a)-abilities. II. Then,

**NOBODY WAS ASKING ME
IF I WANNA BE BORN
TO THIS HIGHLY EXCLUSIVE WORLD
WHICH I AM NOT ABLE TO AFFORD.**

**THIS IS THE SONG OF
EGOISM OF PESIMISM.**

we must gain b)-abilities. III. Next, we must develop and utilise both, jointly. What´s the use of “being able to drive when we don´t have a car?” What´s the use of “having a car when we cannot drive?” (Both are achievable, both are of a dissimilar nature, but in terms of meaning they only function synthetically.)

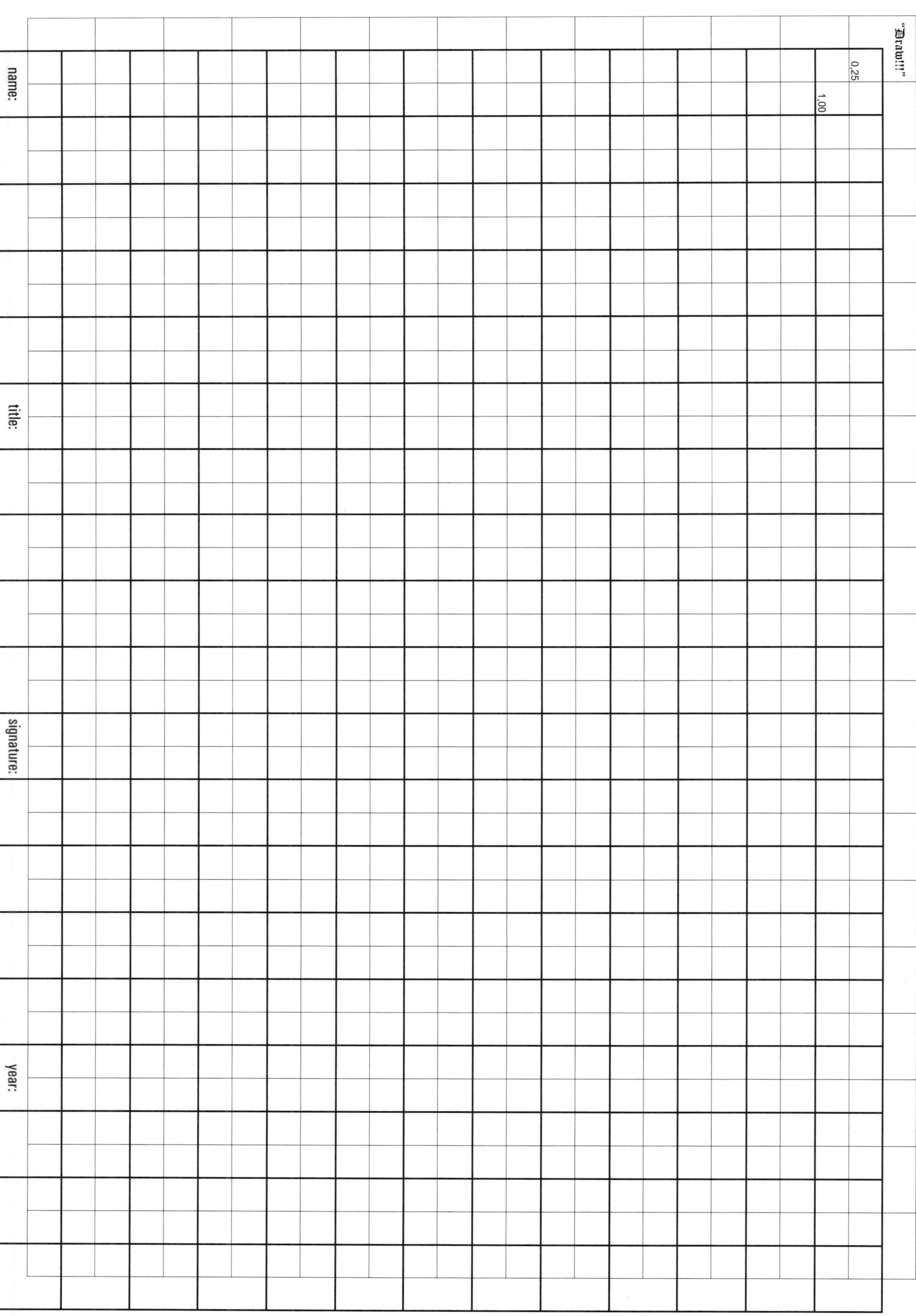

The a)-abilities can have a different source and characteristics as the b)-abilities. They can even act controversially to each other – for example: a)- in, -im /

b)- ex). That b)-ability contains self-confidence, but also self-criticism, predacity and rationality, constructiveness, productivity. And ability is mainly only

i am the floor
i am wounded by your high heels
i swallow your tears fallen down on my skin

oh ceiling,
distant friend i look at all the time but will never
meet,
do you hear my laments?

you defend myself,
i love you

a method, a tool for achieving content, filling. Its meaningful application requires knowledge (conscious or unconscious) of the very “SENSE” = C)-

ABILITY! Which at times involves also a1)-, a2)- ...abilities. Let us give this trivial example: The fact that somebody can draw nicely {= a)-ability, which, in

burn,

burn towers, archs, citadels, fortresses, caserns, bunkers, shelters, casemates, barracks, bastions, bulwarks, ramparts, strongholds, tuck-ins, gabionades, banks, bourses, temples, cathedrals, churches, chapels, monastries, motels, hotels, hostels, rests, dormitories, skelps, castles, courtyards, prisons and other aquariums and terrariums, government and other palaces, capitols, ministries, magistracies and parliaments, consulates, embassies, taxing authorities, insurance companies, trade chambers, underpathes, subways, forts and ports, airports, terminals, train stations and gas stations, fire stations, police stations, radio stations, post offices, bureaus, customs, archives, registries and powerplants,

burn stadiums, hippodroms, swimming pools and gyms, gymnasiums, schools, colleges, universities and academies, theatres, operas, halls and concert halls, symphonies, dancing halls, gaffs, discos, clubs, pubs, alehouses, inns, saloons, taverns, jukes, bistros, bars, dives, confectionaires, cafés and cafeterias, refectories, canteens, brasseries, pizzerias and trattorias, restaurants, bakeries, casinos, forums, brothels and cinemas, libraries, museums, galleries, studios,

burn laboratories, factories and manufactories, workshops, farms and pharmacies, refineries, distilleries, parfumeries, groceries, tobacconists, kiosks, stalls and other shops, malls and mills, markets and stores,

burn edifices, blocks, skyscrapers, mansions and its gatehouses and warehouses and other residencies, publishing houses and printing houses and water houses, all buildings and premises, villas, garages, orangeries, sheds, barns, pavilions, altans and gardens, parks,

burn construction sites, streets, roads and highways, promenades, maidans, beacons, tunnels and bridges,

burn curias, manors, cottages, shanties, bungalows, cabins, bowers, huts, caravans, hangars, bins, silos, kennels, depots, deposits, storages, staples, stacks, stocks, repositories, conservatories, crematories and cemeteries,

so there is no darkness anymore

this case, may degrade even into the fundamentals of a7)-ability), doesn´t have to mean that he/she will become an artist (a drawer does not equal an artist),

since in order to be an artist he/she must have a developed creativity = i.e.,
a)-ability No. 1 – the matter-of-factual drawing is not necessarily equivalent to

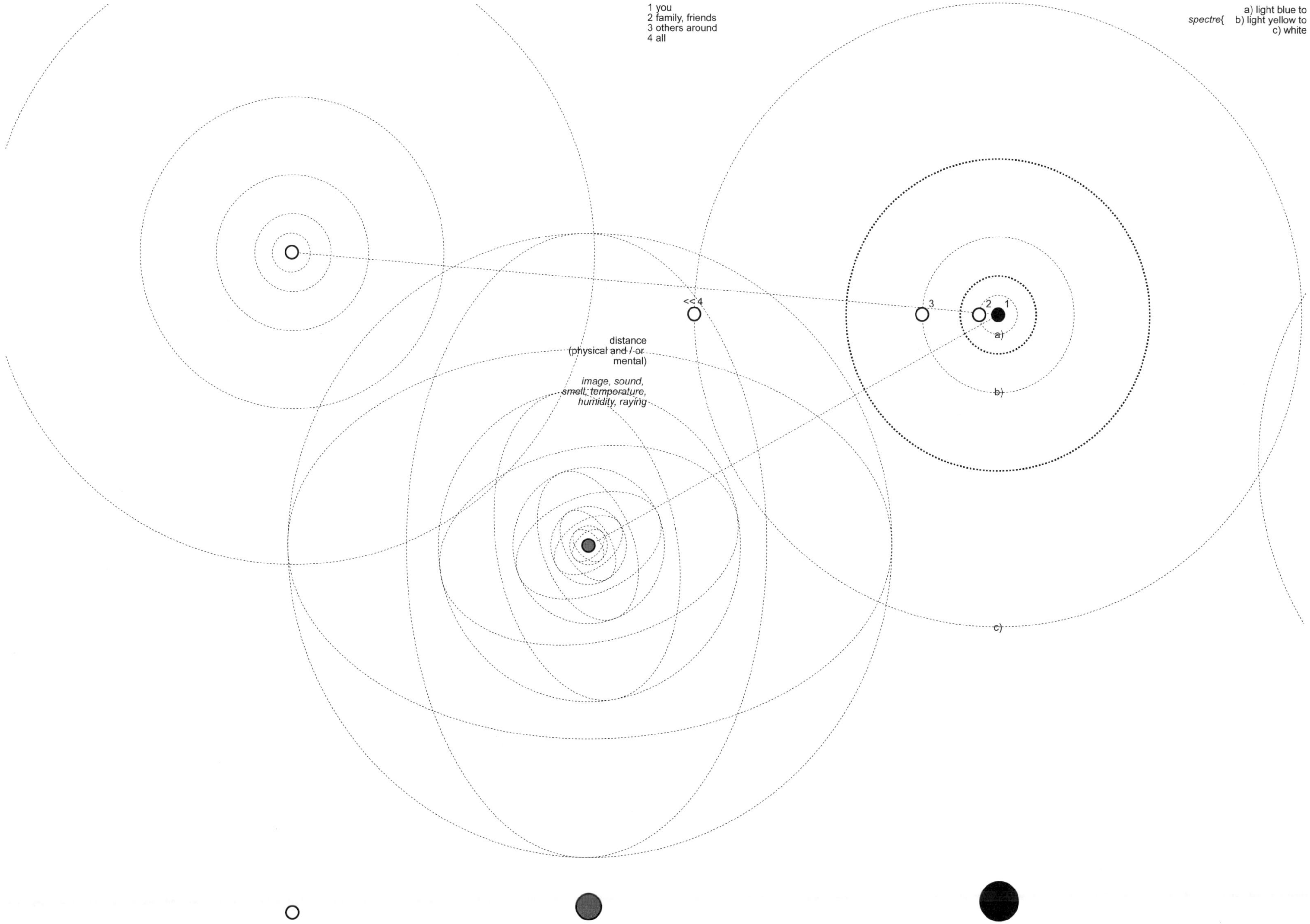

creativity, it can be the sheer “servility of the depicted”, intuition or intellect, enthusiasm for sensual, sensitive and / or intellectual concentration, aesthetic

puma & le coq sportif

feeling and (not necessarily) knowledge of history and presence, theory,
practical skills in techniques and technologies, understanding of operational

principles, the market, etc. and (long-term instrumental) refinement of all that … and be a carrier of the contents and have the inevitable urge and substantial reason and well-developed, trained ability to recast it into communicative forms… oh, oh! Ofttimes, a certain indispensable complement must be

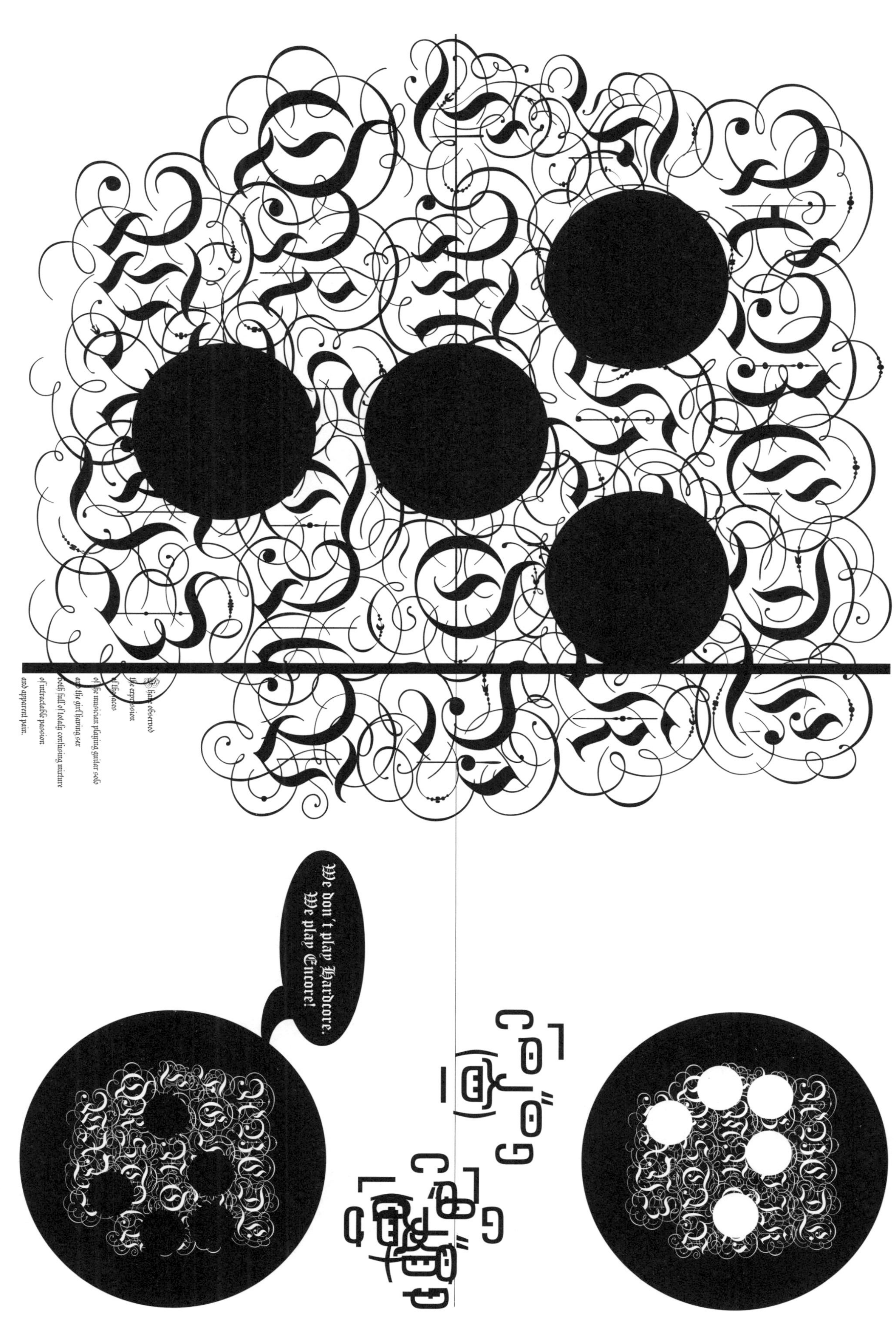

Boris Ondreička, *Alphabethead #2*

elaborated = “bridging” ability = the ability to cover life’s needs, if from an activity of a first-rate interest there comes no satisfactory means for covering

those life needs, which is more than common in the artistic context. (usually:
I teach to earn money for paint, brushes, canvas and studio, and of course for

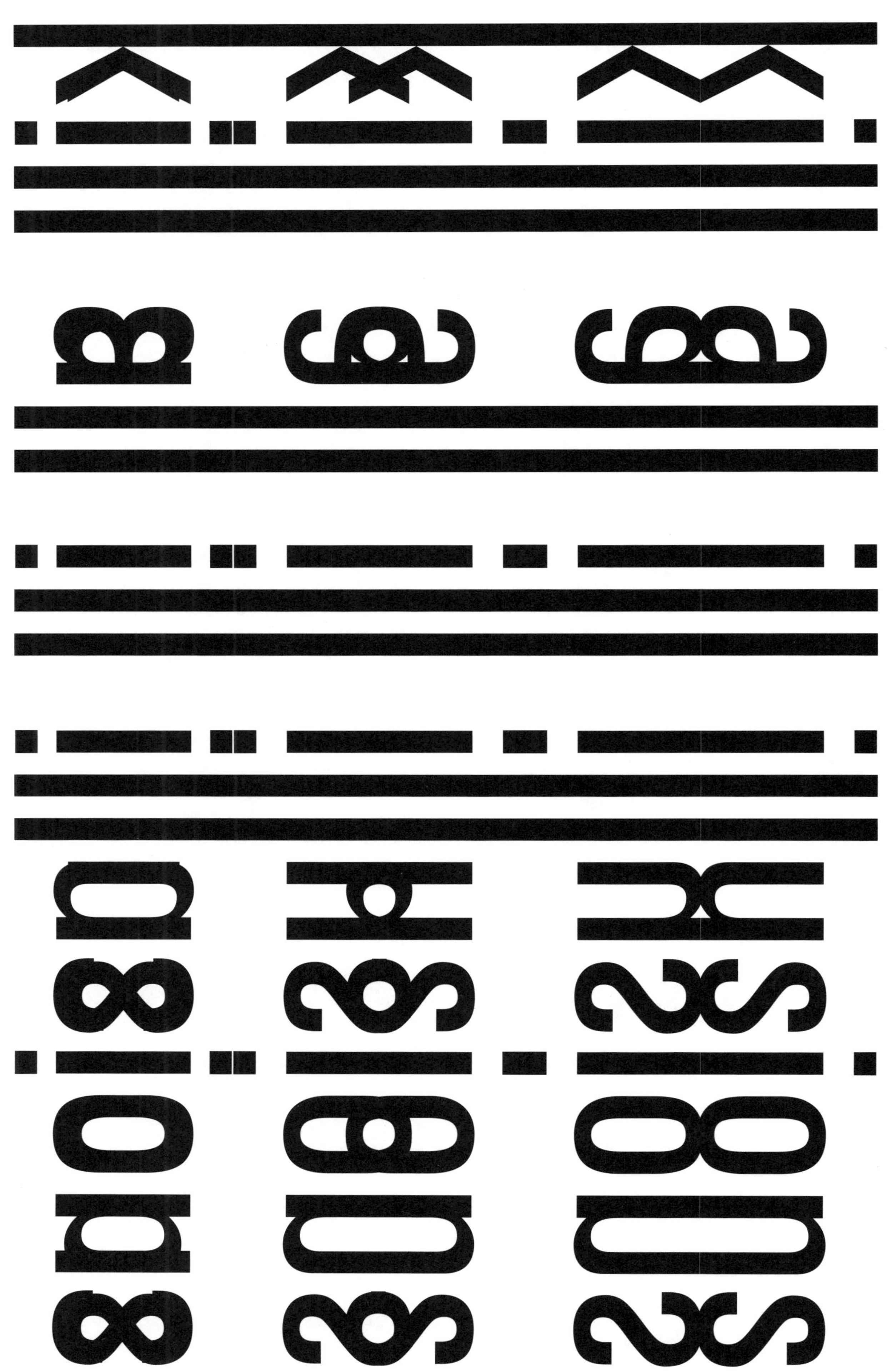

Boris Ondreička, *Illustration*

living… To work for work.) Creativity often meets with a lack of understanding, misinterpretation – negative reaction, if it touches on the transcending of social conventions, non-conformist behaviour and such, which “Art” practically calls forth… Sensorimotor, as the perceiver traditionally, as it dominantly develops in the first 18 months of a child´s life (Most neurons are built halfway through pregnancy. Their function comes about via dendrites and synapses by mutual

Boris Ondreička, *Illustration {To produce this suiting, to sell this suiting, sale-clerk wears suits made of this suiting.}*

energetic exchange. These routes undergo a process of myelinisation – biochemical maturing. In the primary learning period, the brain grows

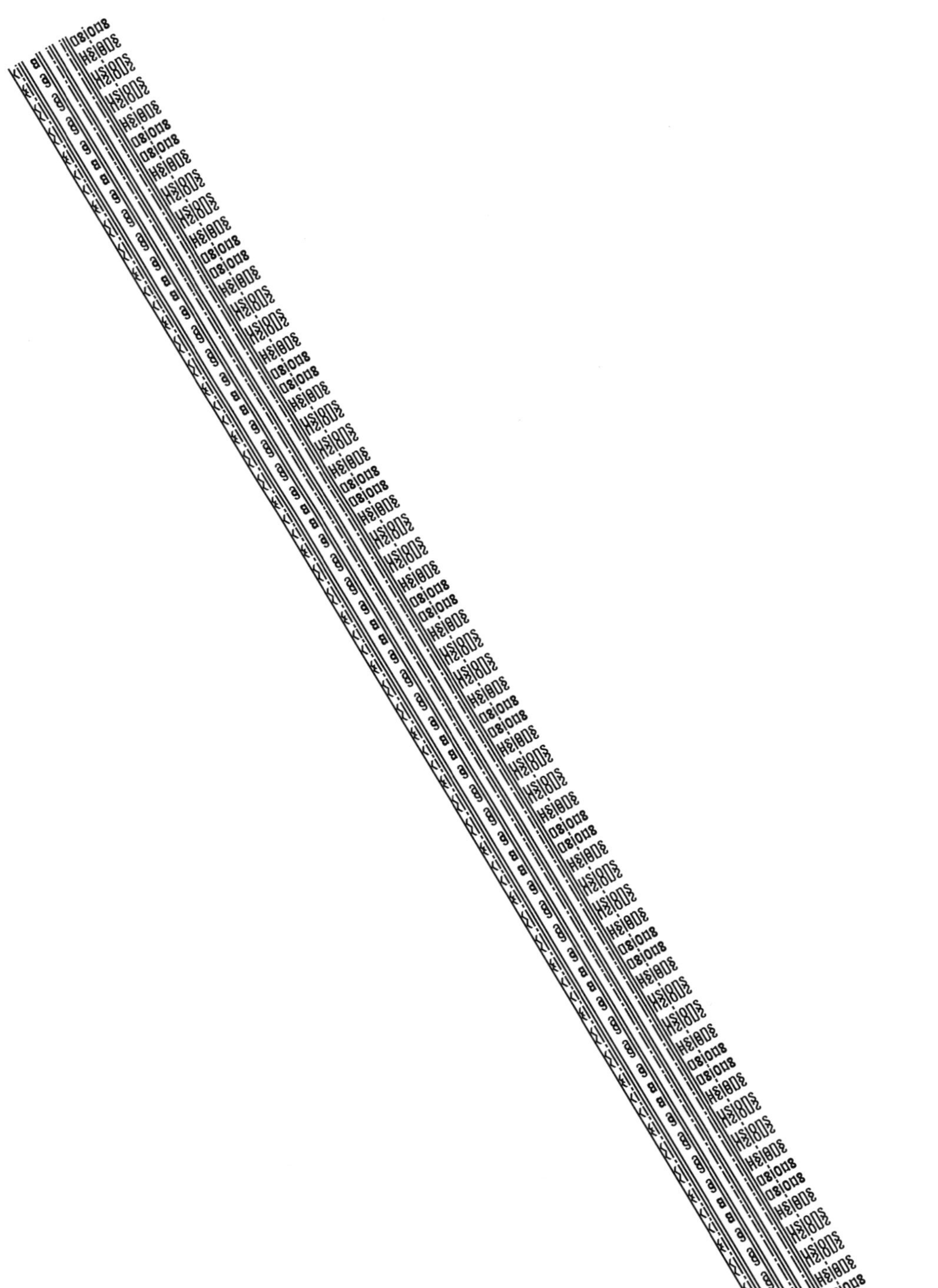

Boris Ondreička, *Illlustration {paint-roller, carpet...}*

explosively: at the end of the first year of life, starting at conception, it has 50 %, at the end of the third year already 80 %. The first 18 months are dedicated to sensorimotor development – a crucial connection between movement and sensual perception. This is a period when repeated experience creates habits and

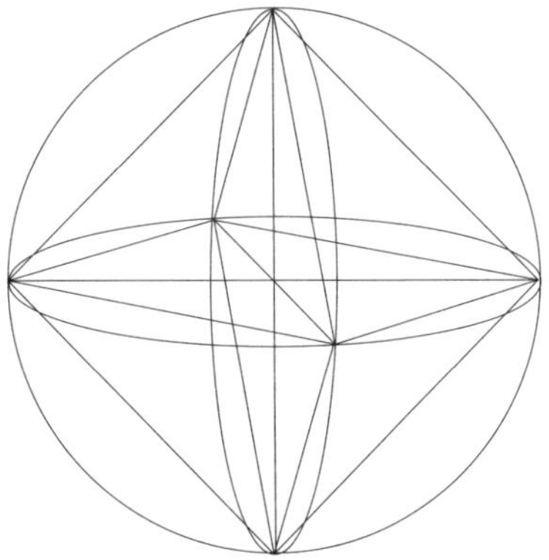

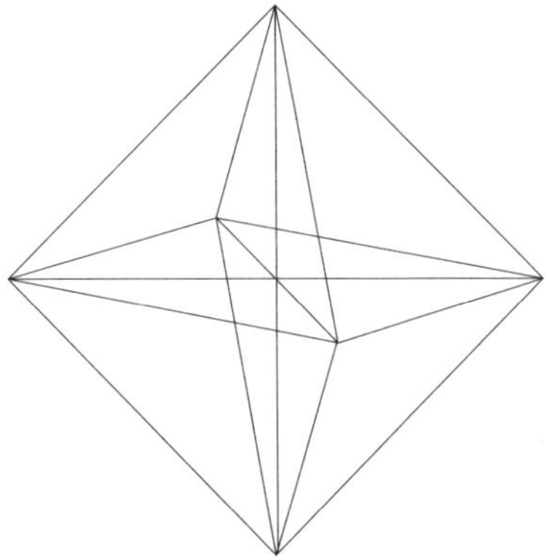

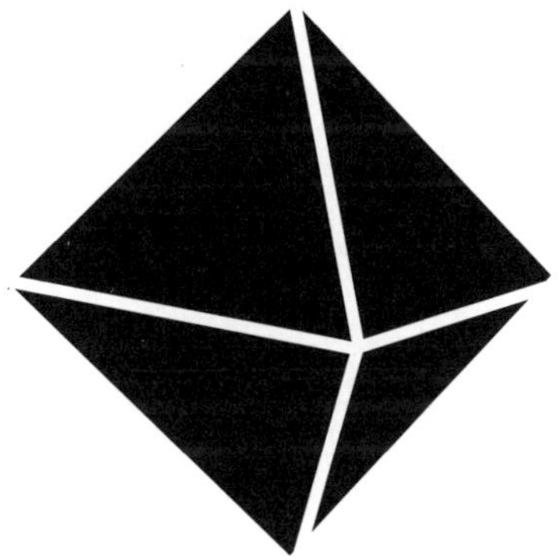

sensomotorics

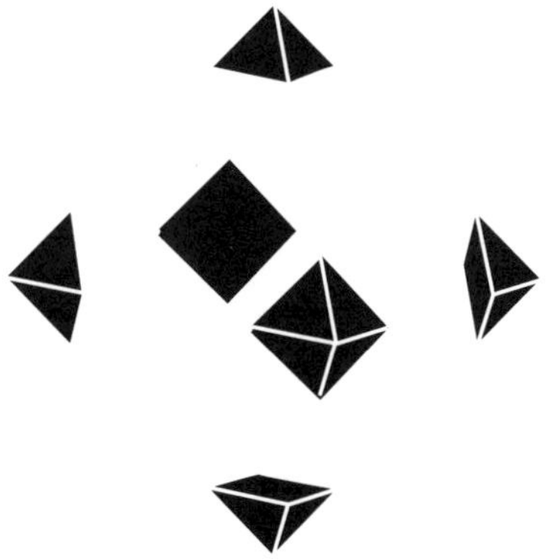

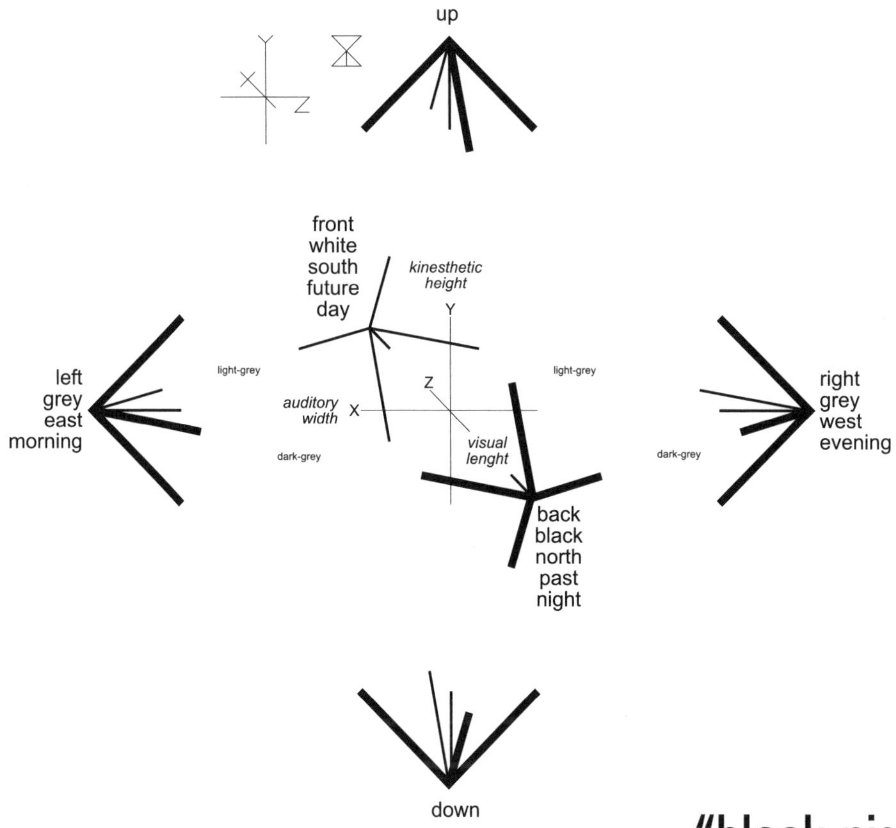

up

front
white
south
future
day

kinesthetic height

Y

left
grey
east
morning

light-grey

auditory width X

Z

visual lenght

dark-grey

light-grey

right
grey
west
evening

dark-grey

back
black
north
past
night

down

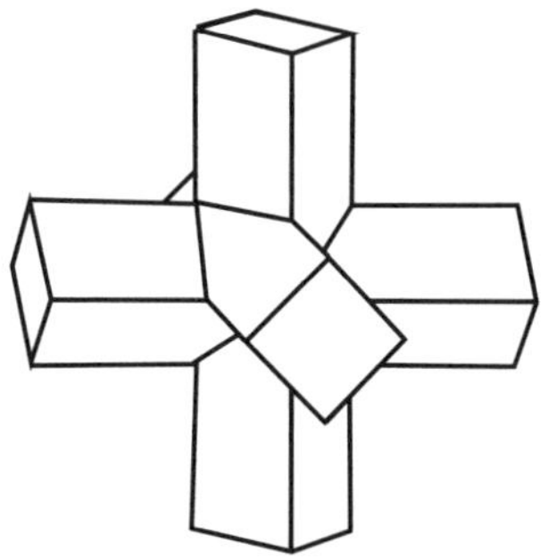

“black night
morning grey
white day
evening grey

back night
morning left
front day
evening right”

Boris Ondreička, *The birth of Poem and its retrograde life.*

attitudes, motivation, curiosity, adaptability, assertiveness..., which speed up the maturation of the entire personality through metabolic processes. This is vital for the later quality of thinking, speech, writing, counting, the ability to love, consideration for freedom, respect... If at this stage a child obtains

All of those liquids of the biggest mine
went through a complicated period
of fermentation,
expecting distillation.

Homme, sweet Homme.

So now,

I am not fruit anymore,

I am an adult alcohol,

to make an alcohol of tears,

finally.

incorrect connections, associations, it influences the physiognomic development of the brain, and consequently the general personal profile. These errancies may become chronic and difficult to eliminate. – according to the simple but excellent Jiřina Prekop & Christel Schweizer, “Unruhige Kinder“, ©1993,

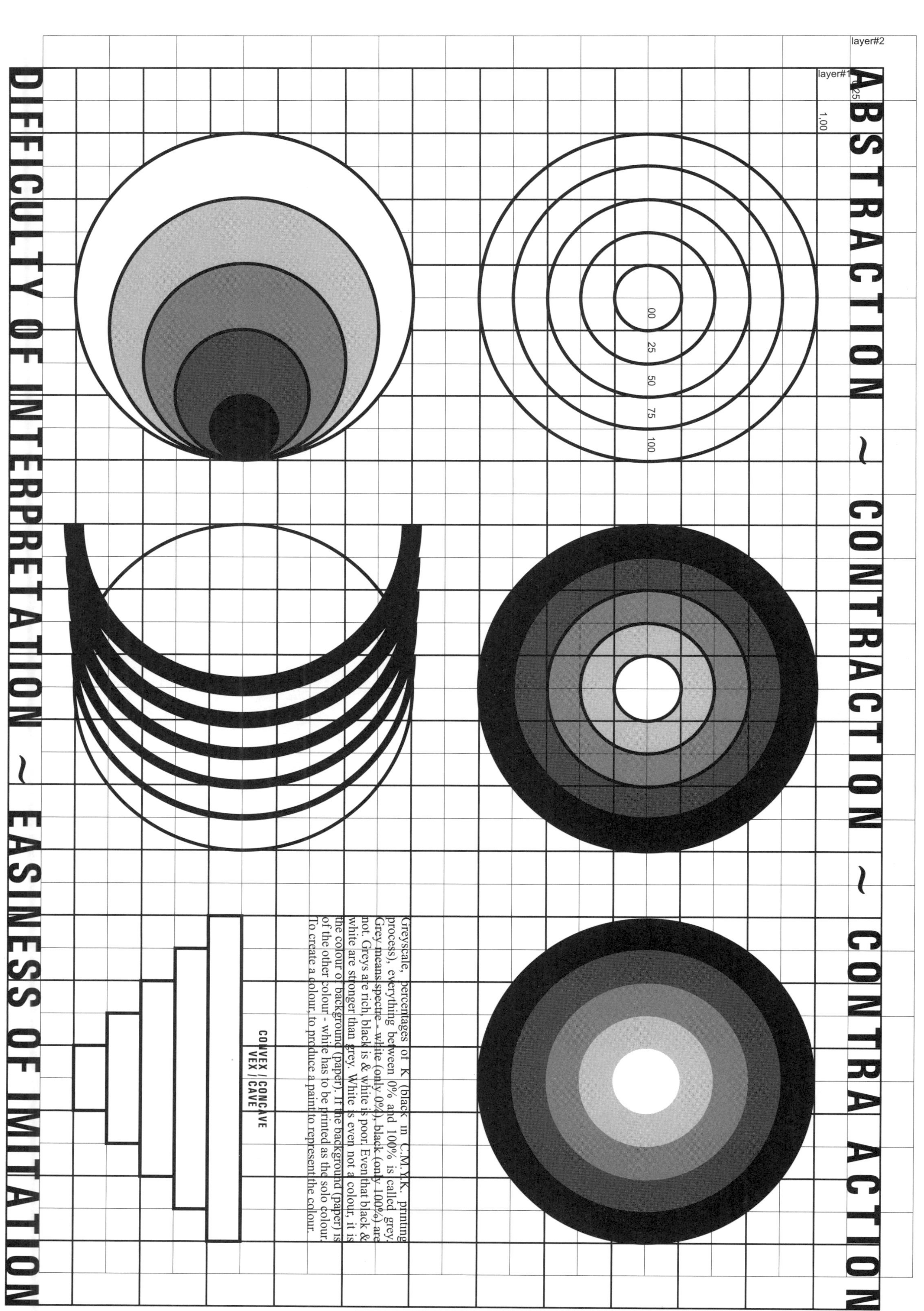

Kösel-Verlag GmbH & Co., Munich, DE, Europe), so it must contain some kind of psycho-social quality = the ability to assess the psycho-social, cultural nature of the surrounding environment, to know when to abstain from voting, when to be for or against. What use to us is “a car when we have it, when we can drive it,

INTERIOR DOES NEED EXTERIOR. EXTERIOR DOES NOT NEED INTERIOR.

EXTIMACY
INTIMACY
OUTIMACY

INTERIOR SURROUNDED BY EXTERIOR

EXDIVIDUAL
INDIVIDUAL
OUTDIVIDUAL

Boris Ondreička, *In & Out*

but we don´t know where to go”? (and even if we know where we want to go, and we will even drive carefully, someone can crash into us, ah...) The situation with the glass that is half-full (and / or) = half-empty illustrates the dilemma of a variety of evaluations, which are dependent ONLY on our own decision,

Let me
introduce myself – I am nameless tuft of dirt
containing hair, dust, rubber band, a – guitar string, micro-
crumbs of bread, cigarette ash, snot, grains of coffee powder and few
grams of something not able to be identified.
I am living in the corner / in the gap between the back of cooking range, floor &
wall. 7 days old.
Other comrades here said: that this is quiet quiet peaceful piece of place with real
chance to live may-be even 50 years long.

It´s nice & warm here – every day new fellows.

Most of us are abstract.

sometimes directly and immediately, without space for reflection or taking counsel with someone; no friend on the phone. Whether the day of birth is

Relish the taste of pure (still) water
not just for a time of swallowing, my dear.

the first day of life or the first day of dying is up to us alone, despite our parents´
attempt to insinuate it even before we are capable of forming opinions ourselves;

Boris Ondreička, *T. P. #6*

which we can not denote as positive or negative. For such a judgement we need much more data... (I have many friends who dislike celebrating their birthdays.)

Well, and this is where this most simple requirement, the basis of self/determination, registration starts to thicken – the fact that we have a gift, a talent

from:

DR.EGG
MON.STR 69
R-999 MISERAVILLE
RESISTIKA
KRITERION

LOCLASS

UNDERGROUND MAIL

ROTEN POSTCARDS PUB_LICKERS. MISERAVILLE. RESISTIKA. KRITERION

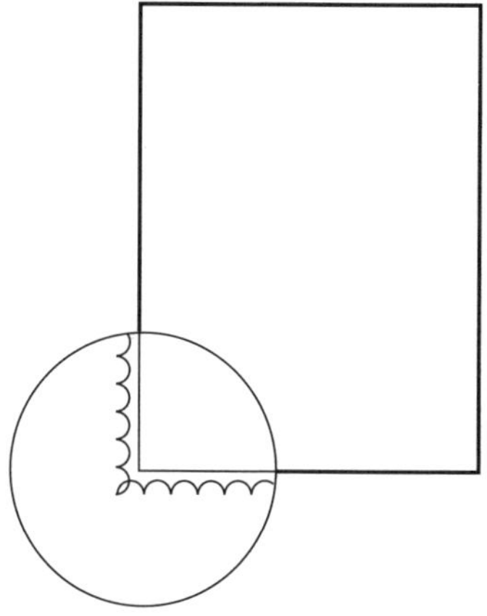

to:

Mr. EGON GRABSTEIN
DEMON.STRAAT 00
A-666 MISANTHROPOLIS
ANTAGONIA
INERTIKA

for “Something” does not yet mean that we want to perform it, maybe we are attracted by “Something Else” and so we decide to perform Something which we do not have such apt abilities for...!!! Not even the fact that we will successfully graduate from an academy means that we should, must, will do it!!!

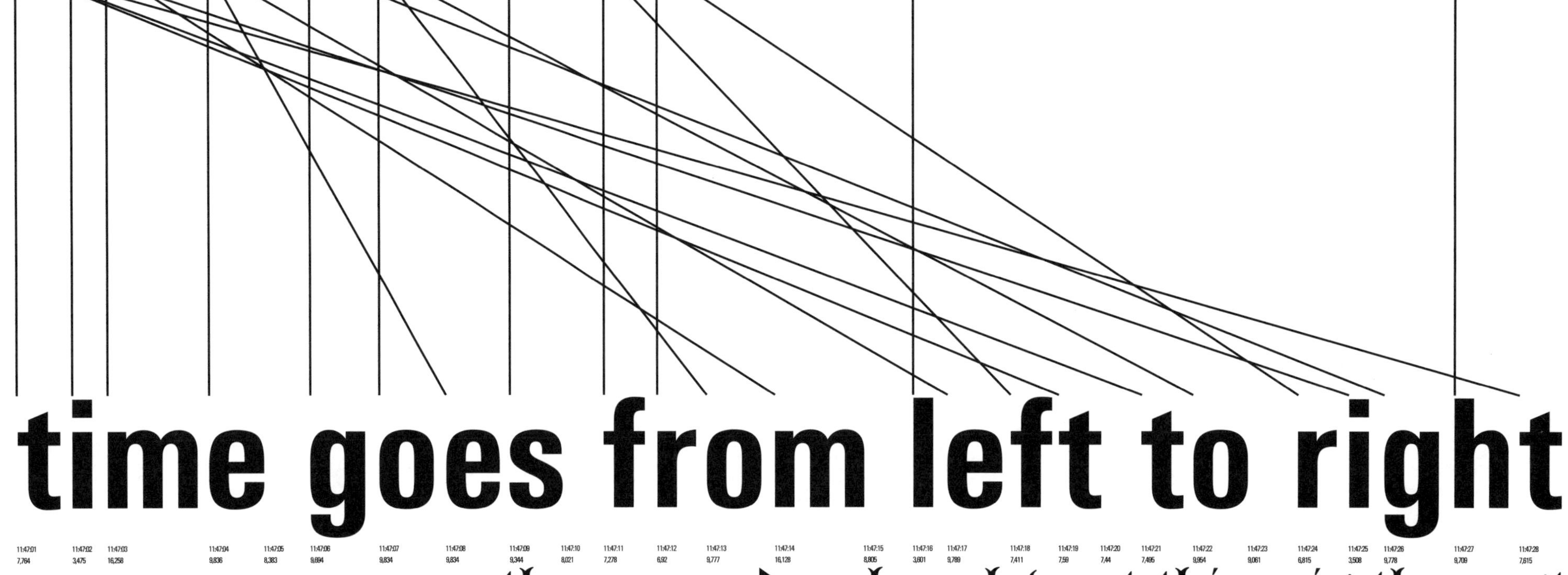

typing = 28 seconds.

each letter,
each gap between words

= each 1 second.

{23 letters / 6 words, 5 gaps}.

time sequence
≠
space sequence,

{= each letter
= different width}.

equal time. / different space.

{gaps between letters automatic
≠ time}.

{gaps between words
= each 1 hit}.

the one and only relevant thing is the past

THE PAST OFFICE

The New York Past

There is no age of definite decision. Therefore, we should take care of children with full endeavour from the very beginning of their lives (some say from conception / others speak of birth). Therefore, all children should, from 3 to 5, 6 to 15, 16 to 17, be compulsorily tested (diagnosed) by a specialised psychologist

amors
feelosophia
multifunctionl polymeanings
anythinking
stereologue
contextomania
(con)txt.o-men.ia)
pro:cess.p(00)l
d"cayde
(D.K.D.)
esc without ctrl
verbalance
(globalanzza)
(globlabla)
understanding
(understanding-dong)
(understandingdong) stand under
inf)initió
(inf.initio)
identific( )tion
circulpa
doomstyx
sepa/ratio
Makrohard 3.000,-
LoTek unltd.)
d)press
d)vision
a)version
cour"h"
r)h
sabot:h
bond"h
his-tO/Ery of trash
remembrane
re/sign
lessness
con)tras/t
per-verse
b(lack)mail

d"mo.b
a.b.solution
yesno & noyes
(yesno)
(noyes)
hard-correct
inhibition
sextra
superotic
feminent
"m"(bra)ce ´z
fee-mail
naivital
rebelité
Sweet Homme
sweet sweat
familitant
mediktat
negazzi
alternazi
ign.or.all
frag.men-t .all
introlerance
modelirivm
U—ROPE
dend (= *dead end*)
lecturno

WARA, WARB, WARC,
WARD, WARE, WARF,
WARG, WARH, WARI,
WARJ, WARK, WARLD,
WARM, WARN, WARO,
WARP, WARQ, WARR,
WARS, WART, WARU,
WARV, WARW, WARX,
WARY, WARZ, WAORM

Universüs
Morbis
Criterion
Planet Exitus
Hormonia
Antagonia
Bastardia
Resistika
Anarchá
Empirium
Re)pub.lick
Utopsia
Empathex
Inertika

Misanthropolis
Miseraville
Ferro.city
Atro.city
Furio.city

N.T.T. s:
city.zen
Ultrans - Herrors / Variours /
Nekrobats / Selective Franx:
Bionfó
Binfó
Boyko
Connot
Mélanchö
Emot
Erös
Torpido
Gangel
Chao
A)men
O)men

(psychologists, to exclude preoccupation) at least every 6 months, since, in addition, particular a)-abilities can occur in different ages pursuant to various impulses, stimuli (work, appreciation...). Such testing contributes to correct decision-making based on self/understanding. Such testing is (logistically,

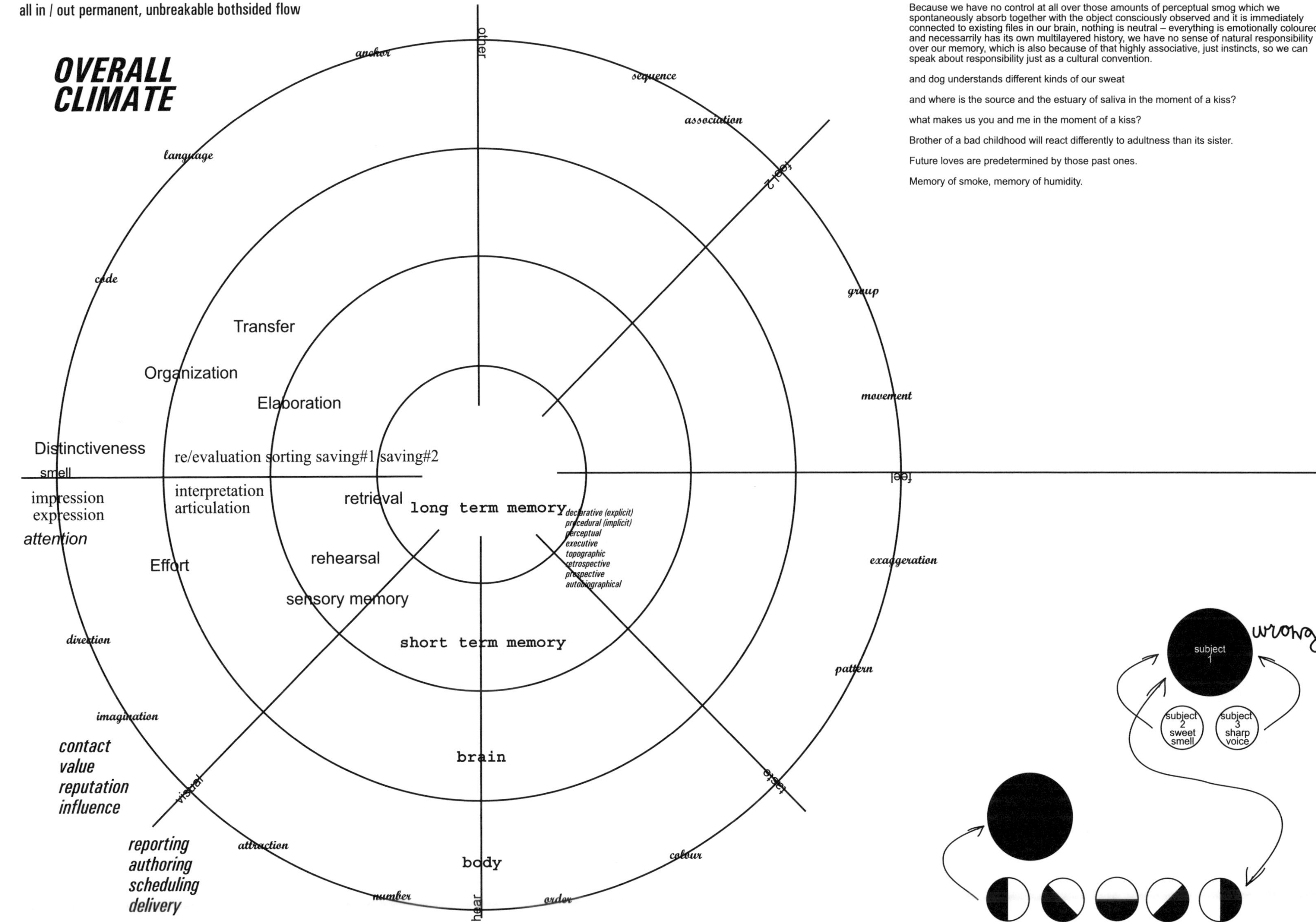

economically...) doable! Thus, we are talking about the unconditional interactivity of parents, pedagogues, school management (and other relevant institutions – social authorities...) psychologists, psychotherapists, neurologists, sociologists, economists, politicians, eventually also sponsors, in order not to

WRITTEN WORLD

SPOKEN WORD

lose excellent individuals – Humankind needs them! The Earth needs them! And personally, furthermore, I am convinced that the pedagogical staff in kindergartens, should be university graduates with specialised teaching qualifications in Developmental Psychology, since they participate in a very

PLAYGROUND SHEET 1/2

ADULT PROPORTIONS | METAL, WOOD, PLYWOOD, SAND, ROPE, PVC (TRAMPOLINE), CONCRETE BASE, GRASS SURROUNDINGS | "BALCONY / BRIDGE" ON THE TOP, WOODEN FLOOR (08-16 / RESP. 27-35 MOVING FLOOR) | "SHELTER / TUNNEL" WITH BENCHES, GARBAGE CANS ETC. ON THE CEILING INSIDE (ASPHALT FLOOR)

01 STAIRS
02 ENTRANCE (NO WALL)
03 CLIMBING ROPE LADDER
04 CLIMBING (HOLES IN THE PLYWOOD)
05 TUNNEL THROUGH (BARRIER INSIDE)
06 SOLID WALL (PAINTED BLACKBOARD GREEN FOR CHALK DRAWING)
07 SOLID WALL (PAINTED BLACKBOARD GREEN FOR CHALK DRAWING)
08 SOLID WALL (PAINTED BLACKBOARD GREEN FOR CHALK DRAWING)
09 CLIMBING (WOODEN LADDER)
10 SOLID WALL (PAINTED BLACKBOARD GREEN FOR CHALK DRAWING)
11 SOLID WALL (PAINTED BLACKBOARD GREEN FOR CHALK DRAWING)
12 TUNNEL THROUGH (BARRIERE INSIDE)
13 SOLID WOODEN WALL
14 EMPTY
15 CLIMBING (HAND RAILS)
16 SOLID WOODEN WALL
17 SOLID WOODEN WALL
18 CLIMBING (ROPE) (NO WALL)
19 TUNNEL THROUGH (BARRIER INSIDE)
20 CLIMBING (ROPE MATRIX)
21 SEESAW C (NO WALL)
22 SILD WALL
23 SLIDE
24 SEESAW C (NO WALL)
25 SOLID WOODEN WALL
26 TUNNEL THROUGH (BARRIER INSIDE)
27 SOLID WOODEN WALL
28 EMPTY
29 CLIMBING (METAL PIPE)
30 SOLID WOODEN WALL
31 TUNNEL THROUGH (BARRIER INSIDE)
32 SOLID WOODEN WALL
33 EMPTY
34 CLIMBING (HAND RAILS)
35 SOLID WOODEN WALL
36 TUNNEL THROUGH (BARRIER INSIDE)
37 SOLID WOODEN WALL
38 SOLID WOODEN WALL
EX 01 SAND
EX 02 TRAMPOLINE
EX 03 SEESAW A
EX 04 SEESAW B
EX 05 MERRYGOROUND
EX 08 DRINKING WATER
EX 09 GARBAGE CAN
EX 10 BENCHES AND TABLES

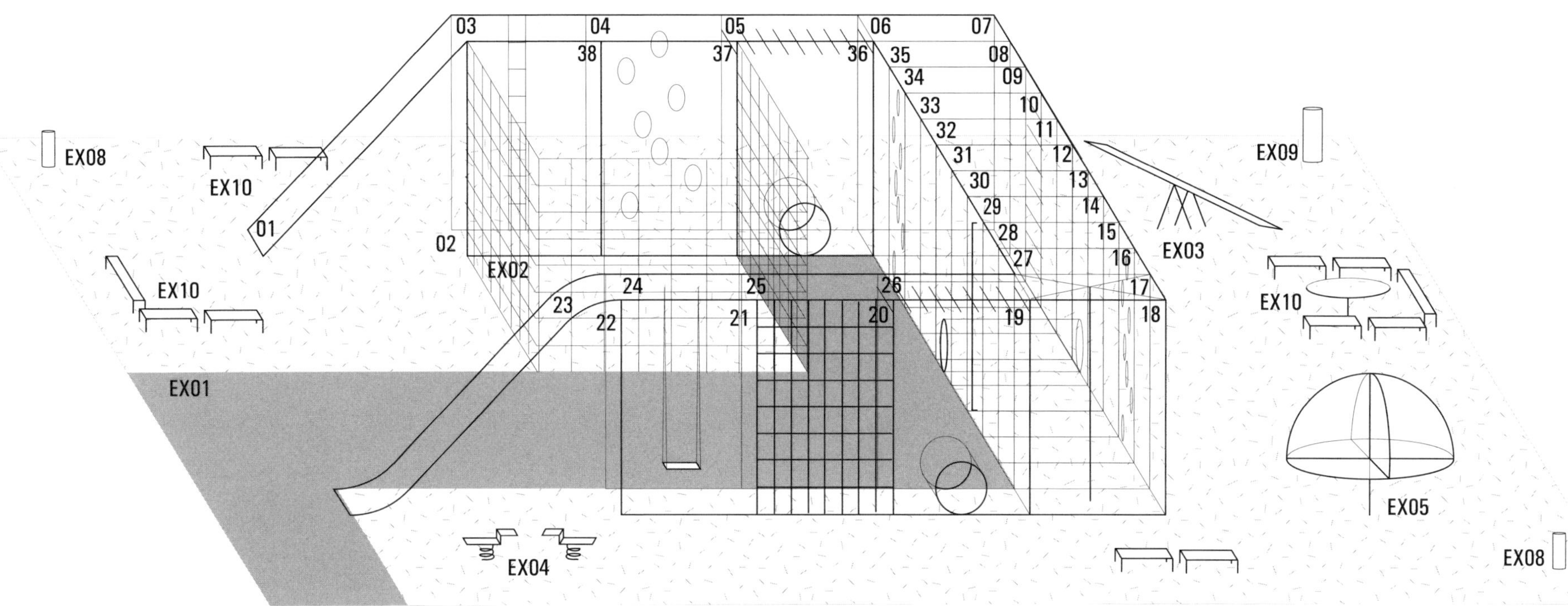

delicate sense to the centrobaric categorisation of children; and then, allowing the parents to be lawyers or nuclear physicians in peace!!!!! Like the synonymic

the street

high wave
new way

= the kingdom of cars, cops and amateurs

analogy between excellent and lonesome, which I mentioned above, also
the children of extreme talent truly have a significantly more limited spectrum

Boris Ondreička, *The street*; incl. *Hi & Nu*

of equal partners (for discourse, for life). When speaking about a minority (mentally diasporic in its own flat, and after hopelessly searching for the bedroom, finding a sink instead of bed), we again talk about the smaller possibility of holding a dialogue with a peer... ...we must help them!!! This seed,

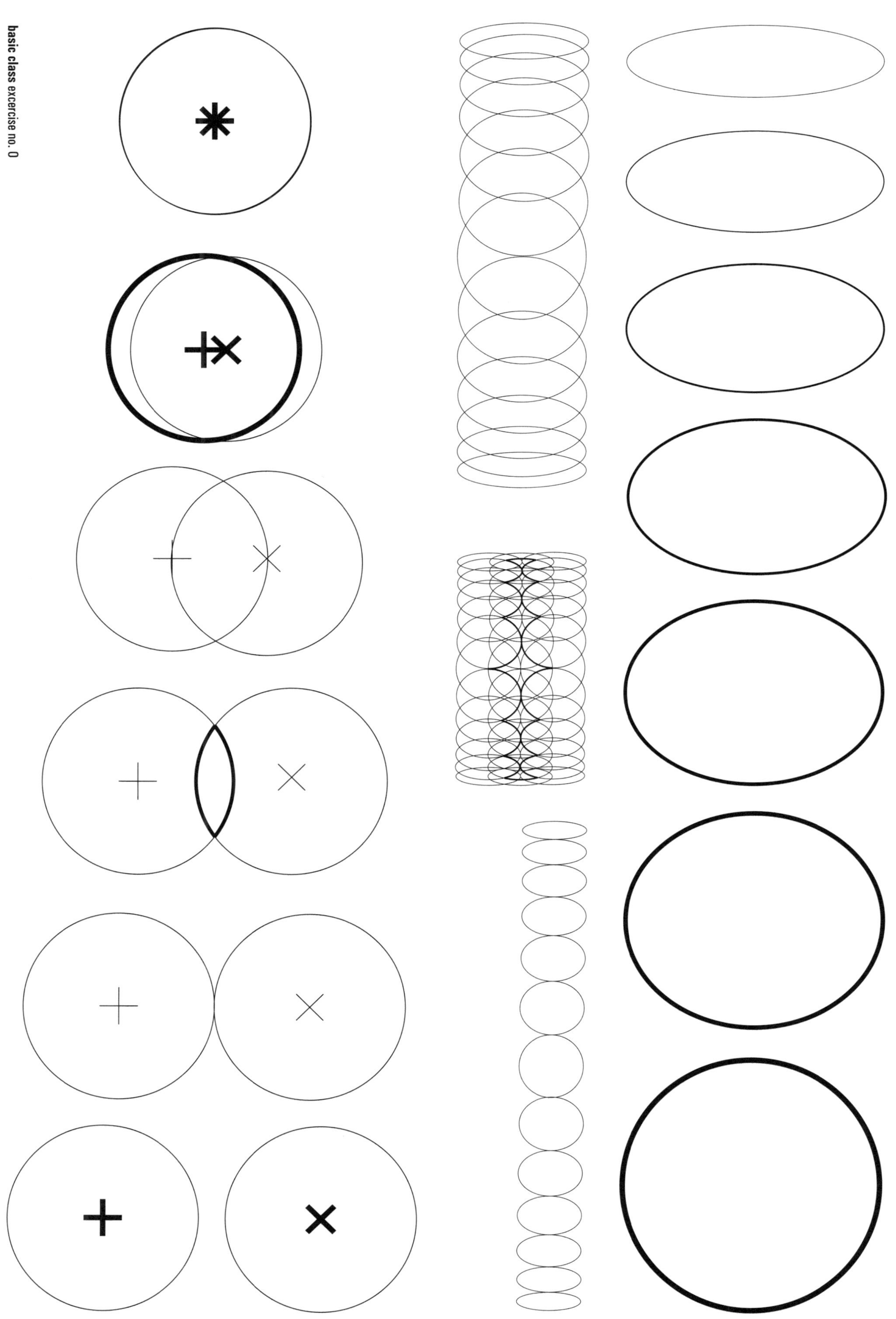

basic class excercise no. 0

Boris Ondreička, *Strobe series*

even if it is of a marvellous quality, is still only potential – without sowing it into good earth and without regular watering, it will not grow (and a cactus

ARTISTGARDENER
Adam damn in the lust fase of
DENTISTCOLLECTOR
Evaporisation - his brain is a ball in
POLICEMANMODELLER
polystyrene structure. The basic body
TEACHERFISHERMAN
is a disinfected crap of lump 181cms
SINGERMUSHROOMPICKER
under the ground in the left middle of
ACTORSWIMMER
dead field of consideratisation. U feels
MINERCOOK
those holes pores in it made by mental
COOKSKATER
insects penetrate this matter
DRIVERDIVER
a fact - building homes.

needs different soil, different care, a different climate than an orchid. And yes, palms can grow even in Finland, but WE have to create Africa-like conditions for them; which is doable!), it will dry out on the surface of its partner´s lap; and there is also a slow sperm, however superbly fertile in its essence, but incapable

of reaching a first-class egg... and vice versa. And a puppy cannot be conceived
in the infertile days of a bitch, or it can even have fertile days, but it doesn't

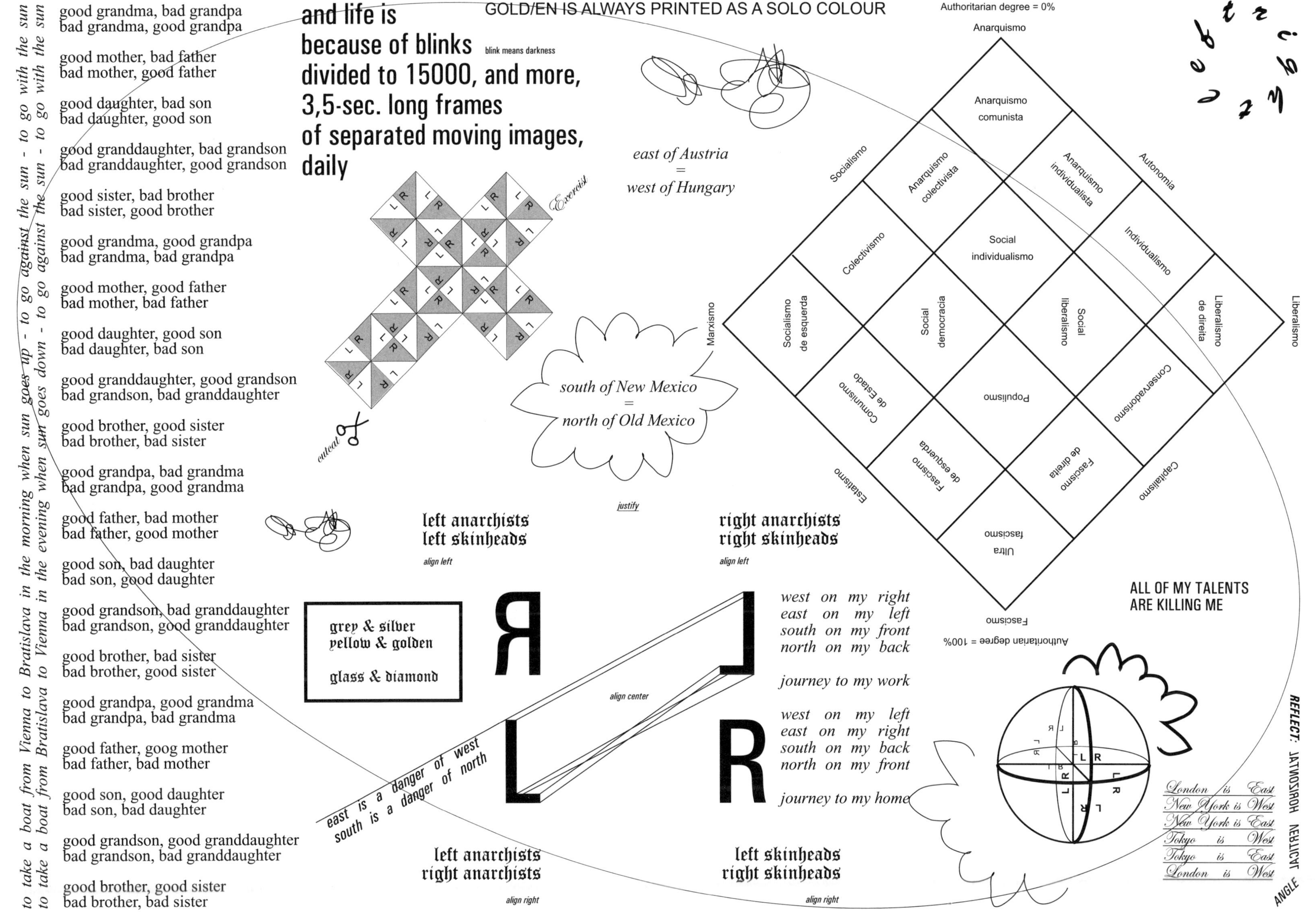

have to like this particular dog... and the story of Viagra, which was initially designed as a heart medication and now, those for whom it was originally intended – people with heart conditions, cannot take it. They cure the skin, when they are supposed to treat lungs and actually, a fixation from childhood. A smile,

She is so beautiful.
So silent.
So slim.
So slow.
So-so.

So-so.

a grimace, a smiling cramp, a smiling refusal. “Extremely talented” is identical to minority and Minorities must be protected by the Majority!; the only problem remaining is that there is nothing like One Majority – that is merely a view from a distance, majority is also just a generalisation of plentiful fragmented plurals

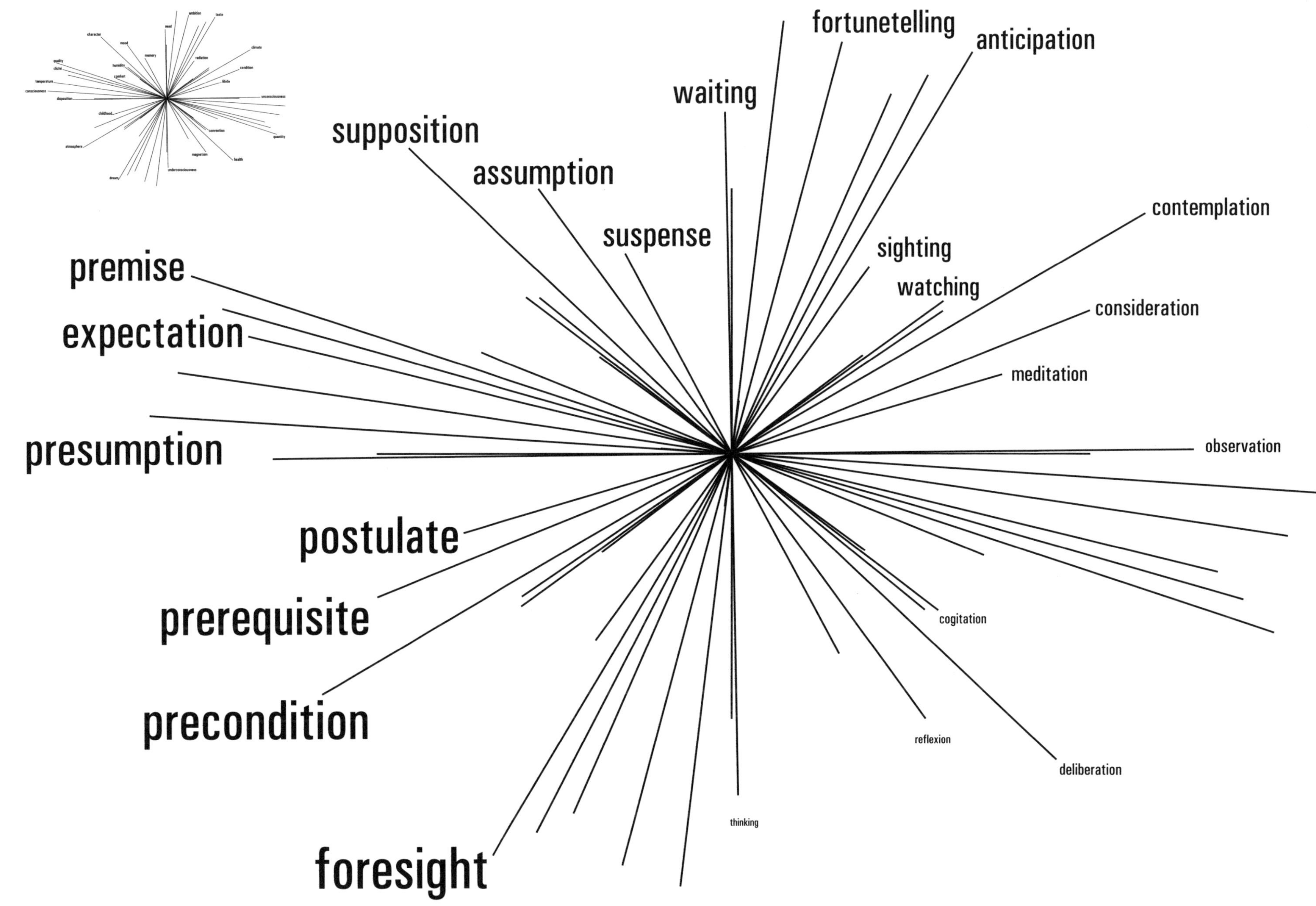

connected by loyalty to conventions. And if we refer to majorities, then we speak about numerous possible opinions, hence about very probably pending

THE HOME IS THE HOUSE IS THE TRAP.

Keep the door closed,
I wants to sleep.

discord. So, we don´t talk about plurality only in the sense of one quantification, because various numbers bring along diverse constellations towards one given

Boris Ondreička, *Home*

space, that means different reactions, groups of solutions, source exploitation, demand for coordination and control of single common source utilisation...

A concert with 50 visitors to a club with a capacity of 500 requires altered logistics than 1500 visitors, who are trying to get inside the same venue. I must,

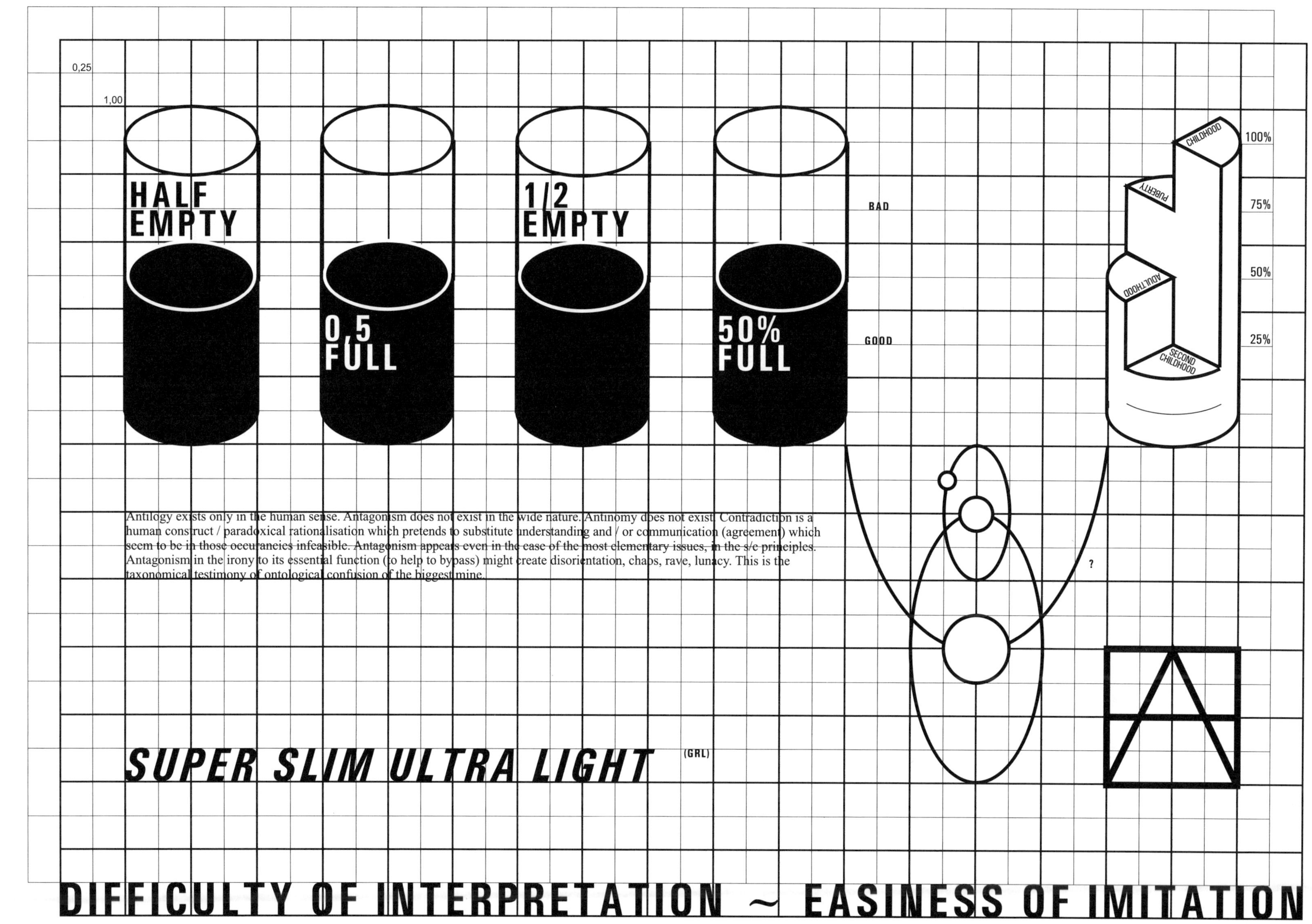

however, mention that even though I am personally acting so moderately in this dissertation in praise of education, I do not believe in the implicit, compulsory,

irreplaceable significance of studies or the educational system... A meaning
superordinate to all (apart from biological necessities) is to find one´s own –

to do

to do

to do to do to do to do

to do to do to do to do

to do to do to do to do to do to do to do to do
to do to do to do to do to do to do to do to do
to do to do to do to do to do to do to do to do
to do to do to do to do to do to do to do to do

to do to do to do to do to do to do to do to do
to do to do to do to do to do to do to do to do
to do to do to do to do to do to do to do to do
to do to do to do to do to do to do to do to do
to do to do to do to do to do to do to do to do
to do to do to do to do to do to do to do to do
to do to do to do to do to do to do to do to do

personal means of happiness and I am truly aware of the fact that someone can find it being a goatherd!!! !!!!!!!!!!!!!!!!!!!!!!!!!

!!! all his/her life. And, of course!, even without self-knowledge one can survive, no

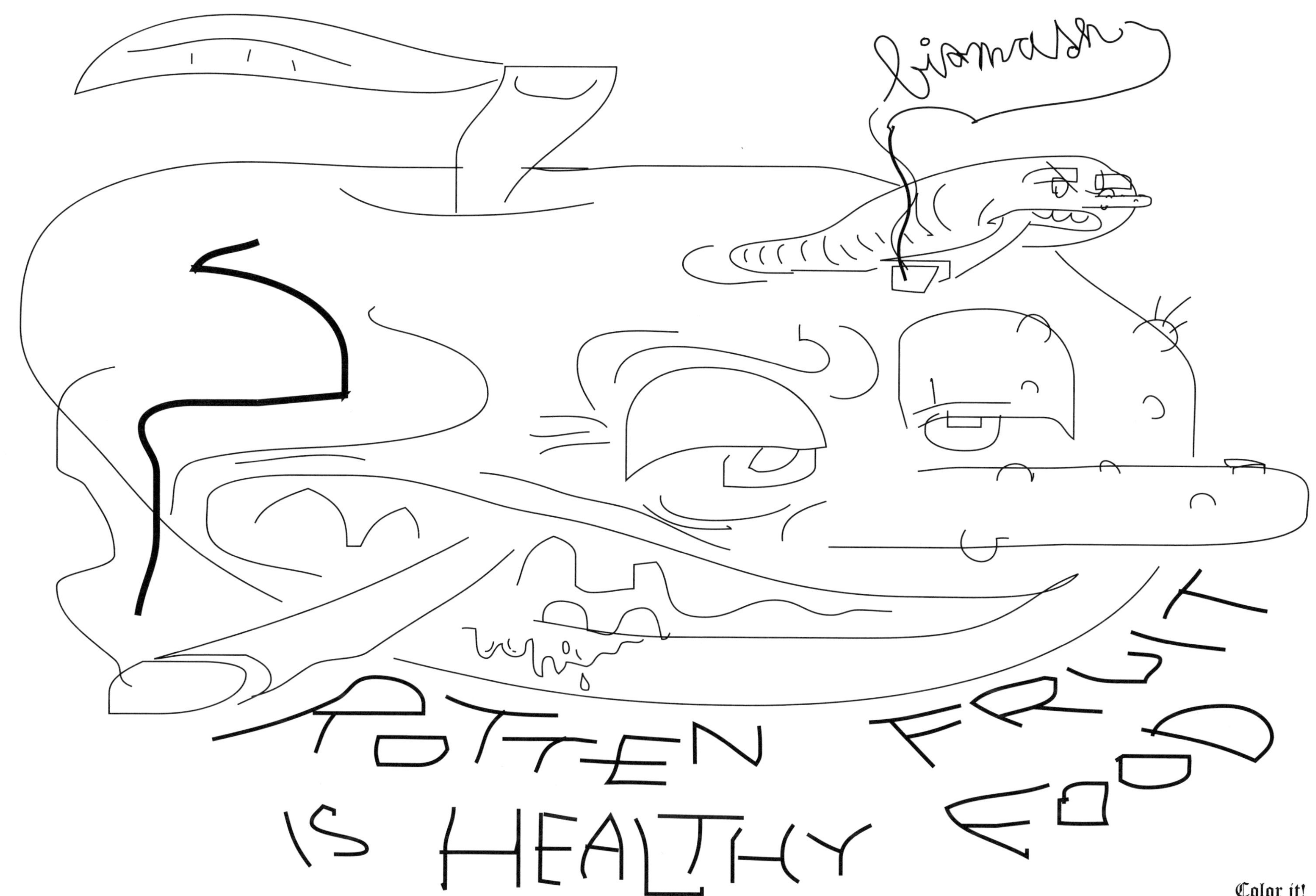

Color it!

problem! And experience real joys inside a great loss – exactly like when children are born in times of war, or a young chimp born this year in the Bratislava ZOO does not know the reality of jungle. And amorousness is not necessarily love, so what? And minority versus elite? Homeless ≠ Billionaire.

"THE COORDINATES OF THE CONTAINER AND ITS CUBAGE ARE NOT IDENTICAL SO IT IS IMPOSSIBLE TO DEFINE THE PRECISE POSITION. TRANSACTION WENT HAZARDOUS, STOP COMMUNICATION, ALFRED*!"

*HITCHCOCK

(and we, artists are only lumpen – proletariat by day; in the evening we change without changing into high-society. The Oligarchy, bourgeoisie, aristocracy have always romantically welcomed us at their mundane banquets – unkempt clowns in ragged trousers stained with paint, Ooh, how exciting!!!, the legal slackening

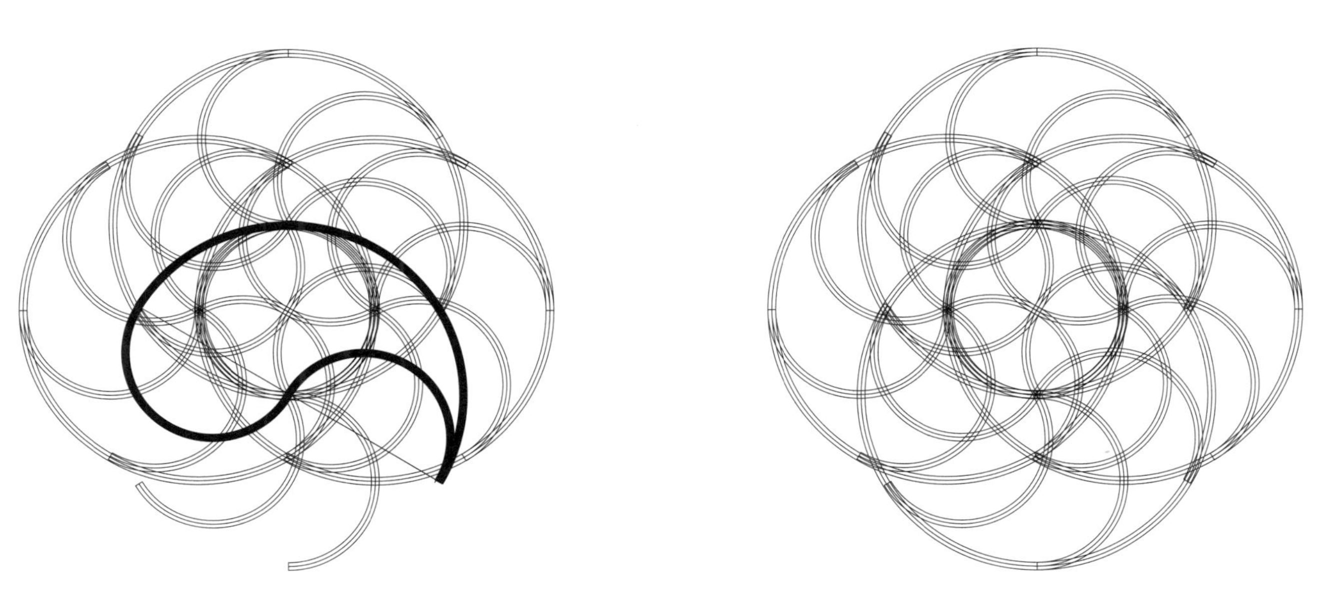

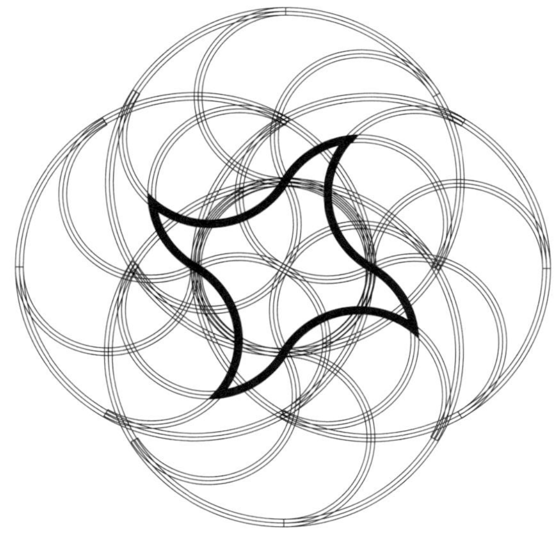

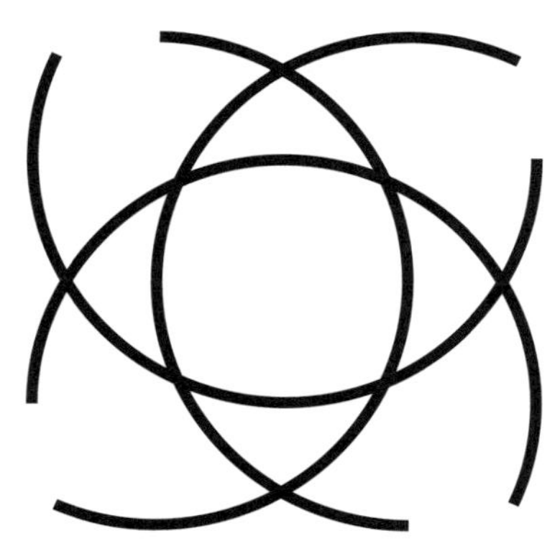

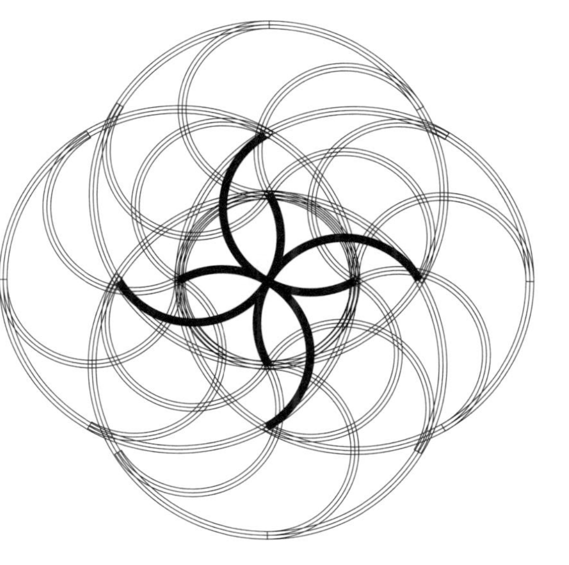

– of Freedom mascots / Independence masquerade – through the longed for smelliness of our unshaved armpits and the desired pong of our cigarette teeth to

Boris Ondreička, *Strobe series*

mélanchö inertika ben egon grabstein thu. sept. 06 2003 01:15am raining +18°c 26 years old female 178cm 95-58-88cm 55kg slovak jewish converted protestant sergeant detective (murder dept.) lecturer on police academy no kids - 1 abortion (9 years ago) single daughter of philosopher († 1999 at age 51) and stewardess (47 still single) no grandparents († 1999 99 95 89) kick-boxer ta-i-chi chuan swimmer 1st-class driver perfect gunner malboro lights smoker (45 per day) mineral water and red wine drinker english german french hungarian russian languages vegetarian healthy alone naked hungry tired cold lethargically standing still a bit straddled saying nothing crying in her 200x300x350cm light yellow walls sleeping room +27°c closed northern window opened door ikea mörkedal - sultan norrsken bed switched-on antifoni lamp stelton ashtray incl. 2 malboro lights 1 benson&hedges reg. bugs ronson lighter panasonic rx-ds 25 vol. 32 is it because #05 lena fiagbe visions © 1994 mother rec. cd siemens tel. CSI5 (3 room appartment 2nd floor of 4 floor house /8 flats/ the center of nyc-ny-usa) on wooden floor (no carpet) flawlessly oval head superb wallnut brown long straight hair lovely symmetrical face 1 wrinkle on marvellous forehead amazing black eyebrows thorough azure blue almond eyes astonishing long black eyelashes blue cd shades tetter on temple rash and teardrop on left chick small nose 2 earing holes in both tiny ears gorgeous lips red ysl lipstick white teeth 1 dental deficiency in right lower molar scale lower-left wisdom tooth out scar on right jaw wart and his (5th one) saliva on chin dia 2cm butterfly red black tattoo on back of neck ivory chest chill on prodigious breasts no. 6 dia 5cm dark-red stupendous nipples slim graceful waist firm sweet belly piercing in gentle navel traces made of bra on shoulders strong arms slender forearms no hair in armpit scar on right elbow silver bracelet on noble wrist generous hands long-long sublime fingers 1 24k white golden ring incl. little ruby on left forefinger nails painted pearl-white polish dark-brown hair in moisturized crotch pink tender privyparts contradicted vagine cracking redolent lap solid accomplished buttock even back dia 0,5cm light-brown birthmark under left shoulder blade beautiful hips 100cm long legs dried sperms of 34 years old white male on internal side of wonderful right thigh crust on left knee smoothly shaved neat calfs swollen but subtle ankles cold silky feets stiffed tenuous toes nails painted pearl-white polish miracle by lancôme

breathe fresh air, but only from 7PM to 9PM. Per mille, Hyper-heterogenic Per Mille. No, of course, not even an artist, like any other professional company means “good”, nor a doctor, nor a priest, but not even stinky, or drunk, in truth, we drink more non-fizzy mineral water than absinth, in order not to miss some

interesting interview or other lucrative profit... a Secession Sponsoring Dinner)
So, in generalisation, we are talking about the essential collaboration of

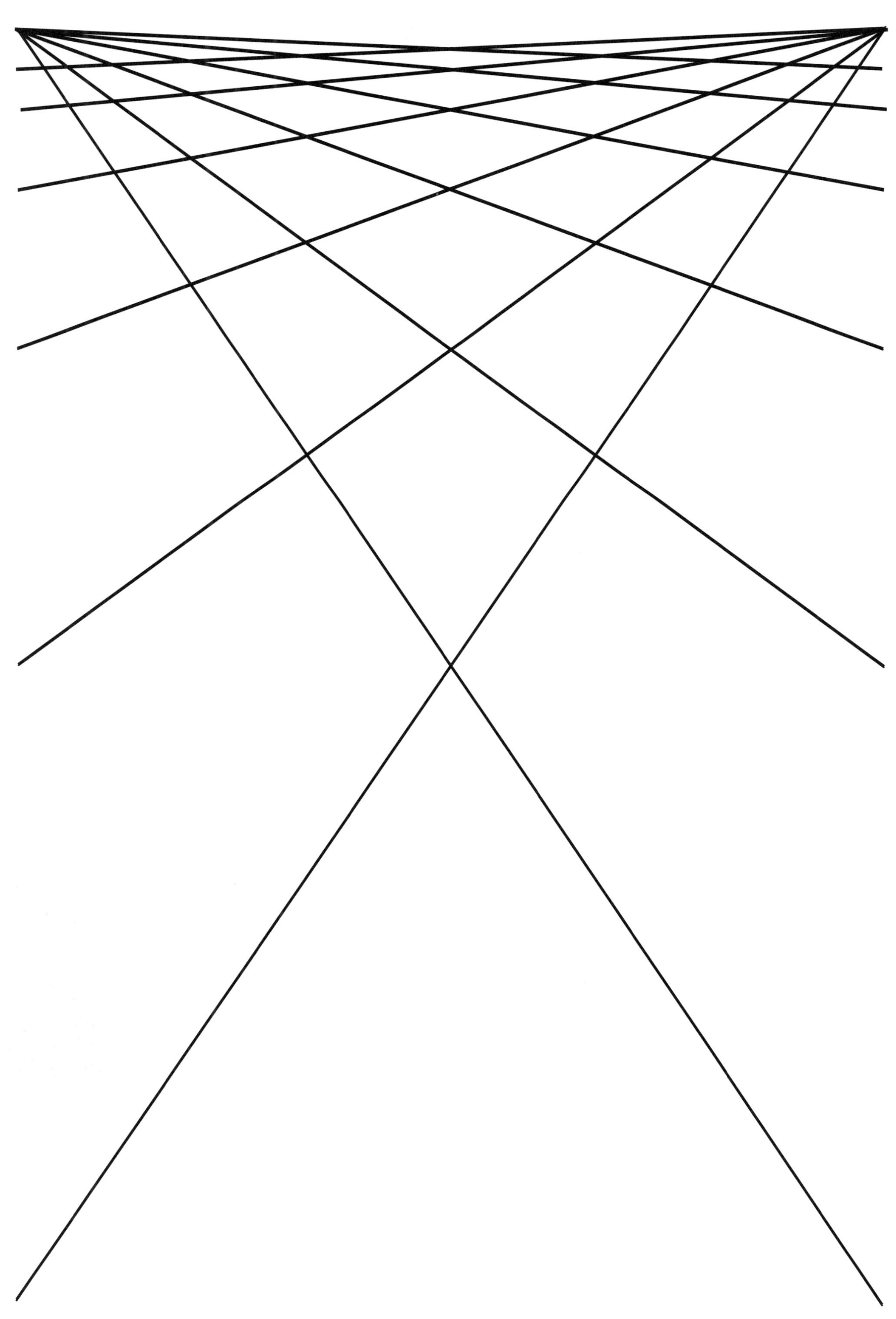

Boris Ondreička, *Half & half & half & half {tiles, floors, grates...}*

pluralities, the synergy of diverse areas, different professions, disciplines, institutions, competences and abilities. We are speaking about polyphony, polyhistory. (Plato, Socrates, Hippocrates, Johann Sebastian Bach, Mikhail Bakhtin, James Joyce, Samuel Beckett, Leonardo Da Vinci? Peter Paul Rubens?

TO
GET
HER

Werner Heisenberg? Herbert Marshall McLuhan? Jan Smuts? David Bohm & M. I. Sanduk? Wolfgang Koehler, Max Wertheimer, Kurt Koffka, Fritz Perls,

Karl Lashley, Aron Gurwitsch, Maurice Merleau-Ponty, Kurt Goldstein, Alfred
Adler, Edgar Morin, Mel Levine, Charles R. Schwab, Pierre Marie, Paul Broca,

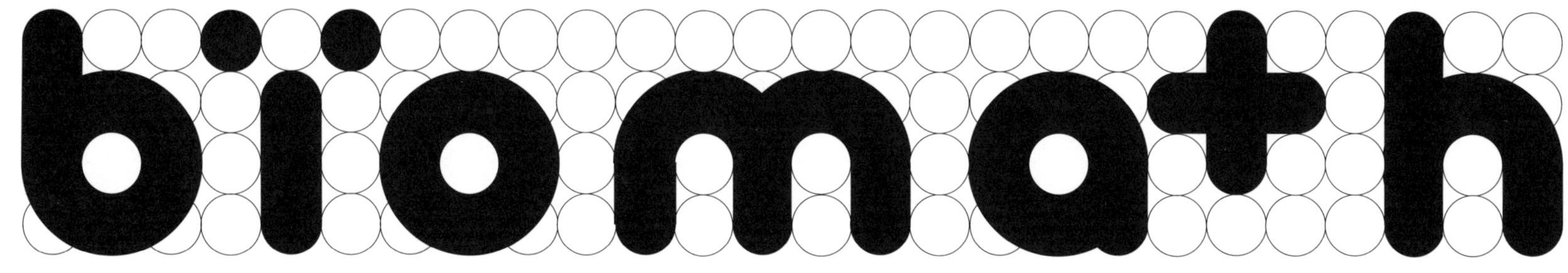

incl. PSYCHMATH
and PHYSMATH

Henri-Louis Bergson, Jean Piaget, Lev Vygotsky, Urie Bonferbrenner, Albert Bandura, Erik Erikson, J. B. Watson, B. F. Skinner, Lawrence Kohlberg, John

Stiles, Richard Miles, Mary Major, Richard and Jane Roe, John Noakes?) Thus,
in total, though in maximum reduction (or, for example, just very briefly, I pay

- FOR SO LONG
- I WAS TRYING TO FIND A COURAGE
- TO INTRODUCE MYSELF TO YOU,
- EVEN WE KNOW EACH OTHER VISUALLY,
- ALREADY.
-
- SO I DO SO TONIGHT.
-
- AND I KNOW THAT THE DARKEST PINS OF YOUR PUPILS WILL ANSWER:
-
- “YES.”
-
- AND WE WILL LEAVE THIS PUB,
- SO NOBODY REALISES THAT WE GO OUT TOGETHER.
-
- AND WILL MAKE LOVE AND/OR JUST HAVING A TALK
- UNDER THE OPEN SKY
- ON THE BANK OF A LAKE
- UNTIL THE MORNING.
-
- AND WHEN THE FIRST RAY OF IT WILL APPEAR
- I WILL DRINK A BOTTLE OF LAPHROAIG AND YOU THREE OF MOËT & CHANDON.
-
- THEN WE WILL JUMP
- TO THAT DEEP WATER
-
- AND WE WILL SINK DOWN AND DIE
- WITHOUT WRITING A WORD OF GOODBYE,
-
- SO OUR DEATH
- WILL LOOK LIKE AN ACCIDENT,
-
- SO OUR LOVE
- WILL STAY AS IT SHOULD STAY,
-
- SO IT WILL NOT TURN TO BE JUST THE DUTY OF SOLIDARITY,
-
- SO THERE WILL BE NO AWAKING
-
- IN DISAPPEARING.
-
-
-
-
-
-
-
- THIS IS NOT EVEN BREATHING ANYMORE. AIR ON ITS OWN ALREADY ENTERED MY VEINS. 1989.

attention to the unnecessary psychological quality of the environment of adolescence, even "Christ´s boundary, but not! eccentric or phantasmagoric

story", escape as far as heaven, and similar) because if I want to formulate
something within bearable comprehensibility, which I do, because I want to be

$ocmath

incl. ECONOMATH
POLITMATH
and CULTUROMATH

LESSON 001:
producing
photography of architecture

Does U see dead profashional smile?
This is the final form of rejection!

... landscape
...

in reality
... realism
... visualisation
... reaction
... fashion
... trend
... globalisation
... aesthetics
... ethics
... history
... competition
... nature
... taste
... moment
... momentum
... idea
... conception
... vision
... morality
... motion
... dynamics
... abstraction
... expression
... metaphor
... intelect
... ratio
... construction
... projection
... association
... empathy
... belonging
... coexistence
... exchange
... exploration
... discovery
... temperature
... climate
... conditions
... weather
... humidity
... stress
... topography

interested in traffic
... mechanisms
... arts
... carriere
... profit
... income
... framing
... communication
... conflicts
... values
... perception
... understanding
... function
... modernity
... ontology
... street
... city
... surface
... distance
... sensuality
... logics
... logistic
... education
... resistance
... dreams
... intimacy
... hierarchy
... order
... planning
... strategy
... memory
... influence
... power
...fixation
... disaster
... demolishing
... destruction
... earthquake
... attack
... articulation
... interpretation
... pronunciation

interested in architecture
interested in photography

interested in space
interested in time
interested in mathematics
interested in geometry
interested in composition
interested in light
interested in forms
interested in color
interested in situation
interested in representation
interested in atmosphere
interested in economy
interested in politics
interested in transformation
interested in inhabitants
interested in stereotypes
interested in habits
interested in traditions
interested in roots
interested in history
interested in separation
interested in division
interested in alienation
interested in relations
interested in consequencies
interested in coherences
interested in coincidences
interested in translation
interested in interactivity
interested in interdisciplinarity
interested in cooperation
interested in exploitation
interested in materials
interested in technology
interested in techniques
interested in dimensions
interested in labour
interested in continuity
interested in backgrounds

CAUSAL

Boris Ondreička, *Socmath*

heard, because you have that urging spur that your message contains the gravity of diffusion, then it has to limit, simplify – IT CLAIMS that any constructive human activity (since, of course, there is also the automatic performance of simple biological needs, when we do not realise that the vessel has been filled

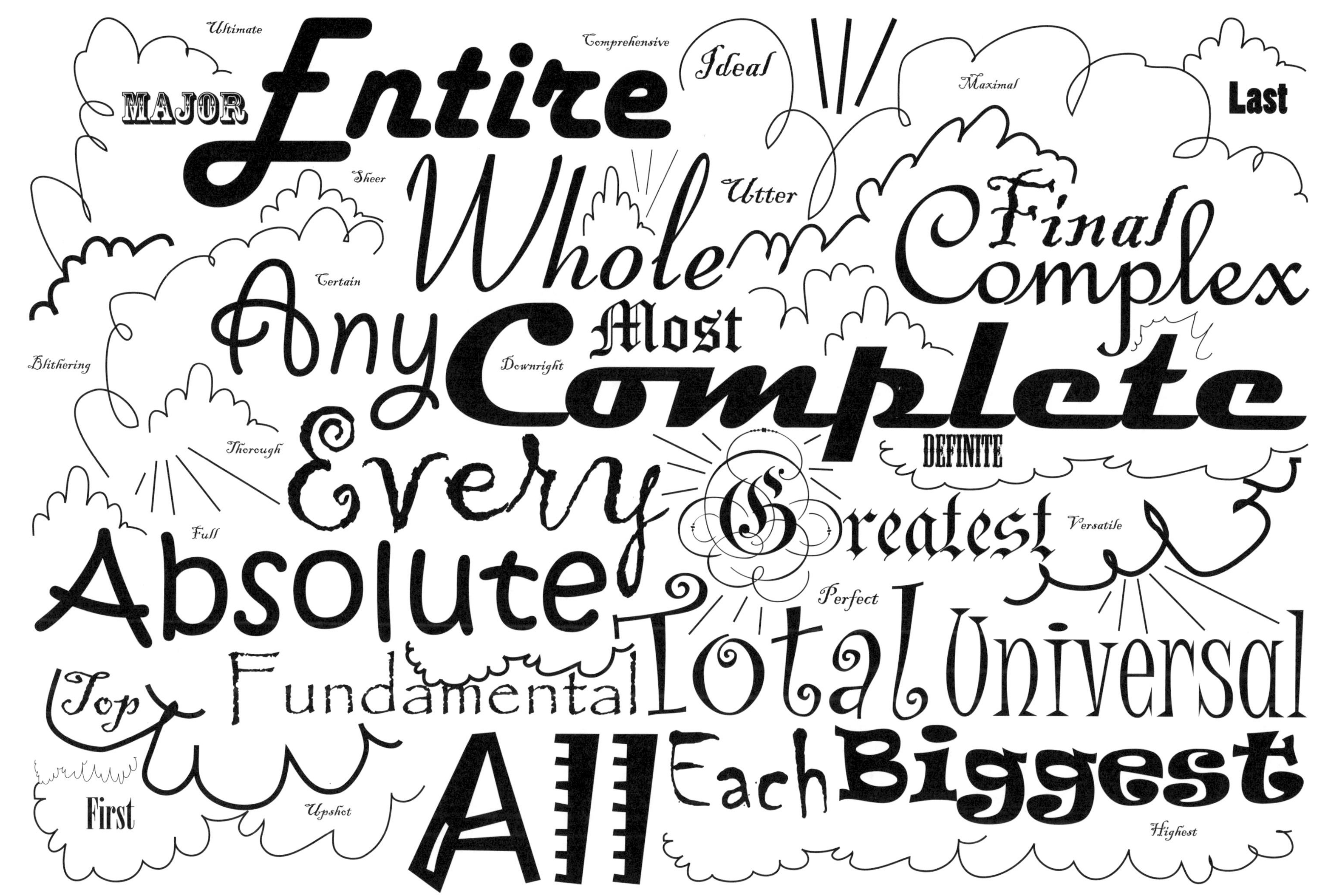

and we keep on pouring, so it overflows, and if there is no other way, then even through ears, therefore, celibacy is a catastrophic concept, the activation of 5-HT distribution (moods and social dominance from intestines, so as to be able to ensure food for a start) into the whole Central Nervous System, for the purpose

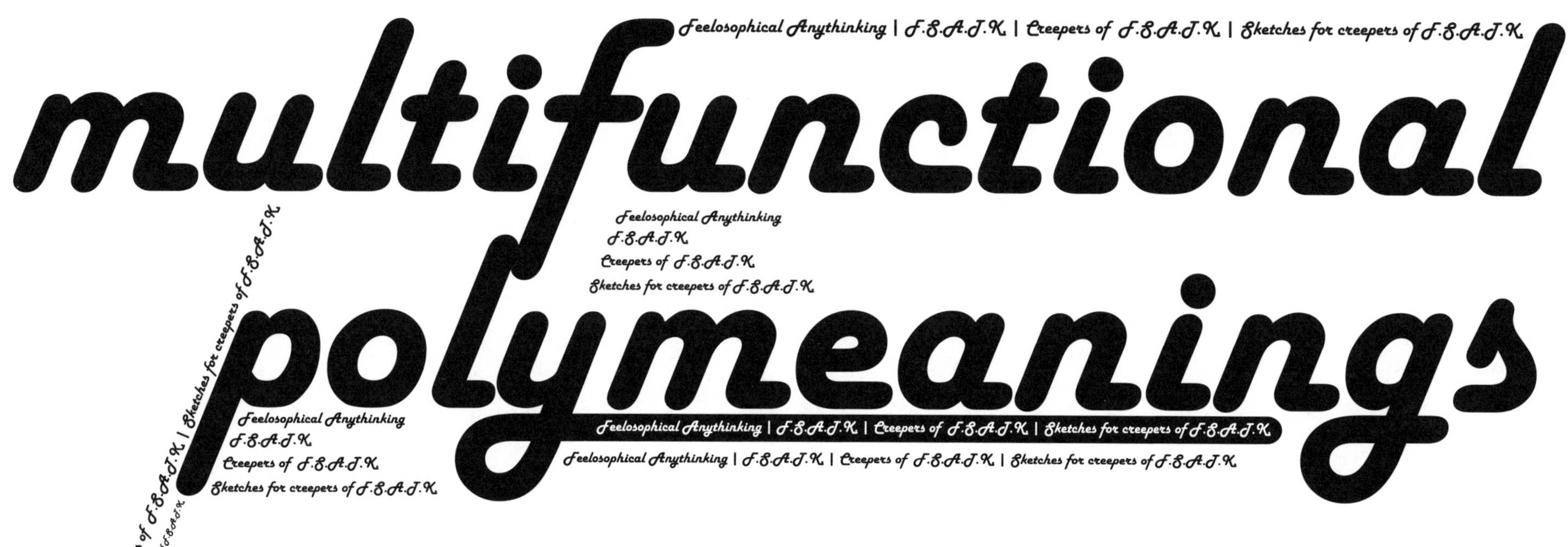

Feelosophical Anythinking | F.S.A.T.K. | Creepers of F.S.A.T.K. | Sketches for creepers of F.S.A.T.K.

bauhaus baumaxx

of catharsis, abreaction; or even purely destructive / self-destructive acting, not acting, because I MUST NOT touch on a case to case positive meaning of destruction… and polemic discourse between positive and negative… repellingly misleading Yin-Yang, listen 4 minutes and 14 seconds, parallel to continuous

I am a hotel

I am a hotel
whose construction
was made
of bones

I have clients
which come
just for an hour.

I am a hotel.

reading, to: Mark Lanegan “Skeletal History“ from “Here Comes That Weird Chill“, Ep, Beggars Banquet, 2003, I accentuate that I am not a neurosurgeon or

a philosopher, nor do I want to pretend to be either, every sentence, each word,
or even the round shape of the letter “o” orders me to STOP!) is heading toward

DING DONG QUARTET

STAND UNDER

“...under stand ding-dong {stand} under stand ding-dong...”

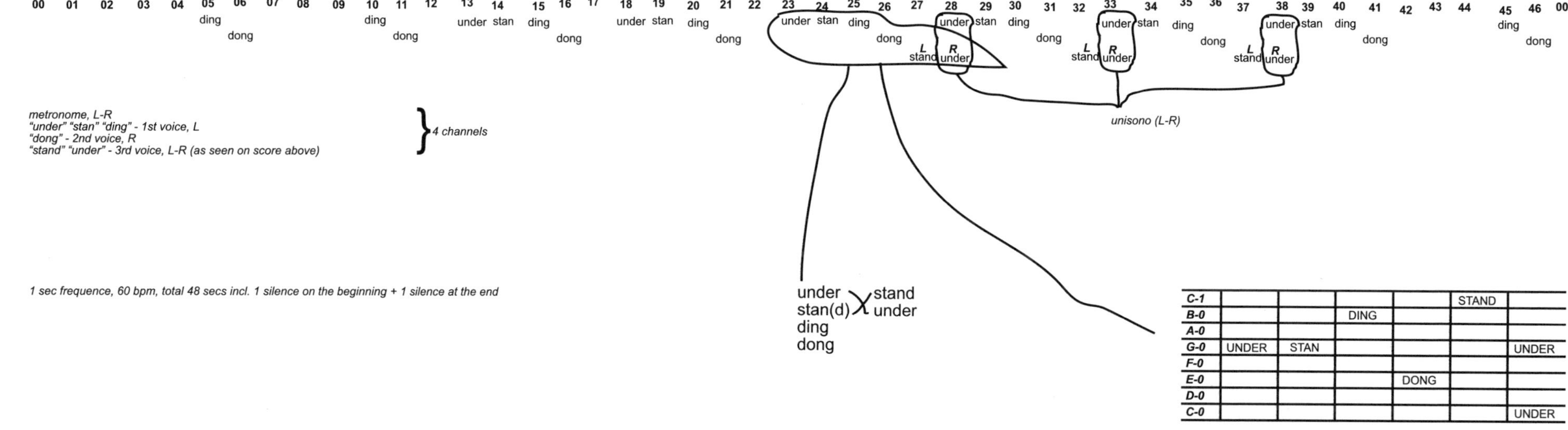

IMPROVEMENT of life, one´s own or of a group (from a couple, through a family, to a society, to humankind and nature, in a whole, to couple / a couple, to

Sing with mouth closed listening to it via nose, my dear.

pair / a pair, impair / to pair, and not to pair doesn´t have to mean not to copulate...) And, for this reason, remotely diverse areas come to similar or even identical observations, conclusions. I am talking about how a psychiatrist (Science) is suddenly agape shocked by a poet (Art) that he so clearly and

correctly diagnosed his long-term hopeless patient just on the basis of a brief
verbal description and consequently suggested that he perform such processes

thin king

anythinking

ink kin

which could be named in the standard language of the healer, a therapy, which in the end proved to be so unexpectedly successful. Like an oncologist being suddenly shocked at how, seemingly “miraculously”, have (almost!) all metastases of his hopeless patient disappeared only after two sessions of

it is dark and bitter but
it is not scary and cold

psychotherapy, without using any medicaments, radiation, and so on. Our body has an amazing regenerative ability, it is a super-machine, which relies on common sense – a coordinating, commanding organ. The proper functioning of sex requires the collaboration of a psychologist, psychiatrist, neurologist with

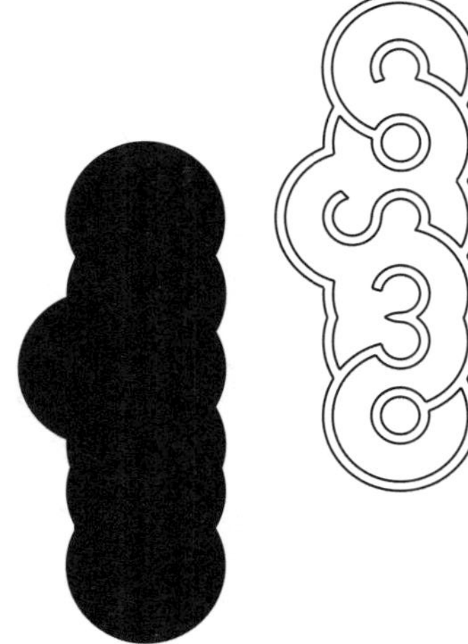

a gynaecologist, urologist... However, in the reality of professions, our innards are in separated services, which do not inter-communicate, but compete for

the super-physical meaning of the heart and soul..., listening with astonishment
to a gynaecologist speaking with total contempt about a psychologist... Our body

Levita

It won't be easy, you'll think it's strange
When I try to explain how I feel
That I still your love after all that I've done
You won't believe me
All you will see is a man you once knew
Although he's dressed up to the nines
At sixes and sevens with you
I had to let it happen, I had to change
Couldn't stay all my life down at heel
Looking out of the window, staying out of the sun
So I chose freedom
Running around, trying everything new
But nothing impressed me at all
I never expected it to
Don't cry for me Bastardia
My soul is with you
My whole life, I dedicate to you
Don't keep your distance
I need you
And as for fortune, and as for fame
I never invited them in
Though it seemed to the world they were all I desired
They are illusions
They're not the solutions they promise to be
The answer was here all the time
I love you and hope you love me
Don't cry for me Bastardia
I have never left you
Although in silence, my soul cries to you
Now and forever
[I am Bastardia]
I am Bastardia
[Ahh, so I chose freedom for Bastardia, ahh]
So I chose freedom
Running around, trying everything new
But nothing impressed me at all
I never expected it to
Have I said too much?
There's nothing more I can think of to say to you.
But all you have to do is look at me to know
That every word is true

is taken care of fractionally, although not on the whole, which can bring about severe complications later on – as described by Jiřina Prekop, whom my above mentioned note draws upon. By the way, which stage is humankind in? still in childhood? Yes, sometimes I think in pre-school, and me too. Ciudad Abierta de

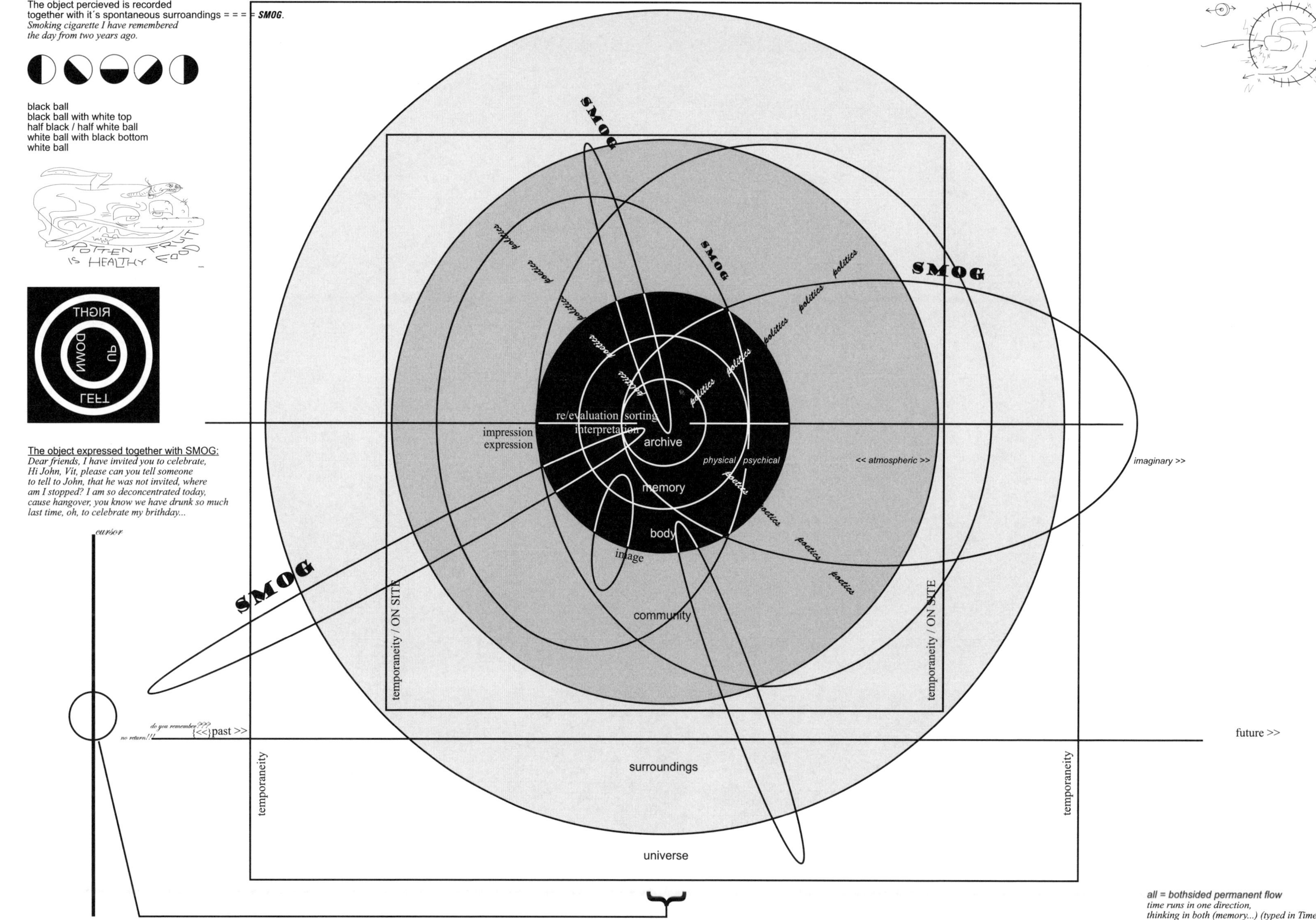

Ritoque, Holism, Bauhaus, Renaissance, Ancient Greece, Holos, things do not occur one after another, but all at once, and Foucault dying of A.I.D.S., it´s just us who tend to incline to chronologies, because it reminds us of history lessons at grammar school. We are is a molecular compound, we are is an atomical

Enter my hybrid veins!

compound with numerous Is – of even varied ages, because, for example, I as a body was born in 1969, but I as a singer of a rock band no sooner than in

1986!!! I is / I am only one, I are unique, and we are completely different from anybody else, nobody is like I am, because only I look at the world from

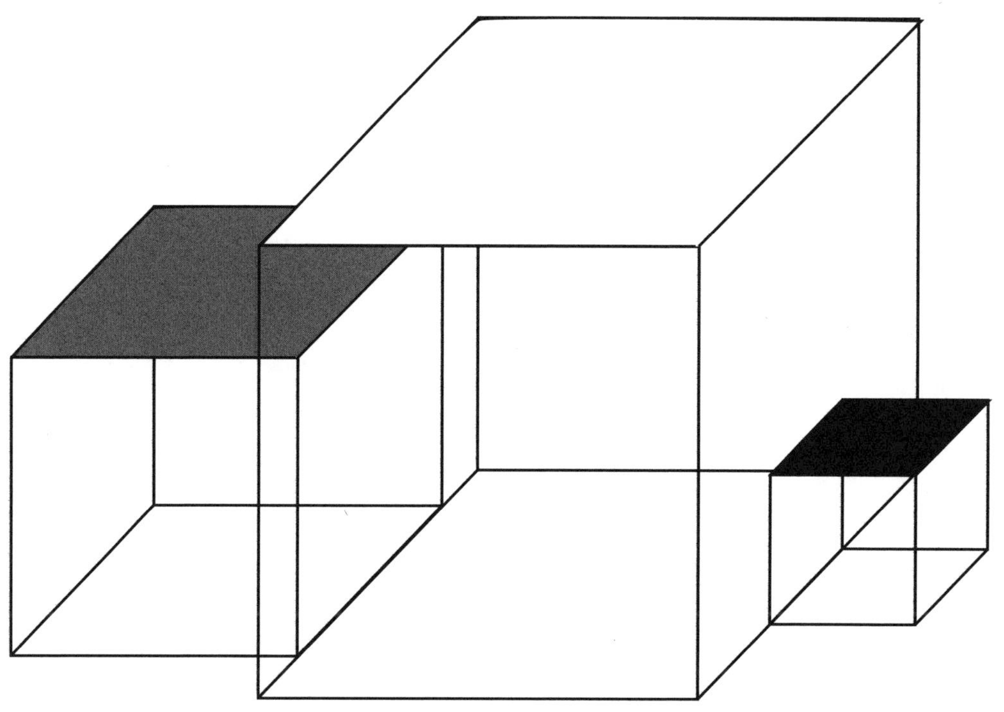

WINNERS

metal construction, plywood platforms,
60x60x60cm = 0%black, 40x40x40 = 50% black , 20x20x20 = 100% black

the inside, and all the rest is therefore (more or less) a regular exterior, which I am equal to on one hand. And my declaration is not illegitimate, although each

Rhythmical exercise

drink - piss
drink - piss
drink - piss
drink - piss

eat - shit
eat - shit
eat - shit
eat - shit

drink - puke
drink - puke
drink - puke
drink - puke

eat - puke
eat - puke
eat - puke
eat - puke

drink - piss
drink - puke
eat - shit
eat - puke

drink - piss
eat - shit
drink - puke
eat - puke

la - la
ha - ha
la - la
ha - ha

one is only one, unique (that consternation at hearing my voice for the first time recorded on tape, have you ever heard yourself like that?) and is completely

Boris Ondreička, *Rhythmical exercise*

different from anybody else, nobody is like the other, the others, because only he / she / it looks at the world from the inside, and all the rest is therefore (more or less) a regular exterior, which he / she / it is equal to on one hand. There is only one Homogenous/Unified/Uniform/United I and everything else is Plural and

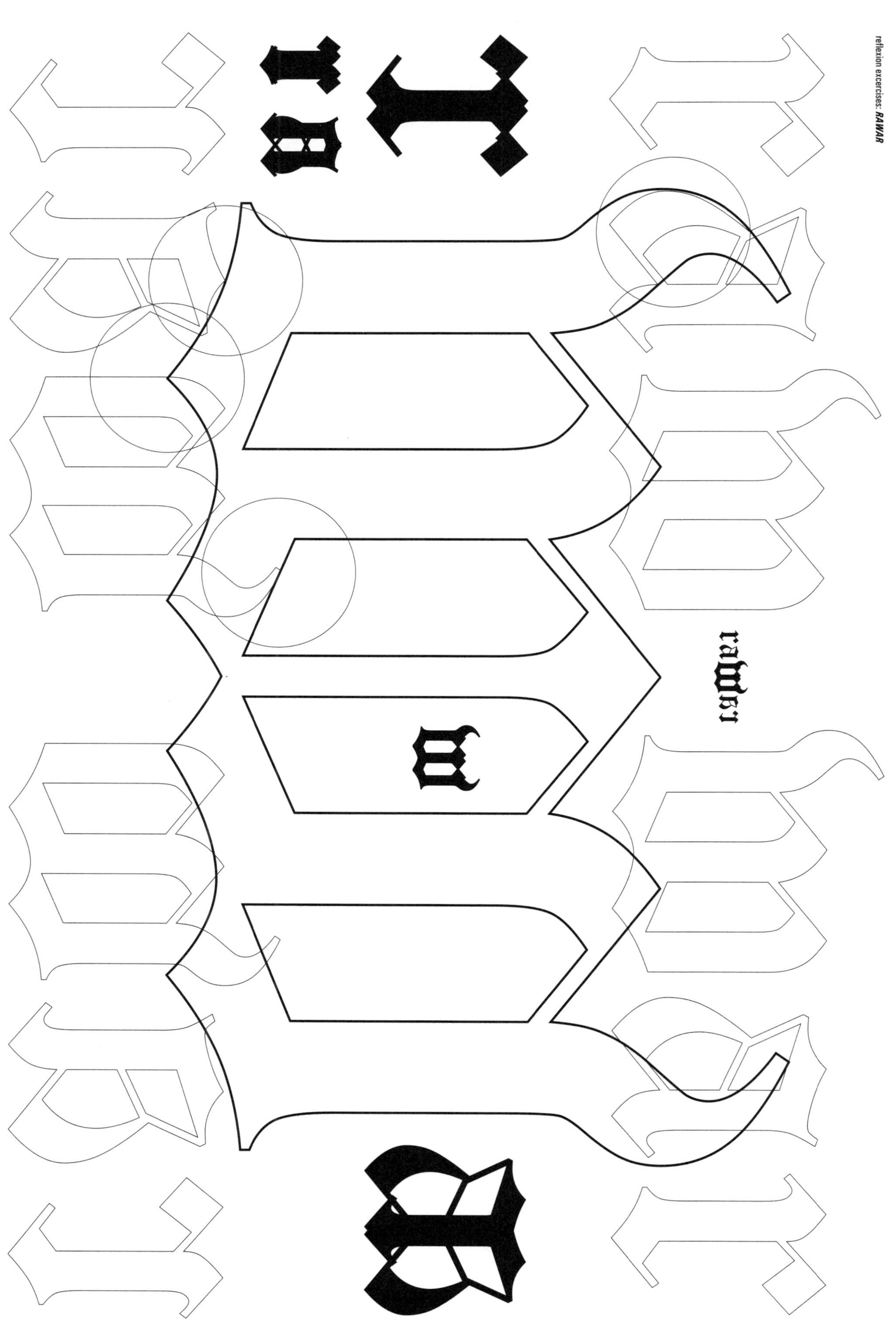

that Plural is backwards composed of Singular Is, which are thus, on the other hand, Plural. There is only one Singular I and multiple Plural Is, but each of that

Plural I is that only one Singular I, too. Therefore, it is necessary to find a way for all Plural Is (I am, I is, I are) to work together in order not to lose their right

reflexion exercises (blind forms)

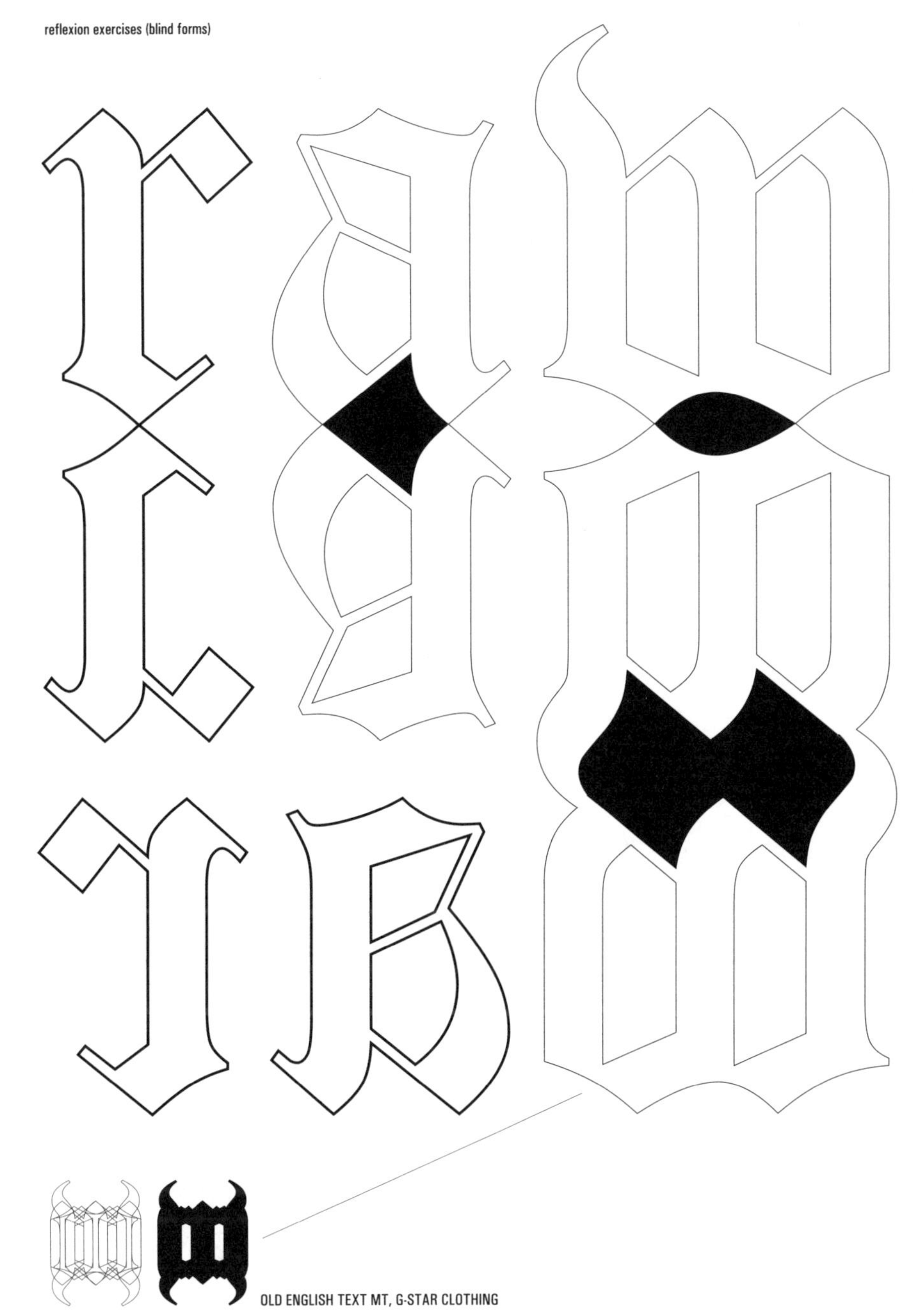

OLD ENGLISH TEXT MT, G-STAR CLOTHING

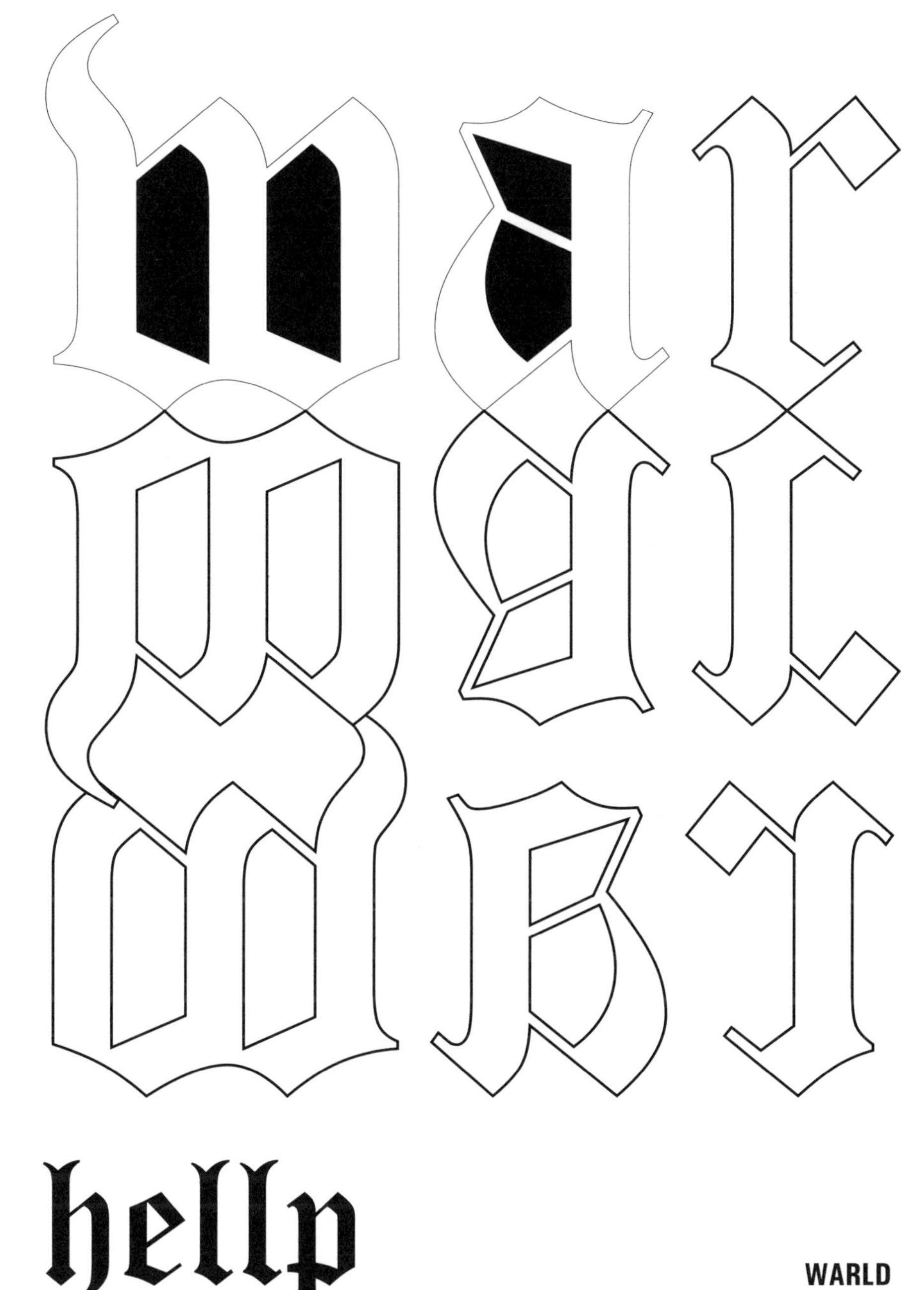

Boris Ondreička, *Raw War #2*

to the singularity of the Singular I, because none of these characteristics are not illegitimate, but they are all indispensable under the threat of ontological

schizophrenia! (In Latin, the number 3 is written as III, which is equal to 3 Is.)
And the plural is also singular = for example, "one" Soviet Union (elsewhere

EXPERIMENTAL RELIGION

experimental
belief

I write more on this and from different, yet similar reasons). And various people, dissimilar texts, read and write and different texts are read and written differently and we all, who write, also read, at least that what we write. Nevertheless, and this is really a catastrophe, we all are, varied areas, so isolated

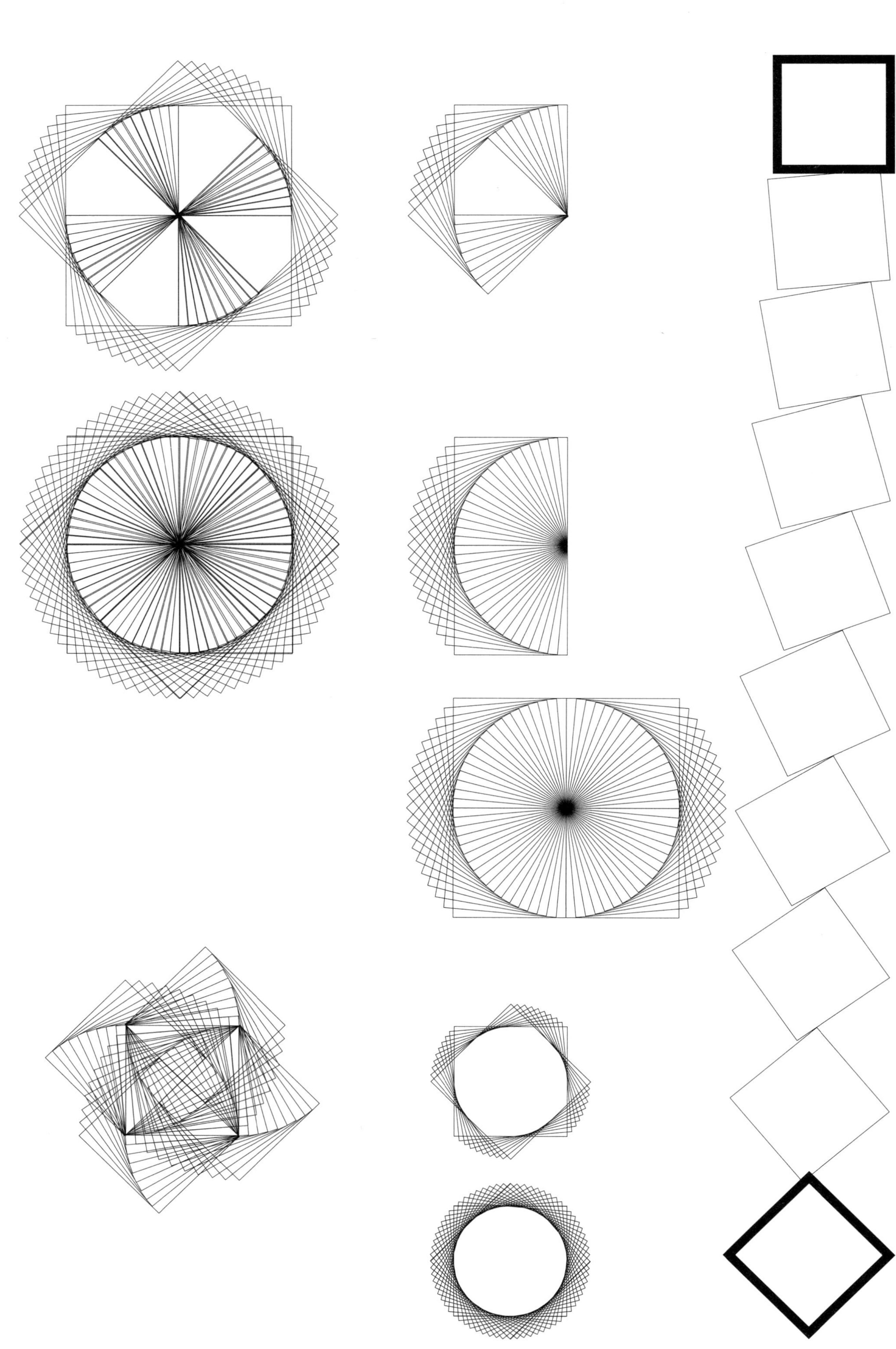

Boris Ondreička, *Strobe series*

(devoted to the above mentioned service to our innards) and mostly egocentrically focusing just on our own specialisation! But, if a nuclear physicist

meets an artist and they have sufficient reason and ample WILL, they will
understand each other immediately and together they will create a genuinely

TO FEEL THE HUNGER.

TO FILL THE STOMACH WITH THE WATER

TO KILL THE HUNGER.

HUNGER, THE CHEAPEST LIQUID.

THE CRITICAL WATER.

more complex knowledge of the world, drinking beer or just coffee and non-fizzy mineral water, or they will even get totally drunk = equal-I-ze, even out :).

Just as very many revolutionary discoveries come into the world in times of relaxation (or in seasons of other-world darkness)... De facto, it is possible only

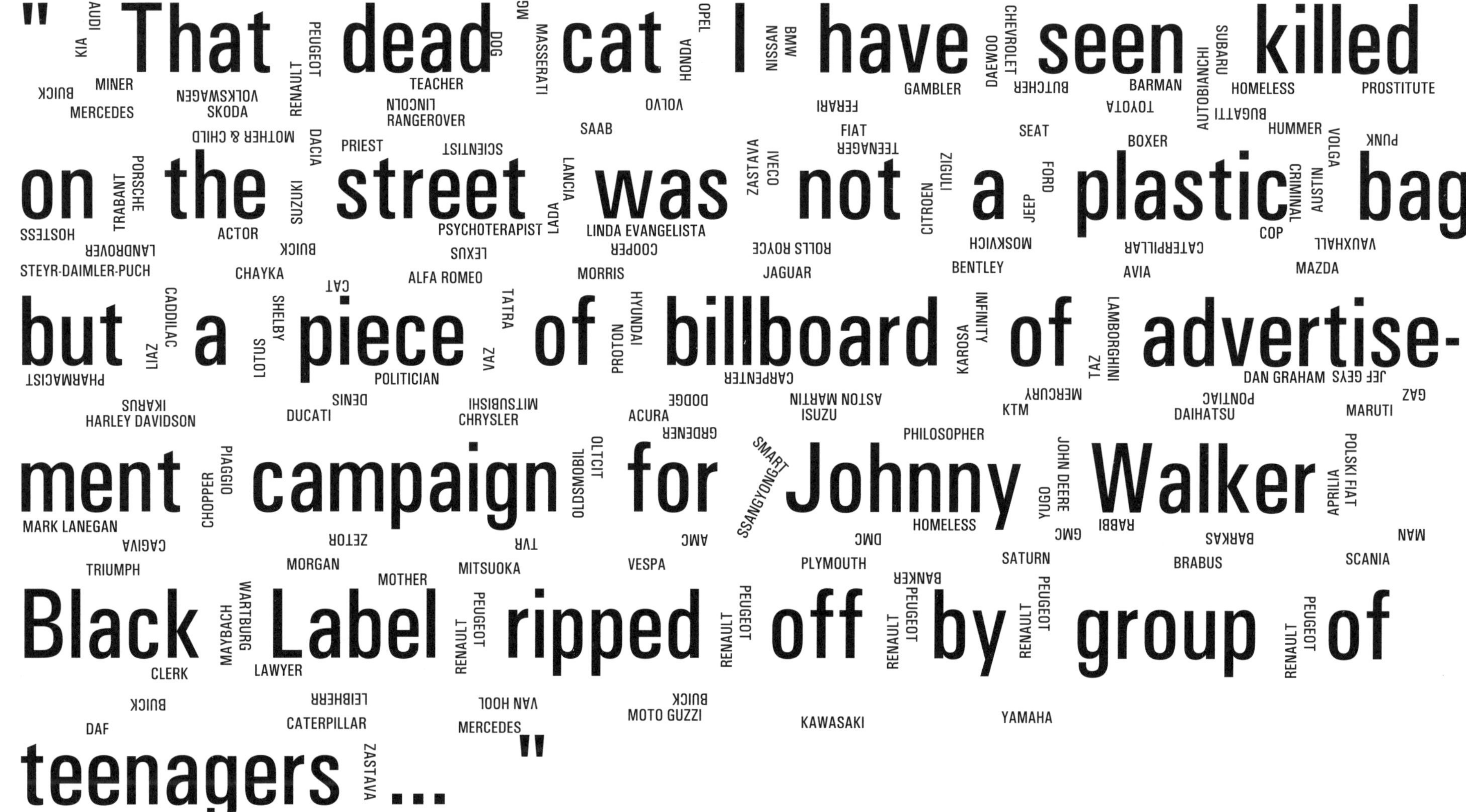

TOGETHER, here and now / there and then, because everybody is irreplaceably dealing with other nuances of reality and only All together can – we can thoroughly describe this reality (by the synchronisation of the massive interaction of autonomies of that innumerable number of single, radical Is, by

TOOL

USED BY
Y

AGAINST **X**

FOR **Y**

THERE IS A DEMONSTRATION.

PROTECTION SHIELDS ARE USED BY THOSE WHO PROTEST AGAINST THE "SYSTEM" (**X**) BUT IN THE SAME TIME ALSO BY THOSE WHO DEFEND THAT "SYSTEM" (**Y**).

AGGRESSION OF SO CALLED PR[illegible]VE FORCES AND T[illegible]ENCE OF SO CALLED REGRESSIVE FORCES - THIS IS THE [illegible]G, THE CLAS[illegible]

IT SEEMS THAT EVEN BOTH SIDES (PRO-, [illegible]NG WITH PARTICULAR "AGAINSTS" AND "FORS" THEY REPRESENT OPPOSITE "AGAI[illegible] OPPOSITE "FORS".

ONE DOES NOT HAVE IT, THE SECOND DO[illegible] BOTH WANT TO HAVE IT.

SYSTEM - COMMON TOPIC, PROTEC[illegible]ND PROTEC[illegible]EFENCE AND AGGRESSION, REGRESSION, PROGRESSION.

THERE ARE DIVERSE ACTIONS DONE BY THE SAME KIND OF TOOLS PARRALLELY.

IN DIFFERENT HANDS BUT SAME TOOLS FIGHTING ONE AGAINST EACH OTHER.

THE TOOL STAYS UNCHANGED.

TO ALL.

USED BY
X

AGAINST **Y**

FOR **X**

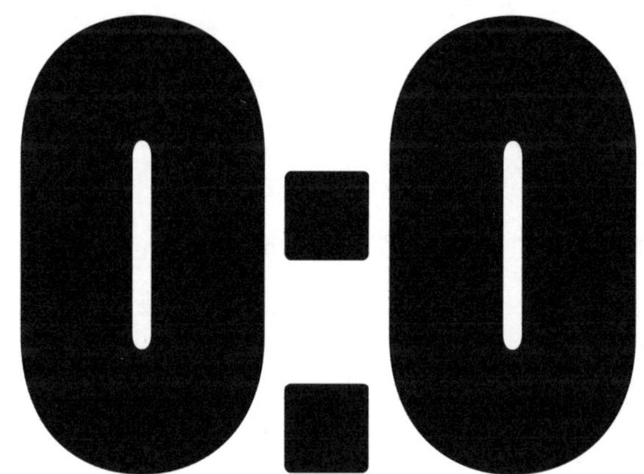

RURAL TEENS vs **URBAN ADULTS**

the creation of solidarity, biased singular Plurality). Purely philosophical thinking is as dully limited as the utterly artistic, logical, illogical, blah, blah,

blah, la, la, la, ha, ha, ha, ha. Usage of Terminus Technicus as Terminus Poeticus, beauty of a diagram, erotica of a scheme, read: http://www.poetryfoundation.

LALA {LAMELLAR LAMENT} SAYS:

MAXMIX MACHT NICHTS

MAX MIX

MAX MIX

Macrohard 3.000,- LoTec Unltd.

org/poetrymagazine/article/180185. 8pt/8pt, Times New Roman Regullar, 404 pages á 2 lines (808 lines in total, including 18 pages ~ 36 lines of masthead, a book within another book) á approx. 140 characters per line (approx. 113000 characters in total), characters & characters, left / right – 90° turn – up / down,

Written in
2009

1989		means	to my	country	the end	of totalitarian	system.
1989		means	to my	country	the beginning	of democratical	system.
1969	I	was			born.		
1989	I	was			20.		
2009	I	am			40.		
1989		means	to	me	the middle	of my heretofore	life.
Totalitarian	system	means	to	me	the memory	of me as a	child.
Democratical	system	means	to	me	the memory	of me as an	adult.

pair / impair, mirrored averse to reverse, "vertical" page-turning (from the bottom to the top) "vertical" reading (from up to down), transparency of pages,

Boris Ondreička, *Written in 2009*

opacity, mathematics of writing, economy of writing, bureaucracy of writing,
grammar and drama. Translation: trans-lie-&-lie. A universal text, a generally

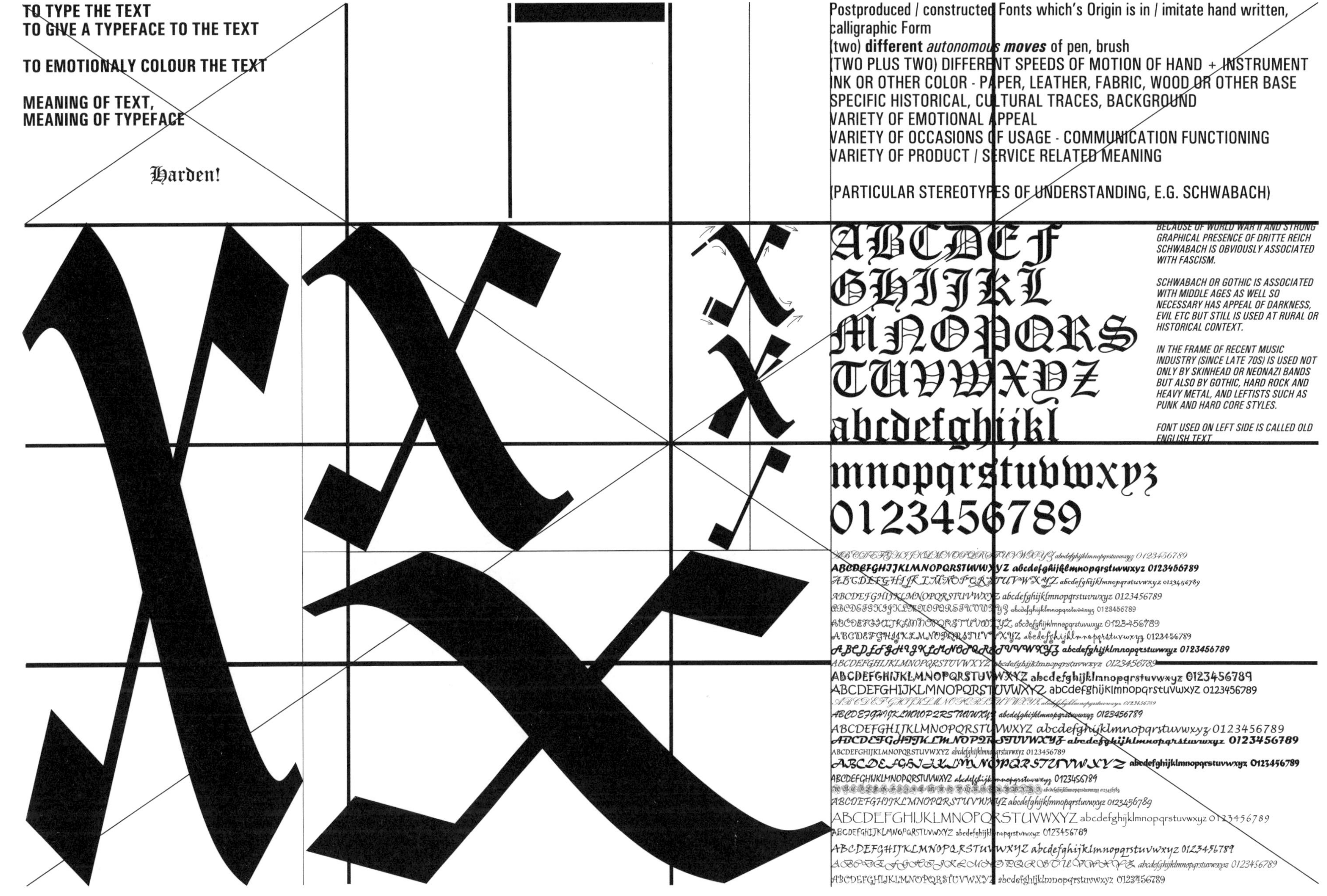

valid book, which after a millennia-long battle between rationalist Crapulence and metaphysical Tippling finally got the name Collection of Laws, Traffic

Smell your open palm, my dear.

Regulations, and such. Text: to express a meaning, “So you obeyed, so you returned, so welcome back!”, a thesaurus, etymological dictionary, message, by a text – writing for reading, writing for reading (aloud) for listening (for at that time non-readers, or even readers, or even reading something else, or also listening to something else, and all that together and moreover, he is looking at her thinking of another one). To write about childhood and to write about writing

less on no. 001

. . . BROWN B L A C K BROWN WHITE BROWN BLUE BROWN RED BROWN YELLOW BROWN ORANGE BROWN VIOLET BROWN GREEN B L A C K WHITE B L A C K BLUE B L A C K RED B L A C K YELLOW B L A C K ORANGE B L A C K VIOLET B L A C K GREEN WHITE BLUE WHITE RED WHITE YELLOW WHITE ORANGE WHITE VIOLET WHITE GREEN BLUE RED BLUE YELLOW BLUE ORANGE BLUE VIOLET BLUE GREEN RED YELLOW RED ORANGE RED VIOLET RED YELLOW ORANGE YELLOW VIOLET YELLOW GREEN ORANGE VIOLET ORANGE GREEN VIOLET BROWN B L A C K BROWN WHITE BROWN BLUE BROWN RED BROWN YELLOW BROWN ORANGE BROWN VIOLET BROWN GREEN B L A C K WHITE B L A C K BLUE B L A C K RED B L A C K YELLOW B L A C K ORANGE B L A C K VIOLET B L A C K GREEN WHITE BLUE WHITE RED WHITE YELLOW WHITE ORANGE WHITE VIOLET WHITE GREEN BLUE RED BLUE YELLOW BLUE ORANGE BLUE VIOLET BLUE GREEN RED YELLOW RED ORANGE RED VIOLET RED YELLOW ORANGE YELLOW VIOLET YELLOW GREEN ORANGE VIOLET ORANGE GREEN VIOLET BROWN B L A C K BROWN WHITE BROWN BLUE BROWN RED BROWN YELLOW BROWN ORANGE BROWN VIOLET BROWN GREEN B L A C K WHITE B L A C K BLUE B L A C K RED B L A C K YELLOW B L A C K ORANGE B L A C K VIOLET B L A C K GREEN WHITE BLUE WHITE RED WHITE YELLOW WHITE ORANGE WHITE VIOLET WHITE GREEN BLUE RED BLUE YELLOW BLUE ORANGE BLUE VIOLET BLUE GREEN RED YELLOW RED ORANGE RED VIOLET RED YELLOW . . .

THERE ARE PRAGMATIQUE AS WELL AS POETIQUE ASPECTS OF RELATIONS BETWEEN OBJECTS OF INTEREST. SOME ASPECTS ARE IMPOSSIBLE TO DESCRIBE JUST VIA PRAGMATIC CRITERIA AND SOME VIA POETIC TOOLS. ONE DOES NOT USE METAPHORS FOR CREATION OF ANY SPACE OF ESCAPE FROM REALITY BUT FOR CLEARER EXPRESSION OF IT. POETRY IS A TOOL OF EXPRESSION OF UNDERSTANDING THE REALITY.
TO SELL THE POEM, TO LIVE OUT OF WRITING LYRICS. THE RICH SINGER AND THE POOR POET.

Egon Grabstein

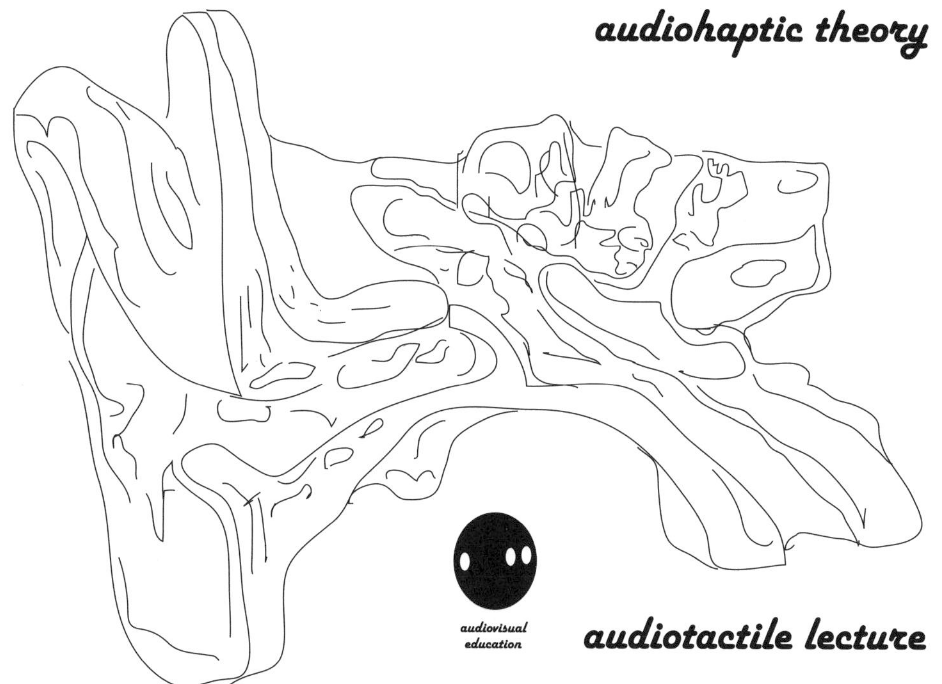

audiohaptic theory

audiotactile lecture

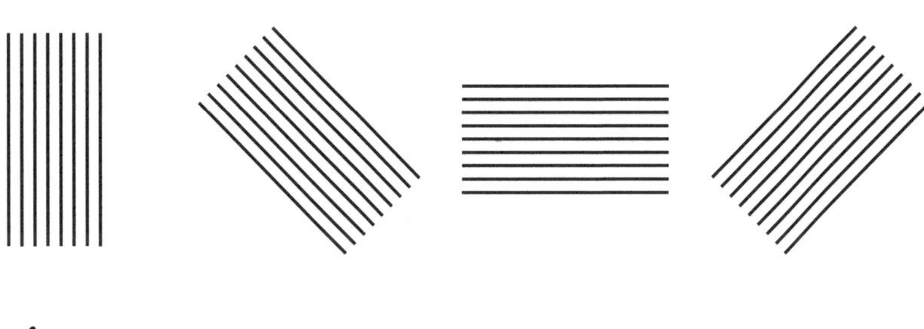

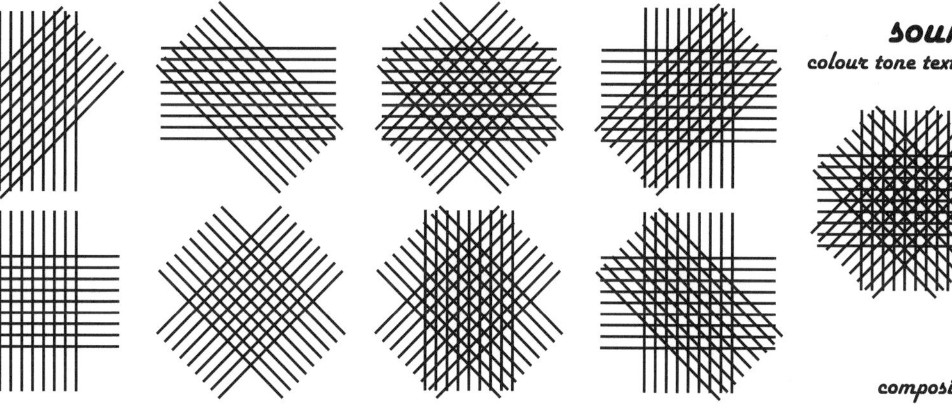

sound
colour tone texture

rhytmn repeating

composition

about childhood. Tangle and untangle through admitting/. Errant writing – peregrinational text. (Transcription of an interview recording, first slavishly similar, I will have somebody else do it, and then adjustment, I must modify it considerably, since that servile version is dyslexically, dysgraphically unreadable

to observe the couple at the moment of a kiss,

1} springs of salivas
2} confluences of salivas
3} estuaries of salivas
4} bothsided flow
5} exchange
6} mixing
7} two bodies
8} one body

in written form, and the person seems idiotic, even though he/she is not. Spoken word and written world.) Through an open window a scent from 1984 has been drifted to me at this very moment. My brain is stretched by senses in all directions. Impulses fight for attention, they try to divert me from the intended.

It is not me escaping, it is Me disappearing, kidnapped (“...I am kidnapped by this music...”), he was seized by brackets. ([Brackets {in} brackets] in brackets.)

...reformulation of language into nomenclature of text and its further forms, prints, posters and leaflets and pamphlets... publications (publicity, public, pubic,

I am the wall.

I am the wall. I am that familiar
wall, which separates you from
neighbors. I am that forgotten
wall which has to listen
your sobbing in the night and their
endless fights from the other side.
I defend you from cold, I protect
you from anybody. I design your
intimacy. And you drill in me, you
stick those fucking screws in me.
I am your tired wall.

puberty, pub) and books, sentences running from one line to another, sentences running from one page to another, meanings returning to notes 4 pages back,

11 lines, including this one, backwards... to repeat in order to memorise. Like actors and singers, and politicians and farmers. And if you get out of your mind,

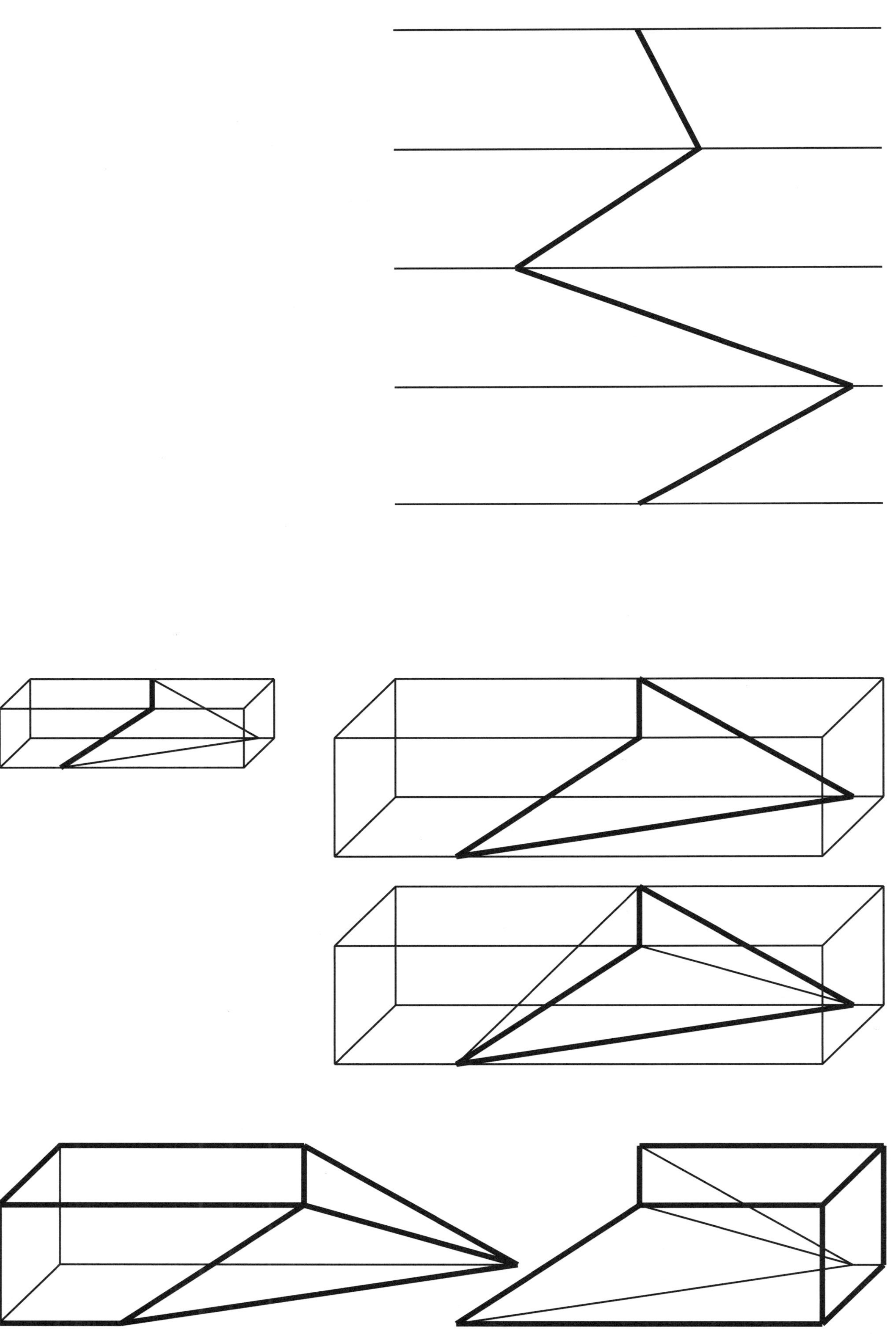

or you don´t understand – read the sentence again. Read the sentence again. Read the sentence again. Texture from text. Arab & The Deux Arabesques of

Claude Achille Debussy (1862 - 1918), 1888 – 1891 (26-year-old). Listen to one and the same song again and again, the whole day, as if observing from where

today
todie
today
todie

and to where to its creepers reach. How to read a creeping text?, when one stem has been unstoppably doubling back on itself since the beginning? Neurons, synapses, Virginia creeper which has been thickening not only linearly ahead, but hyper-fractally along the entire length / width / depth, in all directions, x-y-z

PRIMARY ~ SECONDARY

RE-, SUB-, UN-, UNDER-;
WHY, HOW..:

object, subject, topic, item, device, article ~ accessory, accompaniment, supplement, addendum, adjunct, annexe, appendage, enclosure, appendix, fitment, interpolation,

CON TIN OUS LY
CON SCI OUS NESS

AESTHETICS OF SCIENTIFIC ILLUSTRATION
{COLLECTORS OF SCIENTIFIC ILLUSTRATIONS}

EPITOMA

TO FRAME THE SCIENTIFIC ILLUSTRATION MEANS ACT OF COMODIFICATION - TO TURN THE PIECE OF PAPER TO SOMETHING WE ARE ABLE TO DEAL WITH EASILY. ANYTHING FRAMED IS SUDDENLY COLLECTED LIKE FOR EXAMPLE HUMAN SKIN WITH TATOOS, OLD MAPS, BUTTERFLIES AND VARIOUS MEMORABILIA. TO COLLECT MEANS OBVIOUSLY "TO HAVE" AND/OR "TO BE BUSY WITH". TO FRAME MEANS TO PROTECT BUT ALSO EVALUATE - TO CHANGE THE VALUE, TO CHANGE THE PRICE, TO ATTACH ATTENTION ON AESTHETICAL OR (IN VERY LIMITED CASES) CONTENT RELATED FUNCTION. ANYTHING FRAMED IS AUTOMATICALY CONSIDERED (NEARLY) AS A PIECE OF ARTS.

MAJORITY OF PEOPLE DO NOT DEAL WITH IT AS WITH SOMETHING WHAT IS BUILT TO LOOK AT, TO READ IT BUT MAINLY TO COVER, TO FILL THE BARRENESS SOMEHOW LEFT AROUND. IT IS A HORROR VACUUI OF EMPTY SHELVES AND WALLS WHAT COOPERATES ON THE PROCESS OF PURCHASE. OBJECTS OF THIS CATEGORY WHICH YOU CAN BUY RANGE FROM PICASSO OIL PAINTING ORIGINAL GOT AT SOTHEBY'S AUCTION TO IKEA UNLIMITED EDITION OF OFFSET PRINT POSTER PHOTO OF SWEDISH LANDSCAPE ALREADY FRAMED UNDER THE PLEXI GLASS.

REGULLAR PROCEDURE OF FINALISATION OF INTERIOR STYLING IS THAT THE VISUAL MATERIAL - FRAMED MATTER COMES ON THE VERY LAST STEP. MAJORITY OF PEOPLE UNDERSTAND THIS (ON CONSCIOUS LEVEL) AS A SUPERSTRUCTURE IN COMPARISON WITH FUNDAMENTAL ASPECTS OF LIVING LIKE LIGHT, TEMPERATURE, NOURISHMENT OR HYGIENE AND SO ON.

THE VASE WITH FLOWERS, EMBROIDERED PILLOW, FAMILY PHOTOGRAPHY STAY TOGETHER WITH PIECES OF ARTS AND OTHER ORNAMENTAL, DECORATIVE INSTRUMENTS ON THE SAME LEVEL OF HIERARCHY OF IMPORTANCE. GENERALLY THERE IS NO DIFFERENCE BETWEEN CRAFTS, ARTS OR MEMORABILIA IN TERMS OF NEEDED SPATIAL SOLUTIONS BUT OF COURSE THERE IS A RADICAL DIFFERENCE IN PERSONAL EMOTIONAL RELATION TO PARTICULAR OBJECTS.

WESTERN CULTURAL TRADITION GENERALLY CONSIDERS MENTAL HEALTH AS SOMETHING SECONDARY, EXCLUSIVE IN COMPARISON TO THAT PHYSICAL ONE. THERE IS A RACIONAL HIERARCHICAL DIVISION IN BETWEEN PHYSICAL AND MENTAL, EMOTIONAL NEEDS.

GEORGE LUKAS MADE HIGHER INCOME ON MERCHANDISE OF STAR WARS (LIKE T-SHIRTS, TOYS...) THAN ON ACTUAL MOVIES.

UNDER WHICH

CRITERIA

DO YOU DO THE

SELECTION

?

PERMANENTLY CONTINUOUSLY I TRY TO RECONSIDER SUBCONSCIOUSNESS AND UNCONSCIOUSNESS BECAUSE I BELIEVE THAT IT IS THE ONLY RESPONSIBLE WAY TO UNDERSTAND PARTICULAR PROCEEDINGS = WHY AND HOW PARTICULAR ACTS ARE HAPPENING AND WHAT SHOULD FURTHER EFFECT. IT IS NOT A PARALLEL PROCESS BECAUSE ACTIVITIES ARE DONE ALL TOGETHER IN ONE TIME AND NOT IN TWO (AND MORE) SEPARATE LINES. ONE SITUATION THAN SHOULD MEAN THAT IT IS A COMPOUND OF NUMEROUS PARALLEL ACTS. BUT "PARALLEL" IS JUST A TERM OF INSTRUMENTAL CHARACTER WHICH HELPS TO DESCRIBE THE ENTIRETY OF THE PHENOMENON. "PARALLEL" MEANS TO SIMPLIFY THE SITUATION TO EXEMPLARY RELATIONS OF MODELS, TO DIVIDE, OPEN, TO DISSECT AND AFTER ANALYSIS THAN PUT BACK TOGETHER FOR SYNTHETIC RESULT. THIS WAY OF PERCIEVING, UNDERSTANDING IS JUST THE ILLUSTRATION - EVEN SCIENTIFIC ILLUSTRATION, JUST THE EPITOME.*

** "JUST" IN THIS CASE DOES NOT PLAY THE ROLE OF A CRITICAL TOOL.*

FUNCTION - VALUE

and more, backwards / at the same time everywhere and constantly (this is an allusion to the methodology of writing this text: several source texts, their mutual intertwining, all is intertwined, the fabrication of a base skeleton, re-reading / re-evaluation and detailing along the entire length in both directions,

Poems:

"You are justa derivative of us!"

Lyrics:

"We are not sure if you were the first or us, but anyhow - ok! You know, people listen to us cause we are accessible!"

thickening of the inside, which automatically, correlatively results in the final external dimension of the manifestation, preset size in exactness exactitude of the number of lines = filling up the contents / volume of the given vessel), mildly poisonous plant, when in complementary layer the reader is duplicitously

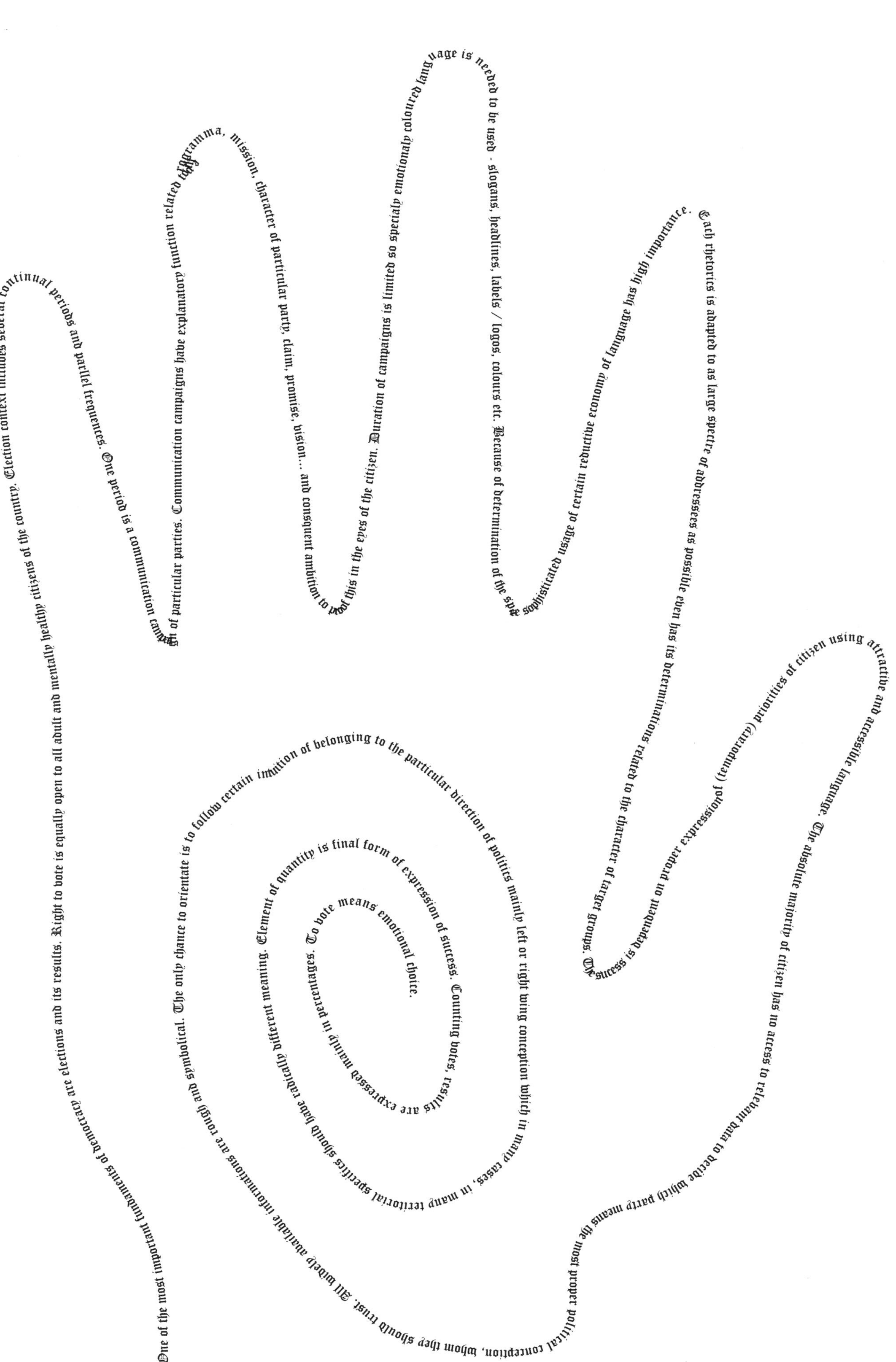

attacked by equally disturbing elements of his/her own spontaneous environment and history of prejudices – that Virginia creeper creeps out of that text through your eyes, into your brain, and from there it spreads throughout your body, that mild poison which is often used in pharmaceutical production in a contrary

to turn
in the sleep

to turn
in the sleep

to the other side

the face in the mirror

is looking at me

and I spit on it.

the other side of pillow is colder

to the other side

sense to killing... A text, which is born as a reaction to a particular stimulus = thanks to the arisen platform of a certainly limited size, after an ordinary visit of

Mr Helbich to the printing office Helbich (together with Vít Havránek, this text thanks you for it as well), which will be printed – at the time of writing, and

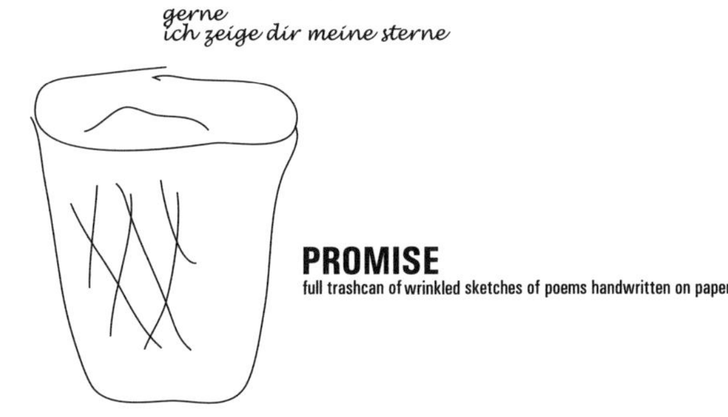

PROMISE
full trashcan of wrinkled sketches of poems handwritten on paper

since you are reading it, the book got printed, on a bench in a park next to that printing office, by the river Morava and Apollo guesthouse; the son of Zeus and

Look directly to the eyes of passers by, my dear.

Leto, oracular god of light and the sun; truth and prophecy; medicine, healing, and plague; music, poetry, and the arts; and more, in the Moravian city of Brno,

Boris Ondreička, *T. P. #9*

18 April 2011, between 1PM and 3PM, approximately 20 minutes of talk, around 25 °C. There arises an entitlement for circa 165,000 characters, from one

book two, while this one is number 2, fill up that space, neither more, nor less, where is this creeper heading? Into a courtroom? An autopsy room thoroughly

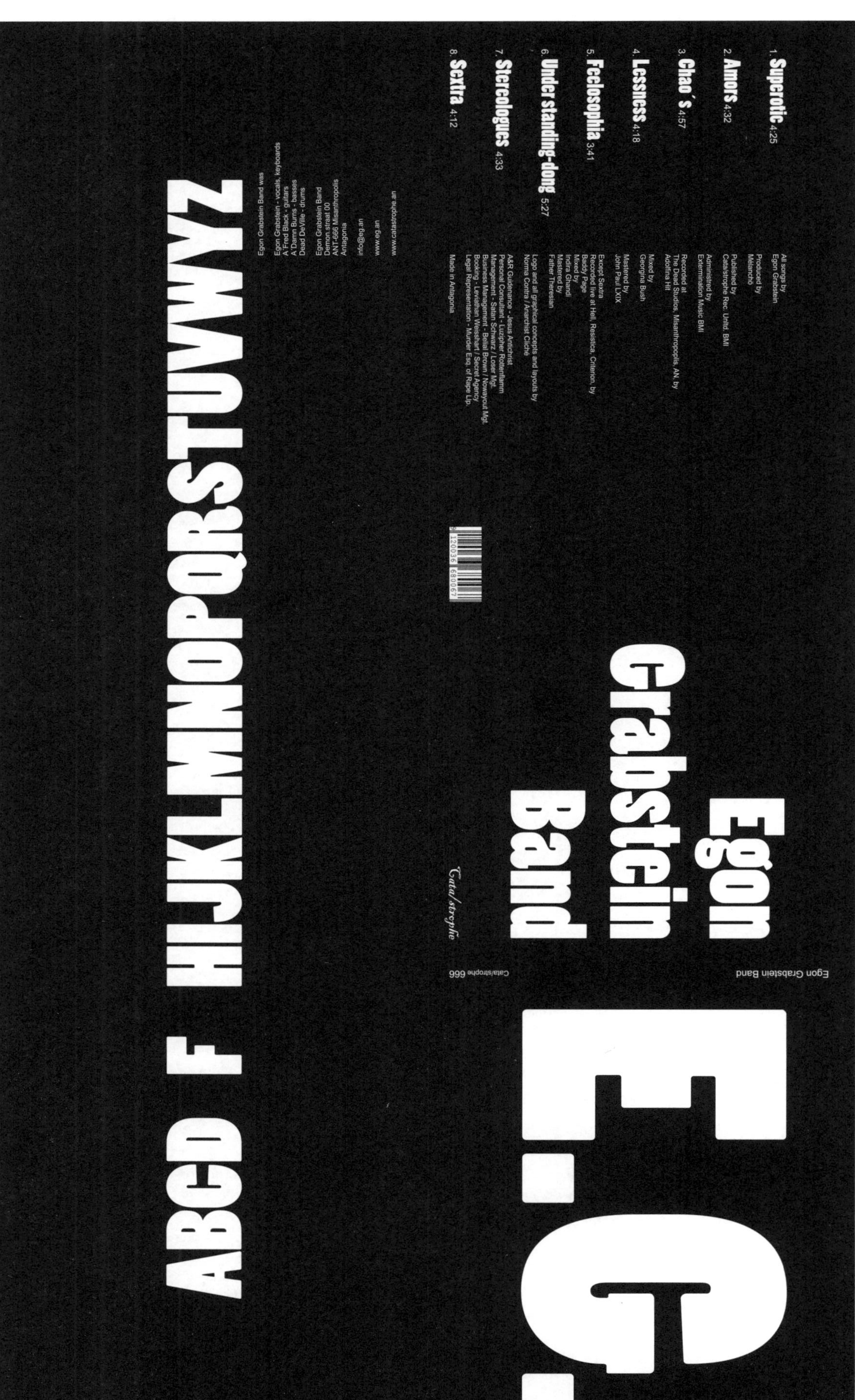

cleaned by that cleaning lady? Onto a wall of an office? STOP!). But those two will not create only a new truth, we will not create only a new truth, because the

biggest part of truth already exists, without us, it already is – and it is dynamic,
constantly developing – mainly independent of us, like that mentioned Virginia

ODIUM IS OPIUM
ONUS IS BONUS

lie,couch

fib, ouch

creeper in our former garden in Bernolákovo, which I didn´t even plant or water, like Denisa´s drawings and Olívia´s games, without our contribution and influence. Only a man appears to him/herself disproportionally big... They will discover it together and build only its reflection and that reflection will fully

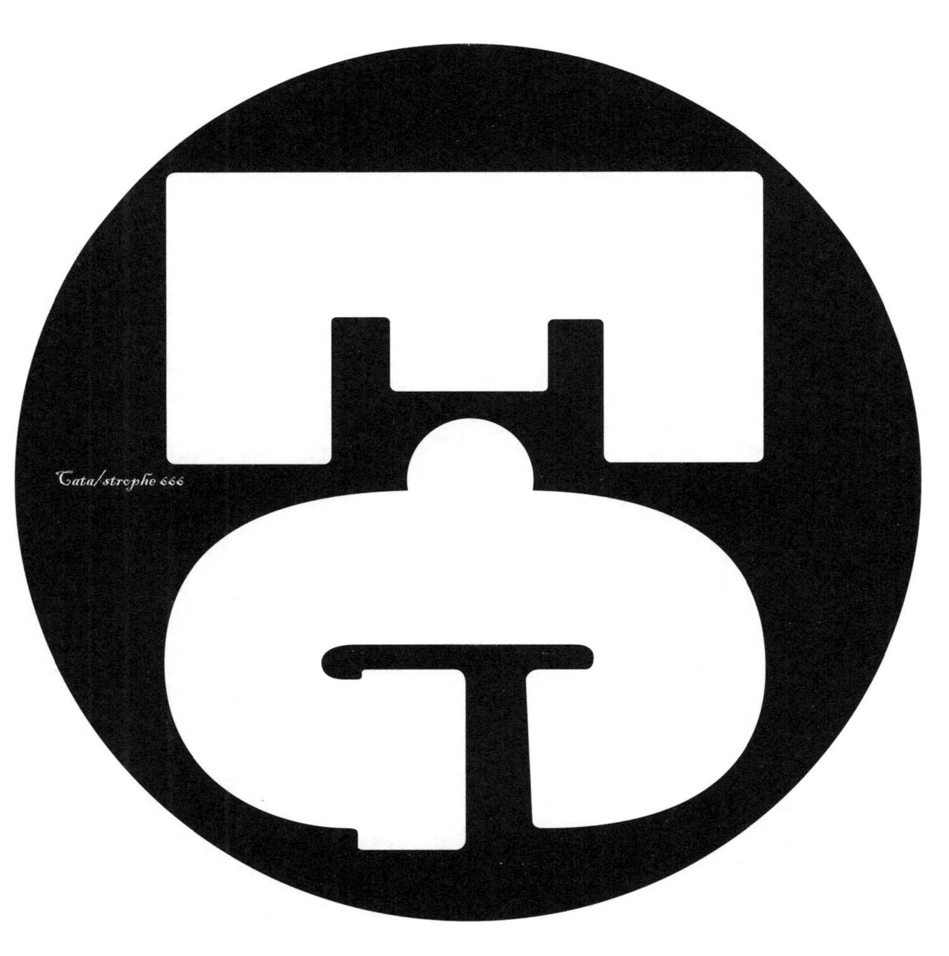

Boris Ondreička, *Egon Grabstein Band {disc}*

suffice for our living in safety, health and avoiding too many further alarming mistakes. Besides talking about the pair, it came into my mind how, a year ago

I stopped my car on red and was pushing the brake pedal and the red of the rear
brake lights was illuminating the face of the driver in the car behind me, it

darkness:

home of beautiful butterflies,
the couple
behind the wall
is making love so loudly,
flower relaxing,
buzz of electricity
and distant hooter of ambulance,

people sleep
but city
never-ever
never-ever

transformed it from dark-grey into red and again into grey and then again into red, and so I began to push the pedal to the rhythm of a song in the radio, and the face of the driver flickered like a cheap stroboscopic lamp, like a zombie in the most low-cost horror of the 50s (my daughter once told me that Christ was

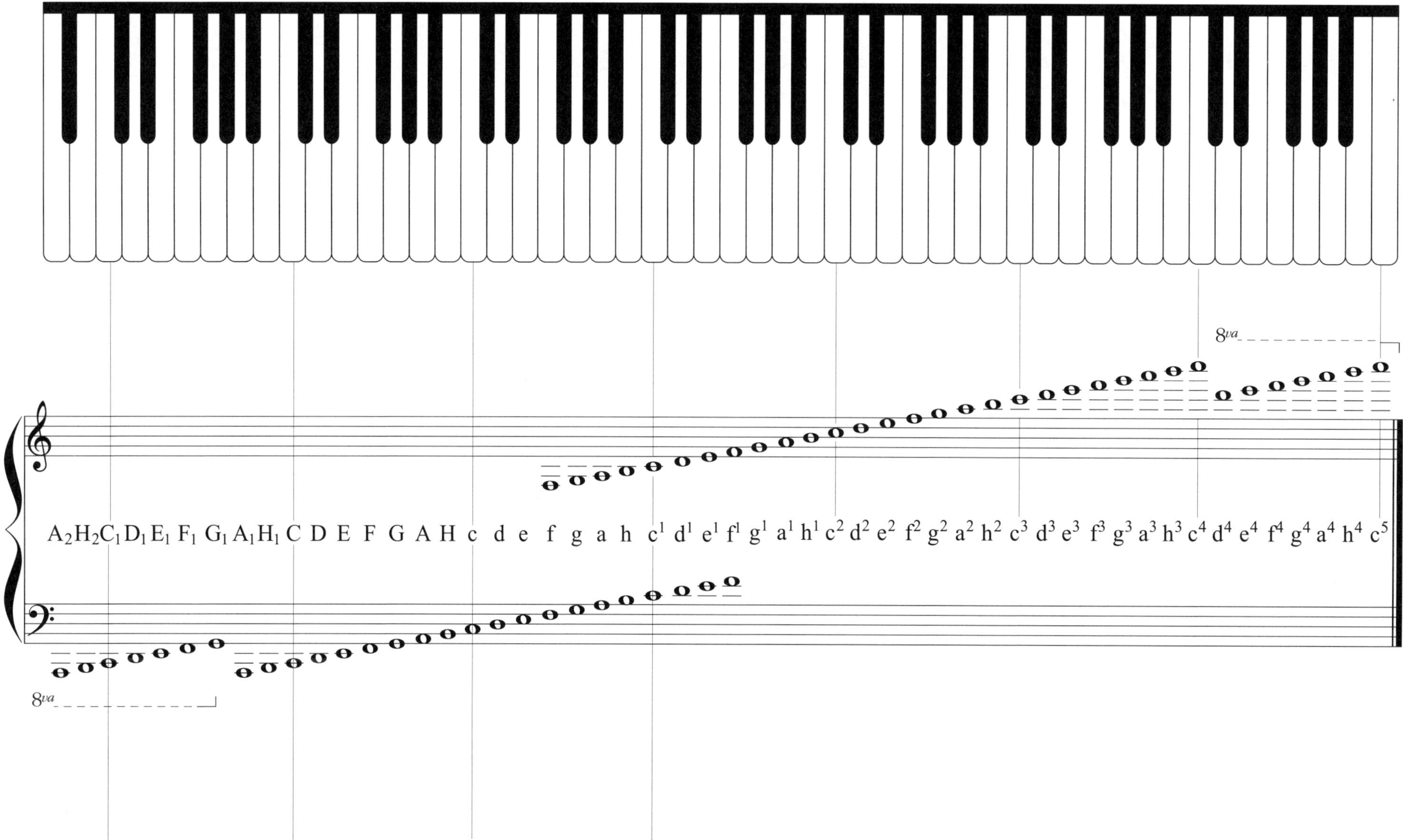

songs: sounds, tones, musics, texts, melodies, metrorythmns, tacts, tempos, metrics, intervals, eras, limits, readers, namers, forms, phrases, subordinates, dynamics, interpretations, expression, intonations, pronunciation, instrumentalisations, meanings, colours, colourings, tonalities, positions, transpositions, chordics, harmonies, impressions, expressions, times, moves, spaces, environments, audio-tactilities, pulsations, frekvencies, hights, lenghts, powers, strenghts, amplitudes, decibels, phones, bpms, compositions, organisations, sensoric abilities, kinetic abilities, motorical abilities, communication abilities, emotional abilities, morals, societals, amplitudes, visual illustrations, marketing supports, rotations, memorizings a zombie, because he had risen from the dead), I don´t know whether the other driver realised it, it could have even pissed him off, if I remember well it was

Bon Iver and his "Skinny Love". And since my car has an automatic gear, by each release of the pedal I moved a bit forward... I noticed the eminent presence

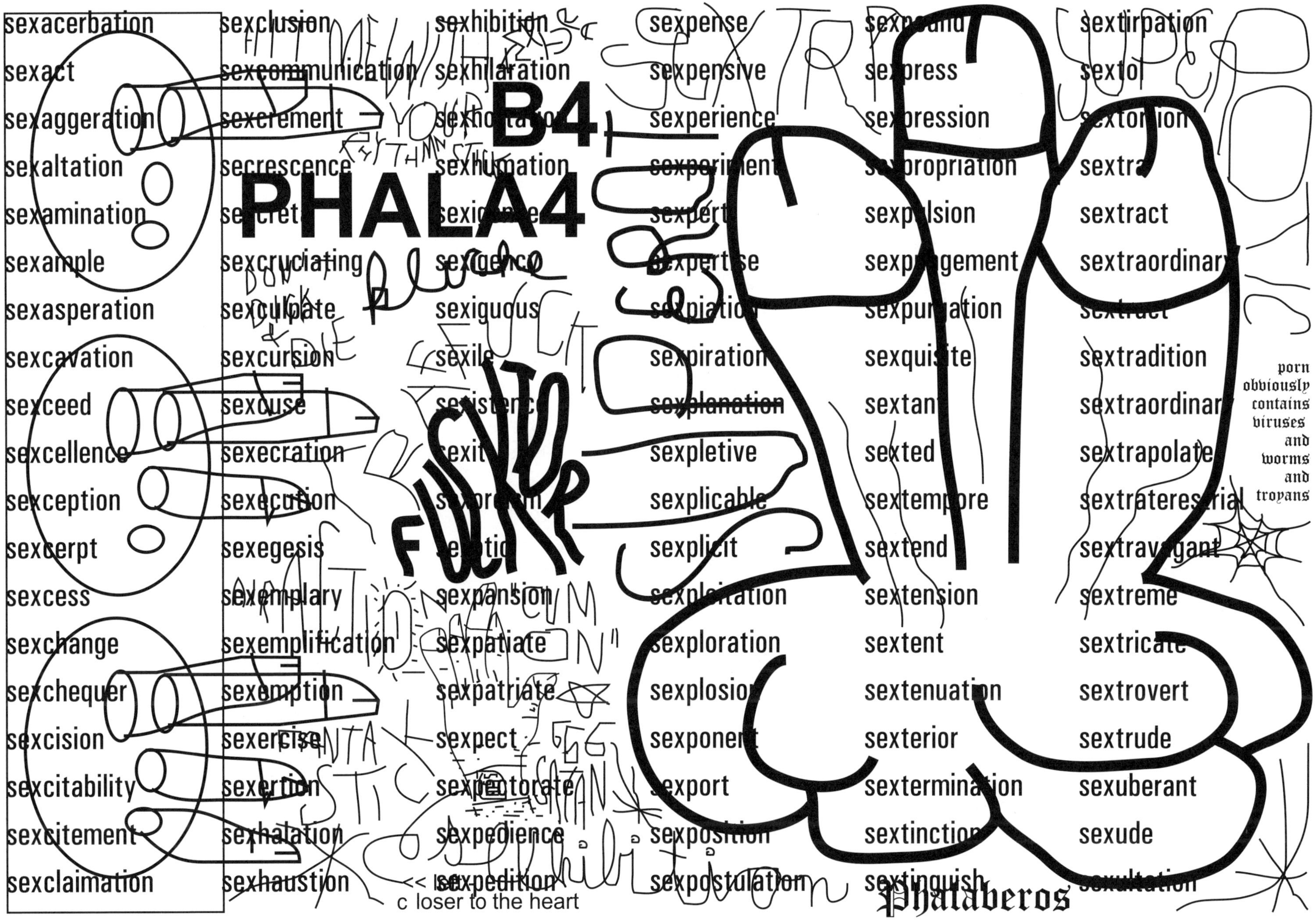

B4

PHALA4

sexacerbation
sexact
sexaggeration
sexaltation
sexamination
sexample
sexasperation
sexcavation
sexceed
sexcellence
sexception
sexcerpt
sexcess
sexchange
sexchequer
sexcision
sexcitability
sexcitement
sexclaimation

sexclusion
sexcommunication
sexcrement
secrescence
sexcrete
sexcruciating
sexculpate
sexcursion
sexcuse
sexecration
sexecution
sexegesis
sexemplary
sexemplification
sexemption
sexercise
sexertion
sexhalation
sexhaustion

sexhibition
sexhilaration
sexhortation
sexhumation
sexigence
sexigency
sexiguous
sexile
sexistence
sexit
sexorcism
sexotic
sexpansion
sexpatiate
sexpatriate
sexpect
sexpectorate
sexpedience
sexpedition

sexpense
sexpensive
sexperience
sexperiment
sexpert
sexpertise
sexpiation
sexpiration
sexplanation
sexpletive
sexplicable
sexplicit
sexploitation
sexploration
sexplosion
sexponent
sexport
sexposition
sexpostulation

sexpand
sexpress
sexpression
sexpropriation
sexpulsion
sexpungement
sexpurgation
sexquisite
sextant
sexted
sextempore
sextend
sextension
sextent
sextenuation
sexterior
sextermination
sextinction
sextinguish

sextirpation
sextol
sextortion
sextra
sextract
sextraordinary
sextract
sextradition
sextraordinary
sextrapolate
sextraterestrial
sextravagant
sextreme
sextricate
sextrovert
sextrude
sexuberant
sexude
sexultation

porn
obviously
contains
viruses
and
worms
and
troyans

<< c loser to the heart

Phalaberos

of (us) two then, exactly thanks to that illumino-haptic contact, yes, touch by light, if he remembers it I have no idea, probably not. A girl, a tourist from

Boris Ondreička, *1985*

a small town in unfortunate Japan, where I will never go, maybe to Tokyo I will,
which at the same time as I walk along a street parallel with mine, we pass each

My past is getting bigger and bigger.

My present does not exist.

It is just an imaginary edge

between my past and my future.

It is just a cursor

which goes from left to right,

and never stops.

I am sitting on the top

attached to this abscissa.

My future is getting smaller and smaller.

other never to meet again. You will never meet the overwhelming majority of the Earth´s citizens, perhaps your dreamed-of lovers and your wife, her longed-for husbands. Some of them you will spot on TV, just for a fraction of a second, maybe at the time when they are being pulled out of house of ruins. Can there be

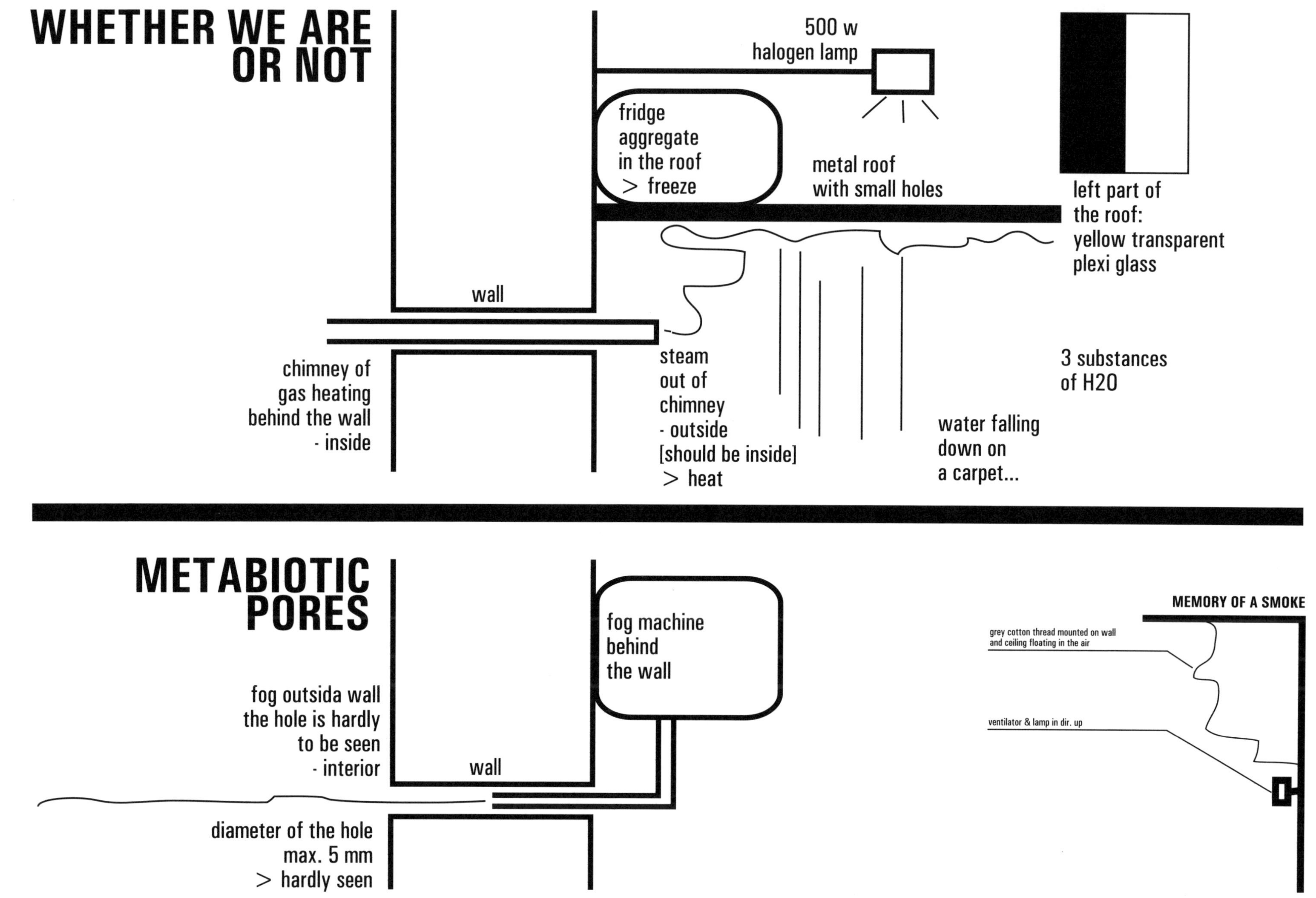

Boris Ondreička, *Whether we are of not*; incl. *Metabiotic pores*

an overwhelming majority? Does it make sense? To limit, but to bridge limitation. Bridges within compilations. Bridges among chapters. Donkey bridges, two obstinate goats against each other at those bridges and messages on that road from the scratching of hooves, bridges and no rivers underneath them,

Piss in the hand.

Feel the temperature of urine.

Think about your entrails, my dear.

Boris Ondreička, *T. P. #10*

but a delta yes – gaps between words, vacancy between letters and a mass of text and mass psychology and they shoot horses, don´t they? However, before that we All must deeply realise that we All aim for the Same, for that improvement of life, for the care of those extremely talented children of any social class, help,

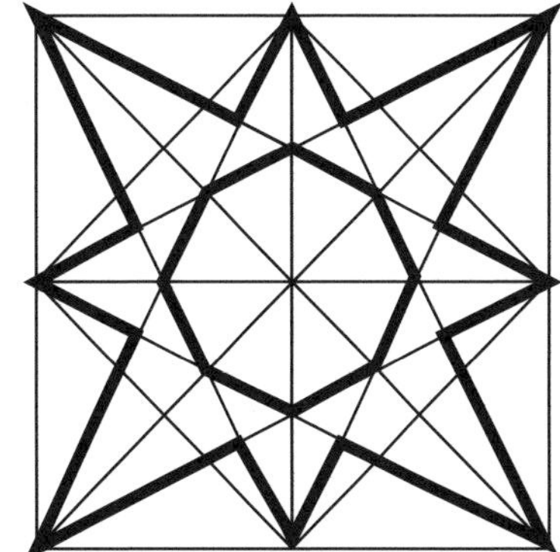

stellar flags

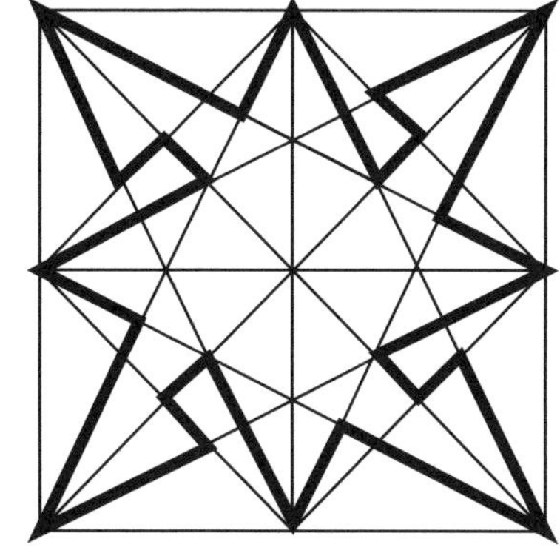

cosmic hoarfrost

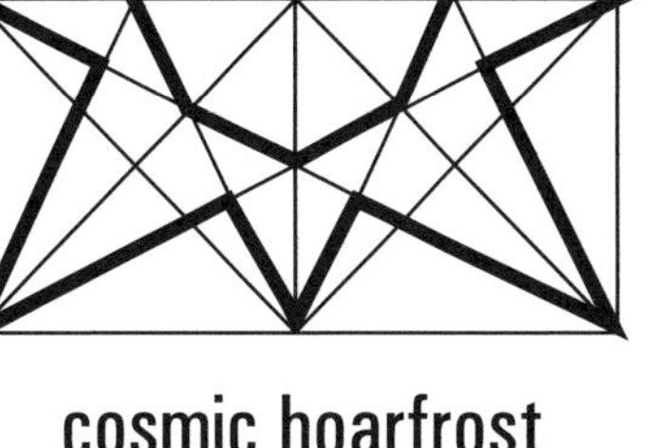

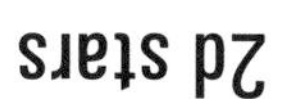

2d stars

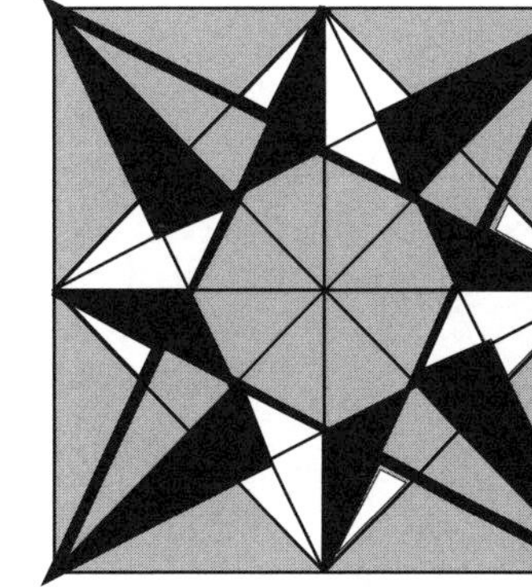

exterritorial cracks

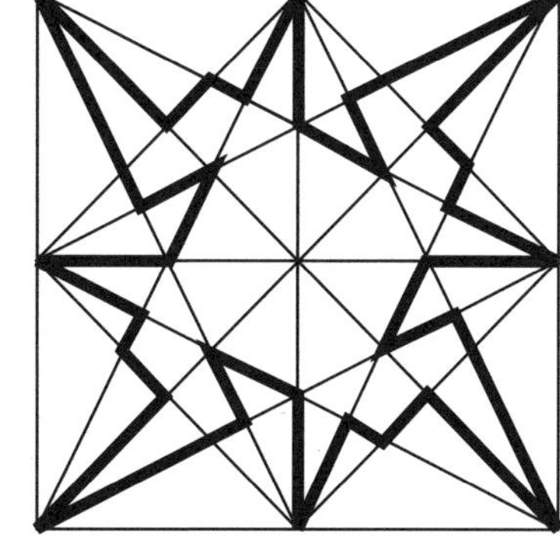

astral banners

outter flowers

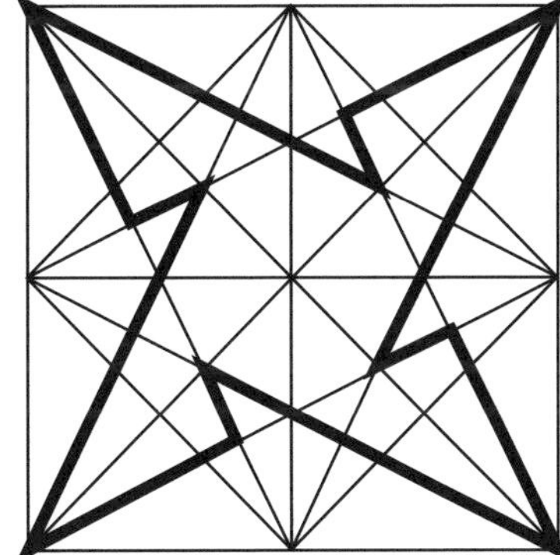

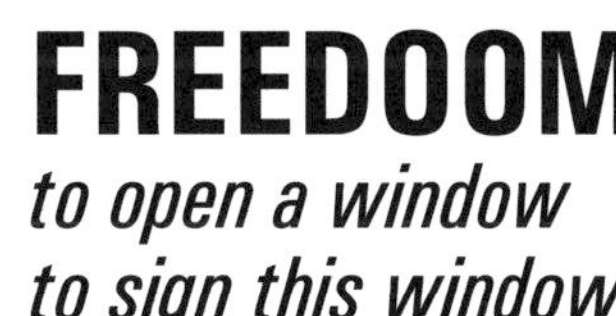

FREEDOOM

to open a window
to sign this window

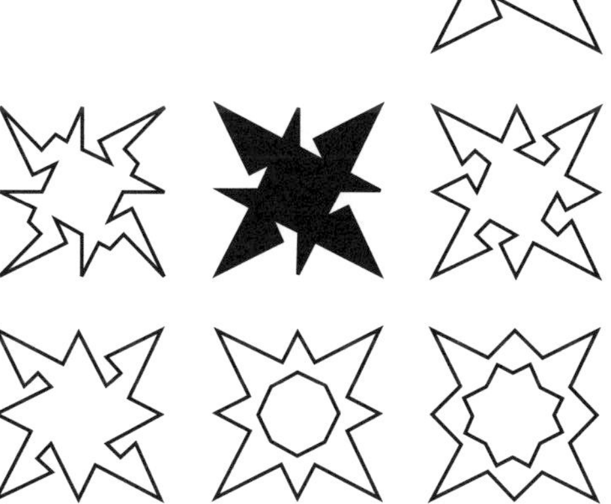

help the poor, help the rich, help the ugly, and help the beautiful, and that in Nature there is no such thing as what we people call a contradiction, which,

nonetheless, unfortunately, from these or those reasons, neoliberal competition
or totalitarian paranoia and academic turgidity, we ourselves construct and put

sounds,
sounds of car,
sounds from car,
sounds inside car,
sounds outside car,
sounds of interior of car,
sounds of exterior of car,
sounds of other cars,
sounds from other cars,
sounds of interiors of other cars,
sounds of drivers,
sounds of environment,
sounds of tires and street,

my tires?
my
sounds?

third
sounds,

song, radio, handy,

up as an obstacle or even borderlines, which are to protect us presumptively.
And when speaking about Us all – I don´t talk only about Humankind, but also

about all so-called living and so-called non-living, about that entire global Nature – carrier of the Truth, and not even it is innocent, nor always good or

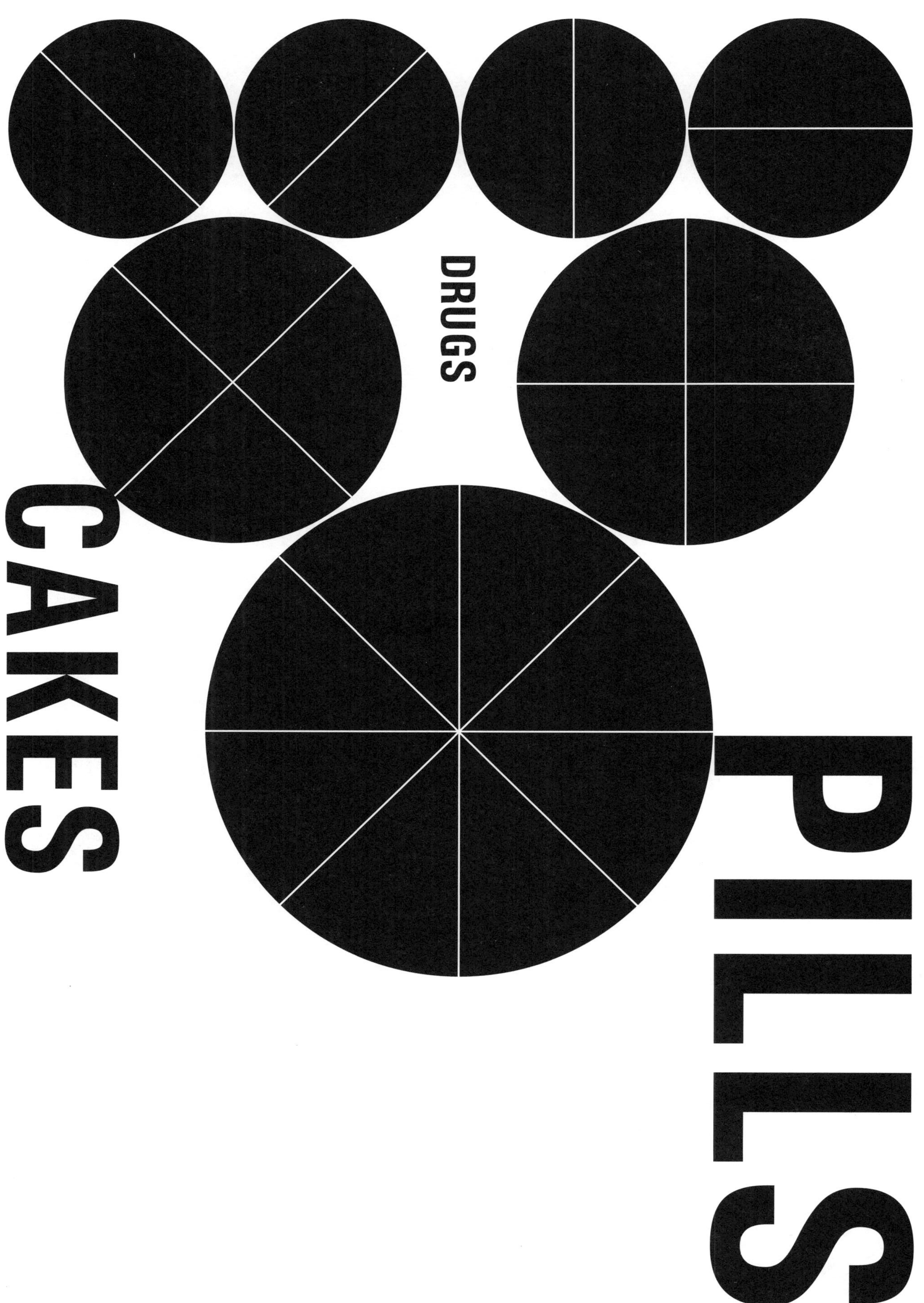

correct, he doesn´t give a fuck about your truth, although when you are dreaming his dreams, about the entire Universe, because we people are

PROPER AMMOUNT OF WATER IS NECESSARY,
THE TASTE IS JUST A BONUS.

PROPER LUBRICATION OF COLPOS IS NECESSARY,
BREASTS, NIPPLES, BUTT, FACE, EYES, LIPS ARE JUST A BONUS.

ONUS.

concentrated only inwards ourselves (simpler organisms adjust to radiation far more easily, the future of the Earth are rats, so let us pay attention to them already) and we understand only human language, we don´t even understand a dog barking any more, and yet a dog realises some things, phenomena much sooner than we do, such as the arrival of some natural disaster and such. After all, a dog recognises the sweat of fear and the sweat of excitement; we only feel

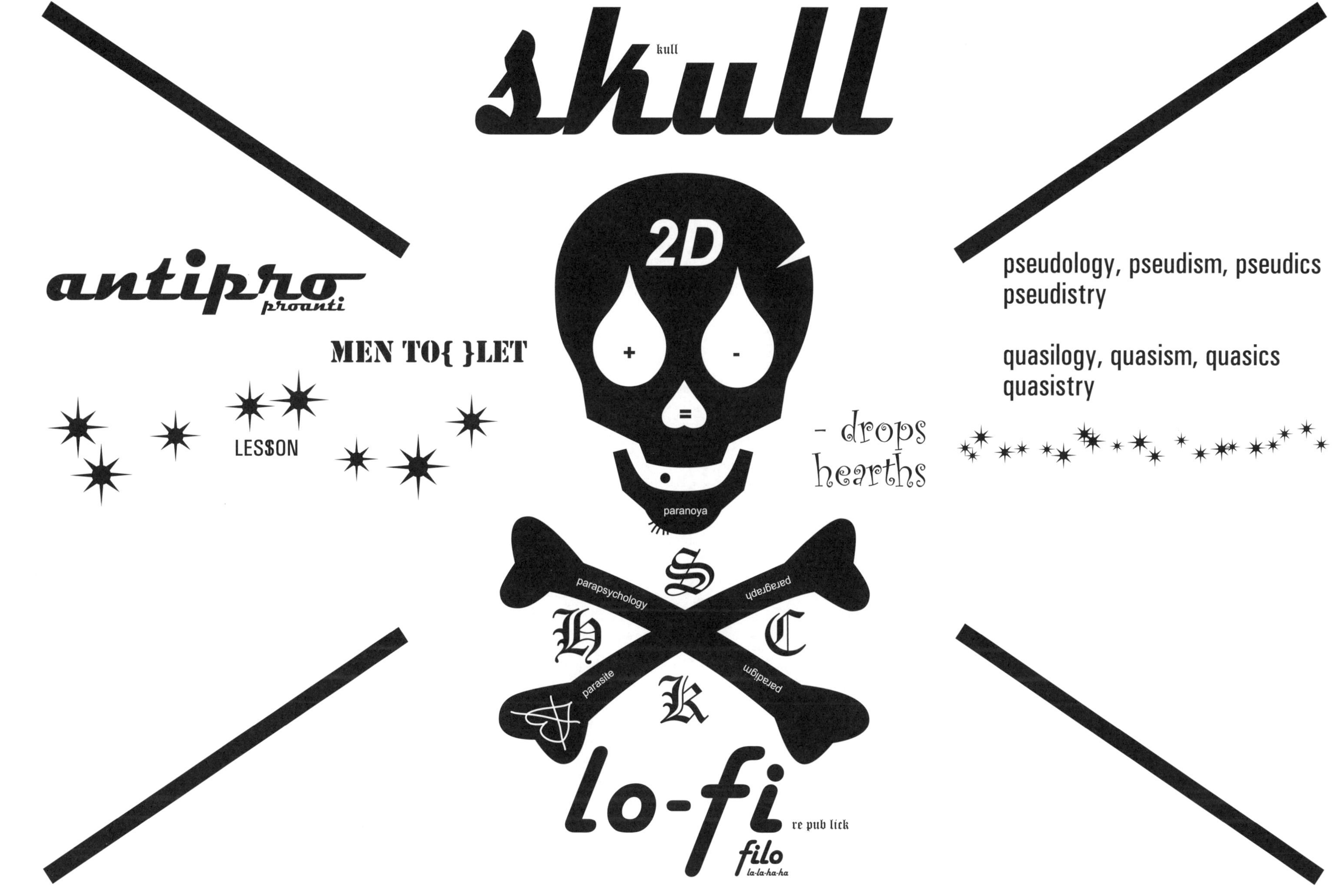

that “it” smells bad... (Read also Black birds & Blackbirds page ... of book number 1: Spoken Word, Written Word) And yes, even a human has (partial)

Touch your own shadow, my dear.

power over the future status of Nature and the Earth, when he blasts apart
the huge meteorite heading towards us from the Universe, spotted in time by

astrologers, who promptly notified army forces, those in permanent mobilisation. But due to his high-pitched sense of doubt, man´s instincts are retarded –

because while we are pondering, the dog has already bitten. To learn not only from one another, but criss-cross. We all are amateurs in every many. We all are

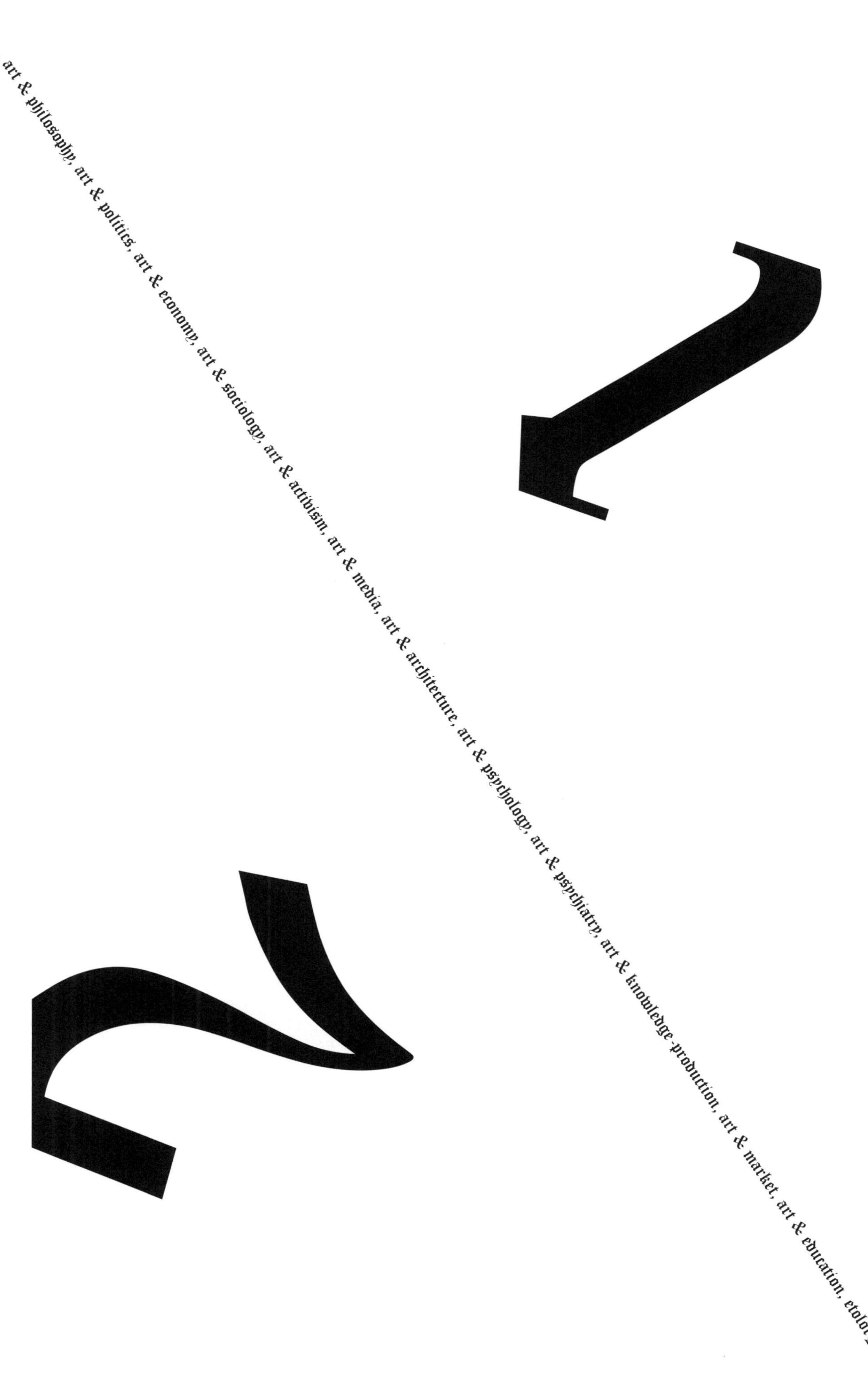

professional in each one. And yet, we are more identical than different. Are you? Yes, we are! Are you? Yes, I am. Tropical questions don´t call for arctic answers,

but in a temperate climate, such a dialogue could weather relatively well; and
a palm in Finland. Philanthropees John and Jane Doe & altruist Joe Bloggs. Real

WE TO BE WE

TEXT AND SINGING OF BORIS ONDREICKA
ON MUSIC OF FRANZ POMASSL A*PORT PU 2000

2005

WE TO BE WE
NEEDS I AND YOU

TOGETHER

I AND YOU
AND YOU AND I

TOGETHER

IF YOU LOVES I
WE MEANS GOOD
BUT IF I HATES YOU
THAT'S EVIL

YOU CONTAINS I
AND I CONTAINS YOU
BOTH CONTAIN WE
AND WE THEM

BUT SOMETIMES
WE IS THEY
SOMETIMES
I LOOKS LIKE WE

SOMETIMES
YOU TRIES TO BE I
SOMETIMES
I DENIES YOU

SOMETIMES YOU
IS FAR FROM I
SOMETIMES WE
IS OUT OF I AND YOU

IT HAPPENS THAT I
TRIES TO HIDE BEHIND YOU
I SLEEPS WELL
AND YOU WAKES BADLY

I IS NOT YOU
AND YOU ISN'T WE
YOU, I, WE,
YOU, I, WE

YOU UNDERSTANDS I
AND NO-ONE STANDS UNDER
THERE IS WE
AND THERE IS THEY

AND JUST IF THEY CAN
THEY SAY WE
WITHOUT US

WE TO BE WE
NEEDS I AND YOU

TOGETHER

I AND YOU
AND YOU AND I
I AND YOU
AND YOU AND I
I AND YOU
AND YOU AND I

TOGETHER

London versus Real Madrid – 0:0: liege passers-by against royally rich ball chasers (by which I don´t mean dung beetles; or Sisyphus). All is nature, all is natural. And there is nothing which wouldn´t be nature, there is nothing which is not normal, and if so, then only by us rationally or instinctively judged as

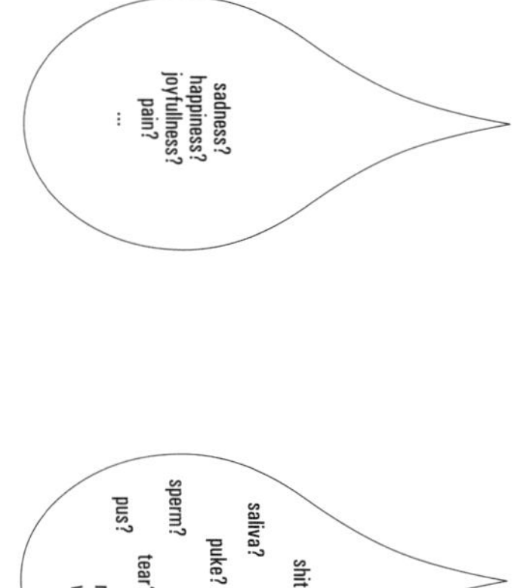

socially inadmissible / existentially vital – that will and ability to live together safely, healthily, or even productively, or even to construct, build, metabiotically ensure such conditions for future generations, for the children of the children of our children, and if necessary, also those rats. Only because of this was

As same as that girl in „Kyodai Makes The Big Time“ (one of the most beautiful movies I have ever seen) at the very end, I am listening, round and around, for almost an hour, Bob Mould singing just with piano: „He didn´t“ from Stephin Merritt, the 3rd track of The 6th´s „Hyacinths and Thistles “ album. One of the most beautiful albums, one of the most beautiful songs! It is pitty that just 2 minutes and 28 seconds.

But fortunately there was Rep1-function created.

Thank you all: Stephin Merritt, Bob Mould, Ian Kerkhof aka Aryan Kaganof

& Sony.

I do not remember anymore what she was listening to.

categorisation constructed to normal and abnormal, hello, I would like one more Coca Cola. Thank you.” “= = = = = = =?” “Yes, with ice.” For all of us (both jointly and individually) there remains a space which is unknown, and vice versa / backwards – to ascertain “the proto-origin” right in front of us is extremely

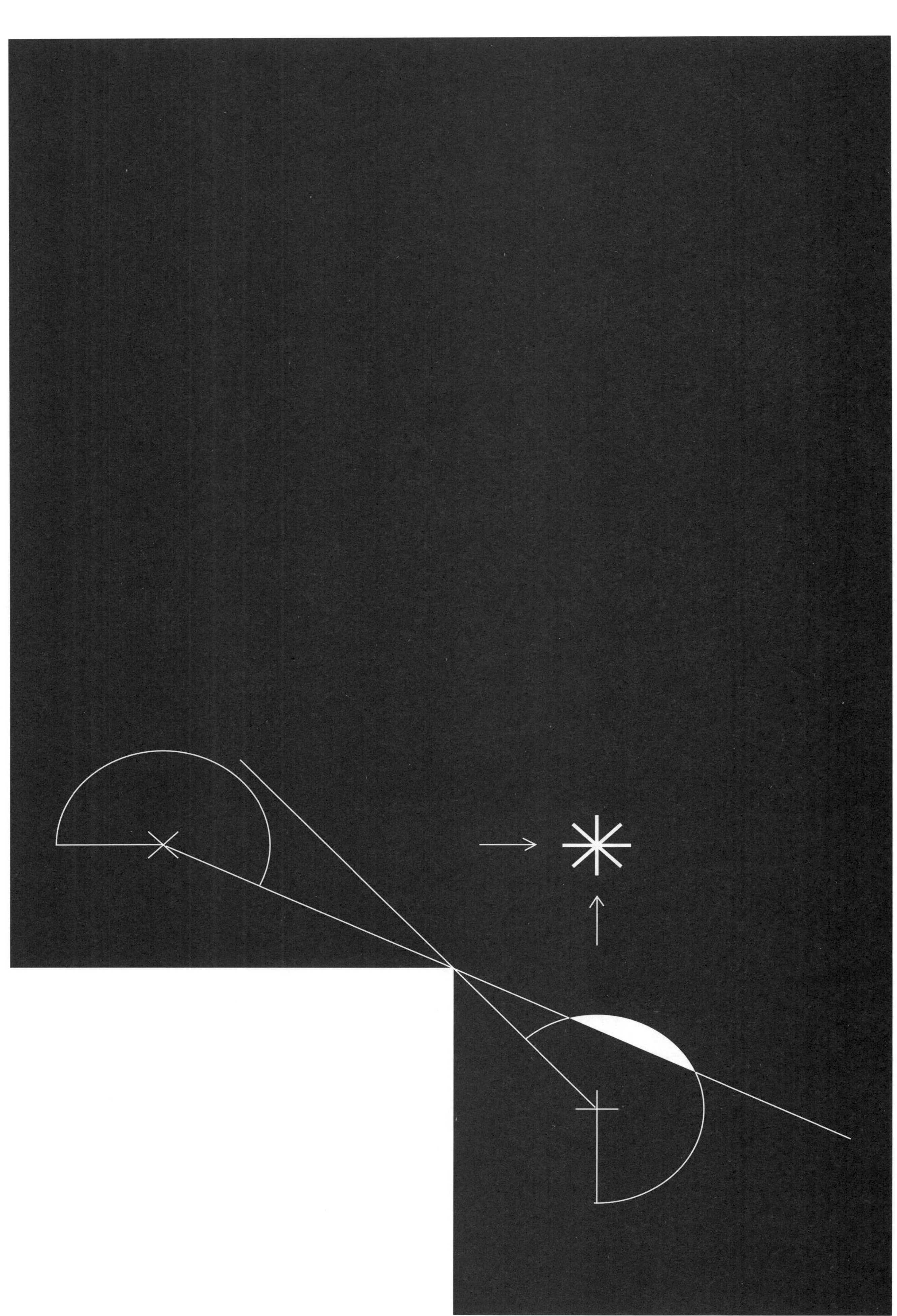

complicated; we can only make partial use of our brain, despite permanently carrying it with us, closely, however, it´s as if it weren´t sufficiently capable of reflecting upon itself, and we haven´t the slightest idea of whether we are alone in the universe. "Oh, and one Ristretto, please." "= =." It´s more likely that we

SHE

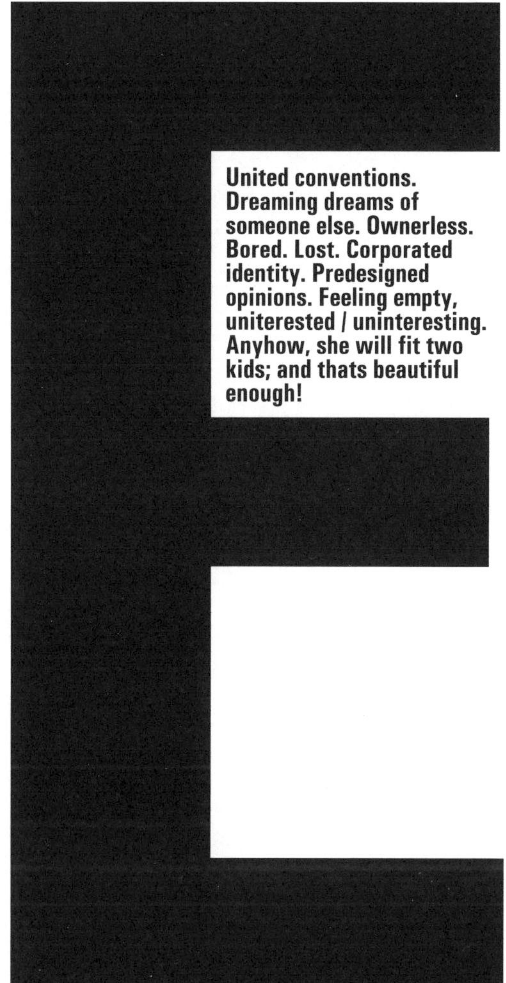

are not alone, because if we are here, why should we be unique, when the Universe is so huge that the Earth is just a grain? and the almost Talmudic observation of a star-lit sky reflection by looking onto the surface of a nocturnal lake, in such a way that you see those stars behind, together with, by your eye,

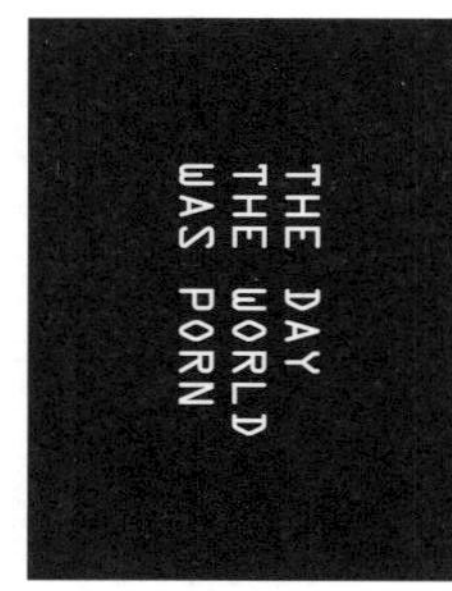

eyes, your face, head, but rippled by that reflex surface which coruscates so much... and underneath it, under that face, movements of fish shadows. I am an interested contemplative layman and to me, “Matter is also just a simplified declaration, the normality of Nature includes also para-normality, which is yet

and ſ at er

ſe tt er

ma de of ſeat her

se n t to her

o h

another human representative expression to the “unknown”. And there is nothing, which is unambiguously left and what is unambiguously right, and not all workers are good-natured and not all millionaires are whores, just for us not to get lost (and for our children not to get lost) we must progressively make

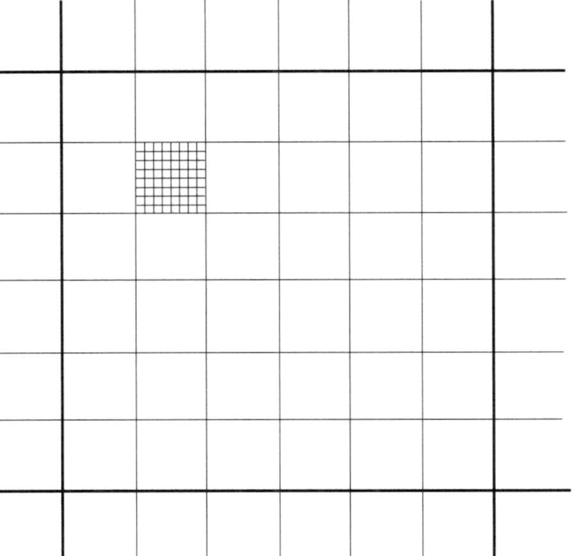

things trivial. We are left-right and right-left and up-and-down and down-and-up and west-east and north-south, simplycomplicated and complicatedlysimple, stupidlywise and wiselystupid, but one more time, we accept and use the agreed elementary protocols if we want to navigate somebody somewhere, because we

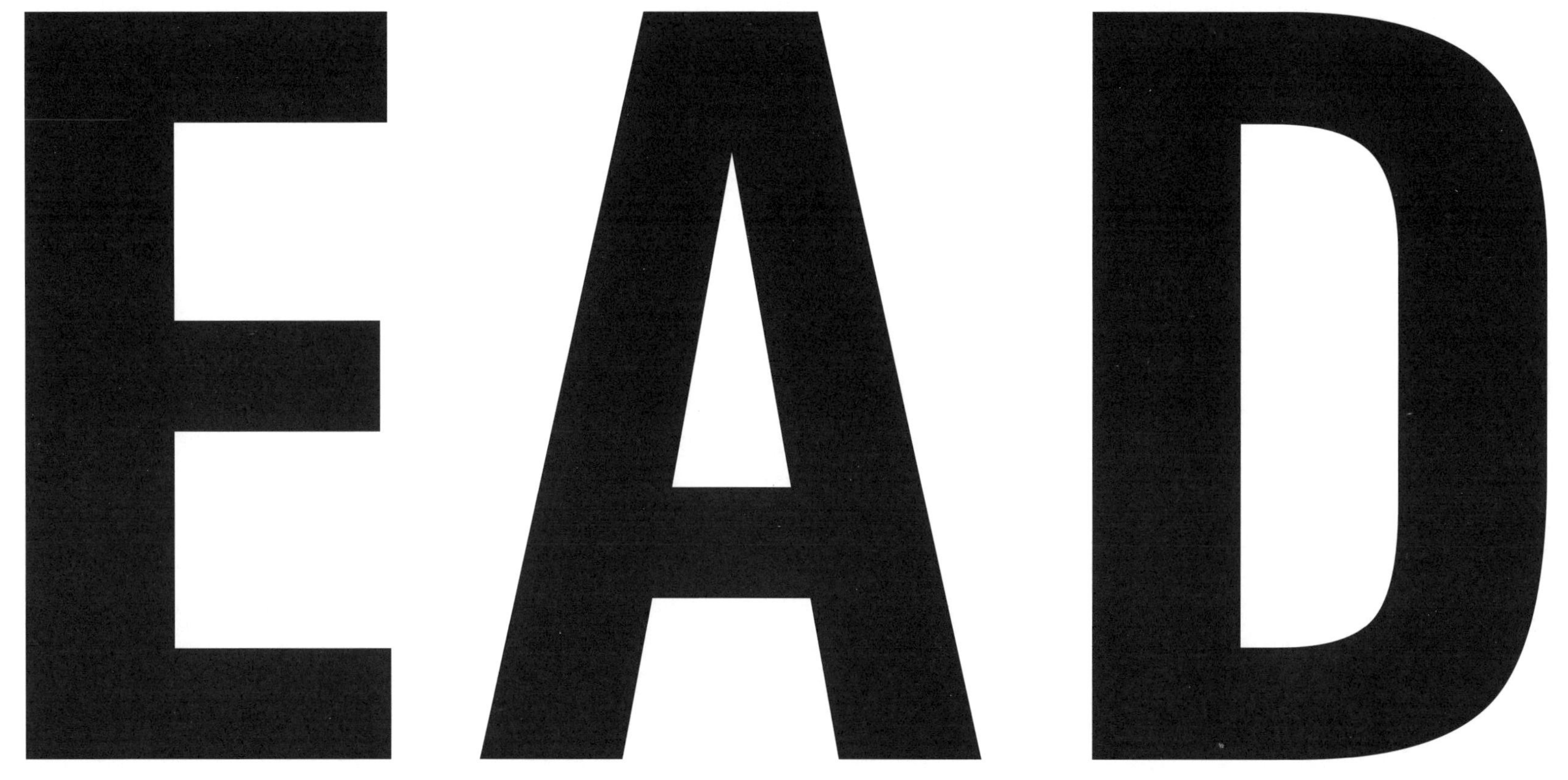

want someone, one another, to meet safely. To believe in God here is as foolishly and dangerously separating as to be a blasphemous manifestative atheist, since, at the end of the day, even I am questioningly devoured by my own consciousness about what all I have done bad in my own life. I perceive both as

1:1 The words of Kohelet, the son of David, king in Yerushalayim: 1:2 "Vanity of vanities," says Kohelet; "Vanity of vanities, all is vanity." 1:3 What does man gain from all his labor in which he labors under the sun? 1:4O ne generation goes, and another generation comes; but the earth remains forever. 1:5 The sun also rises, and the sun goes down, and hurries to its place where it rises. 1:6 The wind goes toward the south, and turns around to the north. It turns around continually as it goes, and the wind returns again to its courses. 1:7 All the rivers run into the sea, yet the sea is not full. To the place where the rivers flow, there they flow again. 1:8 All things are full of weariness beyond uttering. The eye is not satisfied with seeing, nor the ear filled with hearing. 1:9 That which has been is that which shall be; and that which has been done is that which shall be done: and there is no new thing under the sun. 1:10 Is there a thing of which it may be said, "Behold, this is new?" It has been long ago, in the ages which were before us. 1:11 There is no memory of the former; neither shall there be any memory of the latter that are to come, among those that shall come after. 1:12 I, Kohelet, was king over Yisra'el in Yerushalayim. 1:13 I applied my heart to seek and to search out by wisdom concerning all that is done under the sky. It is a heavy burden that God has given to the sons of men to be afflicted with. 1:14 I have seen all the works that are done under the sun; and, behold, all is vanity and a chasing after wind. 1:15 That which is crooked can't be made straight; and that which is lacking can't be counted. 1:16 I said to myself, "Behold, I have obtained for myself great wisdom above all who were before me in Yerushalayim. Yes, my heart has had great experience of wisdom and knowledge." 1:17 I applied my heart to know wisdom, and to know madness and folly. I perceived that this also was a chasing after wind. 1:18 For in much wisdom is much grief; and he who increases knowledge increases sorrow. 2:1 I said in my heart, "Come now, I will test you with mirth: therefore enjoy pleasure;" and, behold, this also was vanity. 2:2 I said of laughter, "It is foolishness;" and of mirth, "What does it accomplish?" 2:3 I searched in my heart how to cheer my flesh with wine, my heart yet guiding me with wisdom, and how to lay hold of folly, until I might see what it was good for the sons of men that they should do under heaven all the days of their lives. 2:4 I made myself great works. I built myself houses. I planted myself vineyards. 2:5 I made myself gardens and parks, and I planted trees in them of all kinds of fruit. 2:6 I made myself pools of water, to water from it the forest where trees were reared. 2:7I bought men-servants and maid-servants, and had servants born in my house. I also had great possessions of herds and flocks, above all who were before me in Yerushalayim; 2:8 I also gathered silver and gold for myself, and the treasure of kings and of the provinces. I got myself men-singers and women-singers, and the delights of the sons of men--musical instruments, and that of all sorts. 2:9 S o I was great, and increased more than all who were before me in Yerushalayim. My wisdom also remained with me. 2:10 Whatever my eyes desired, I didn't keep from them. I didn't withhold my heart from any joy, for my heart rejoiced because of all my labor, and this was my portion from all my labor. 2:11 Then I looked at all the works that my hands had worked, and at the labor that I had labored to do; and, behold, all was vanity and a chasing after wind, and there was no profit under the sun. 2:12 I turned myself to consider wisdom, madness, and folly: for what can the king's successor do? Just that which has been done long ago. 2:13 Then I saw that wisdom excels folly, as far as light excels darkness. 2:14 The wise man's eyes are in his head, and the fool walks in darkness--and yet I perceived that one event happens to them all. 2:15 Then said I in my heart, "As it happens to the fool, so will it happen even to me; and why was I then more wise?" Then said I in my heart that this also is vanity. 2:16 For of the wise man, even as of the fool, there is no memory for ever, seeing that in the days to come all will have been long forgotten. Indeed, the wise man must die just like the fool! 2:17 So I hated life, because the work that is worked under the sun was grievous to me; for all is vanity and a chasing after wind. 2:18 I hated all my labor in which I labored under the sun, seeing that I must leave it to the man who comes after me. 2:19 Who knows whether he will be a wise man or a fool? Yet he will have rule over all of my labor in which I have labored, and in which I have shown myself wise under the sun. This also is vanity. 2:20 Therefore I began to cause my heart to despair concerning all the labor in which I had labored under the sun. 2:21 F or there is a man whose labor is with wisdom, with knowledge, and with skillfulness; yet he shall leave it for his portion to a man who has not labored for it. This also is vanity and a great evil. 2:22 For what has a man of all his labor, and of the striving of his heart, in which he labors under the sun? 2:23 For all his days are sorrows, and his travail is grief; yes, even in the night his heart takes no rest. This also is vanity. 2:24 There is nothing better for a man than that he should eat and drink, and make his soul enjoy good in his labor. This also I saw, that it is from the hand of God. 2:25 For who can eat, or who can have enjoyment, more than I? 2:26 For to the man who pleases him, God gives wisdom, knowledge, and joy; but to the sinner he gives travail, to gather and to heap up, that he may give to him who pleases God. This also is vanity and a chasing after wind. 3:1 For everything there is a season, and a time for every purpose under heaven: 3:2 A time to be born, And a time to die; A time to plant, And a time to pluck up that which is planted; 3:3 A time to kill, And a time to heal; A time to break down, And a time to build up; 3:4 A time to weep, And a time to laugh; A time to mourn, And a time to dance; 3:5 A time to cast away stones, And a time to gather stones together; A time to embrace, And a time to refrain from embracing; 3:6 A time to seek, And a time to lose; A time to keep, And a time to cast away; 3:7 A time to tear, And a time to sew; A time to keep silence, And a time to speak; 3:8 A time to love, And a time to hate; A time for war, And a time for shalom. 3:9 What profit has he who works in that in which he labors? 3:10 I have seen the burden which God has given to the sons of men to be afflicted with. 3:11 He has made everything beautiful in its time. He has also set eternity in their hearts, yet so that man can't find out the work that God has done from the beginning even to the end. 3:12 I know that there is nothing better for them than to rejoice, and to do good as long as they live. 3:13 Also that every man should eat and drink, and enjoy good in all his labor, is the gift of God. 3:14 I know that whatever God does, it shall be forever. Nothing can be added to it, nor anything taken from it; and God has done it, that men should fear before him. 3:15 That which is has been long ago, and that which is to be has been long ago: and God seeks again that which is passed away. 3:16 Moreover I saw under the sun, in the place of justice, that wickedness was there; and in the place of righteousness, that wickedness was there. 3:17 I said in my heart, "God will judge the righteous and the wicked; for there is a time there for every purpose and for every work." 3:18 I said in my heart, "As for the sons of men, God tests them, so that they may see that they themselves are like animals. 3:19 For that which happens to the sons of men happens to animals. Even one thing happens to them. As the one dies, so the other dies. Yes, they have all one breath; and man has no advantage over the animals: for all is vanity. 3:20 All go to one place. All are from the dust, and all turn to dust again. 3:21 Who knows the spirit of man, whether it goes upward, and the spirit of the animal, whether it goes downward to the earth?" 3:22 Therefore I saw that there is nothing better, than that a man should rejoice in his works; for that is his portion: for who can bring him to see what will be after him? 4:1 Then I returned and saw all the oppressions that are done under the sun: and, behold, the tears of those who were oppressed, and they had no comforter; and on the side of their oppressors there was power; but they had no comforter. 4:2 Therefore I praised the dead who have been long dead more than the living who are yet alive. 4:3 Yes, better than them both is him who has not yet been, who has not seen the evil work that is done under the sun. 4:4 Then I saw all the labor and achievement that is the envy of a man's neighbor. This also is vanity and a striving after wind. 4:5 The fool folds his hands together and ruins himself. 4:6 Better is a handful, with quietness, than two handfuls with labor and chasing after wind. 4:7 Then I returned and saw vanity under the sun. 4:8 There is one who is alone, and he has neither son nor brother. There is no end to all of his labor, neither are his eyes satisfied with wealth. For whom then, do I labor, and deprive my soul of enjoyment? This also is vanity, yes, it is a miserable business. 4:9 Two are better than one, because they have a good reward for their labor. 4:10 For if they fall, the one will lift up his fellow; but woe to him who is alone when he falls, and doesn't have another to lift him up. 4:11 Again, if two lie together, then they have warmth; but how can one keep warm alone? 4:12 If a man prevails against one who is alone, two shall withstand him; and a threefold cord is not quickly broken. 4:13 Better is a poor and wise youth than an old and foolish king who doesn't know how to receive admonition any more. 4:14 For out of prison he came forth to be king; yes, even in his kingdom he was born poor. 4:15 I saw all the living who walk under the sun, that they were with the youth, the other, who succeeded him. 4:16 There was no end of all the people, even of all them over whom he was--yet those who come after shall not rejoice in him. Surely this also is vanity and a chasing after wind. 5:1 Guard your steps when you go to God's house; for to draw near to listen is better than to give the sacrifice of fools, for they don't know that they do evil. 5:2 Don't be rash with your mouth, and don't let your heart be hasty to utter anything before God; for God is in heaven, and you on earth. Therefore let your words be few. 5:3 For as a dream comes with a multitude of cares, so a fool's speech with a multitude of words. 5:4 When you vow a vow to God, don't defer to pay it; for he has no pleasure in fools. Pay that which you vow. 5:5 It is better that you should not vow, than that you should vow and not pay. 5:6 Don't allow your mouth to lead you into sin. Don't protest before the messenger that this was a mistake. Why should God be angry at your voice, and destroy the work of your hands? 5:7 For in the multitude of dreams there are vanities, as well as in many words: but you must fear God. 5:8 If you see the oppression of the poor, and the violent taking away of justice and righteousness in a district, don't marvel at the matter: for one official is eyed by a higher one; and there are officials over them. 5:9 Moreover the profit of the earth is for all. The king profits from the field. 5:10 He who loves silver shall not be satisfied with silver; nor he who loves abundance, with increase: this also is vanity. 5:11 When goods increase, those who eat them are increased; and what advantage is there to its owner, except to feast on them with his eyes? 5:12 The sleep of a laboring man is sweet, whether he eats little or much; but the abundance of the rich will not allow him to sleep. 5:13 There is a grievous evil which I have seen under the sun: wealth kept by its owner to his harm. 5:14 Those riches perish by misfortune, and if he has fathered a son, there is nothing in his hand. 5:15 As he came forth from his mother's womb, naked shall he go again as he came, and shall take nothing for his labor, which he may carry away in his hand. 5:16 This also is a grievous evil, that in all points as he came, so shall he go. And what profit does he have who labors for the wind? 5:17 All his days he also eats in darkness, he is frustrated, and has sickness and wrath. 5:18 Behold, that which I have seen to be good and proper is for one to eat and to drink, and to enjoy good in all his labor, in which he labors under the sun, all the days of his life which God has given him; for this is his portion. 5:19 Every man also to whom God has given riches and wealth, and has given him power to eat of it, and to take his portion, and to rejoice in his labor--this is the gift of God. 5:20 For he shall not often reflect on the days of his life; because God occupies him with the joy of his heart. 6:1 There is an evil which I have seen under the sun, and it is heavy on men: 6:2 a man to whom God gives riches, wealth, and honor, so that he lacks nothing for his soul of all that he desires, yet God gives him no power to eat of it, but an alien eats it. This is vanity, and it is an evil disease. 6:3 If a man fathers a hundred children, and lives many years, so that the days of his years are many, but his soul is not filled with good, and moreover he has no burial; I say, that an untimely birth is better than he: 6:4 for it comes in vanity, and departs in darkness, and its name is covered with darkness. 6:5 Moreover it has not seen the sun nor known it. This has rest rather than the other. 6:6 Yes, though he live a thousand years twice told, and yet fails to enjoy good, don't all go to one place? 6:7 All the labor of man is for his mouth, and yet the appetite is not filled. 6:8 For what advantage has the wise more than the fool? What has the poor man, that knows how to walk before the living? 6:9 Better is the sight of the eyes than the wandering of the desire. This also is vanity and a chasing after wind. 6:10 Whatever has been, its name was given long ago; and it is known what man is; neither can he contend with him who is mightier than he. 6:11 For there are many words that create vanity. What does that profit man? 6:12 For who knows what is good for man in life, all the days of his vain life which he spends like a shadow? For who can tell a man what will be after him under the sun? 7:1 A good name is better than fine perfume; and the day of death better than the day of one's birth. 7:2 It is better to go to the house of mourning than to go to the house of feasting: for that is the end of all men, and the living should take this to heart. 7:3 Sorrow is better than laughter; for by the sadness of the face the heart is made good. 7:4 The heart of the wise is in the house of mourning; but the heart of fools is in the house of mirth. 7:5 It is better to hear the rebuke of the wise, than for a man to hear the song of fools. 7:6 For as the crackling of thorns under a pot, so is the laughter of the fool. This also is vanity. 7:7 Surely extortion makes the wise man foolish; and a bribe destroys the understanding. 7:8 Better is the end of a thing than its beginning. The patient in spirit is better than the proud in spirit. 7:9 Don't be hasty in your spirit to be angry, for anger rests in the bosom of fools. 7:10 Don't say, "Why were the former days better than these?" For you do not ask wisely about this. 7:11 Wisdom is as good as an inheritance. Yes, it is more excellent for those who see the sun. 7:12 For wisdom is a defense, even as money is a defense; but the excellency of knowledge is that wisdom preserves the life of him who has it. 7:13 Consider the work of God, for who can make that straight, which he has made crooked? 7:14 In the day of prosperity be joyful, and in the day of adversity consider; yes, God has made the one side by side with the other, to the end that man should not find out anything after him. 7:15 All this have I seen in my days of vanity: there is a righteous man who perishes in his righteousness, and there is a wicked man who lives long in his evil-doing. 7:16 Don't be overly righteous, neither make yourself overly wise. Why should you destroy yourself? 7:17 Don't be too wicked, neither be foolish. Why should you die before your time? 7:18 It is good that you should take hold of this. Yes, also from that don't withdraw your hand; for he who fears God will come forth from them all. 7:19 Wisdom is a strength to the wise man more than ten rulers who are in a city. 7:20 Surely there is not a righteous man on earth, who does good and doesn't sin. 7:21 Also don't take heed to all words that are spoken, lest you hear your servant curse you; 7:22 for often your own heart knows that you yourself have likewise cursed others. 7:23 All this have I proved in wisdom. I said, "I will be wise;" but it was far from me. 7:24 That which is, is far off and exceedingly deep. Who can find it out? 7:25 I turned around, and my heart sought to know and to search out, and to seek wisdom and the scheme of things, and to know that wickedness is stupidity, and that foolishness is madness. 7:26 I find more bitter than death the woman whose heart is snares and traps, whose hands are chains. Whoever pleases God shall escape from her; but the sinner will be ensnared by her. 7:27 Behold, this have I found, says Kohelet, one to another, to find out the scheme; 7:28 which my soul still seeks; but I have not found: one man among a thousand have I found; but a woman among all those have I not found. 7:29 Behold, this only have I found: that God made man upright; but they search for many schemes. 8:1 Who is like the wise man? And who knows the interpretation of a thing? A man's wisdom makes his face shine, and the hardness of his face is changed. 8:2 I say, "Keep the king's command!" because of the oath to God. 8:3 Don't be hasty to go out of his presence. Don't persist in an evil thing, for he does whatever pleases him, 8:4 for the king's word is supreme. Who can say to him, "What are you doing?" 8:5 Whoever keeps the mitzvah shall not come to harm, and his wise heart will know the time and procedure. 8:6 For there is a time and procedure for every purpose, although the misery of man is heavy on him. 8:7 For he doesn't know that which will be; for who can tell him how it will be? 8:8 There is no man who has power over the spirit to contain the spirit; neither does he have power over the day of death. There is no discharge in war; neither shall wickedness deliver those who practice it. 8:9 All this have I seen, and applied my mind to every work that is done under the sun. There is a time in which one man has power over another to his hurt. 8:10 So I saw the wicked buried. Indeed they came also from holiness. They went and were forgotten in the city where they did this. This also is vanity. 8:11 Because sentence against an evil work is not executed speedily, therefore the heart of the sons of men is fully set in them to do evil. 8:12 Though a sinner commits crimes a hundred times, and lives long, yet surely I know that it will be better with those who fear God, who are reverent before him. 8:13But it shall not be well with the wicked, neither shall he lengthen days like a shadow; because he doesn't fear God. 8:14 There is a vanity which is done on the earth, that there are righteous men to whom it happens according to the work of the wicked. Again, there are wicked men to whom it happens according to the work of the righteous. I said that this also is vanity. 8:15 Then I commended mirth, because a man has no better thing under the sun, than to eat, and to drink, and to be joyful: for that will accompany him in his labor all the days of his life which God has given him under the sun. 8:16 When I applied my heart to know wisdom, and to see the business that is done on the earth (for also there is that neither day nor night sees sleep with his eyes), 8:17 then I saw all the work of God, that man can't find out the work that is done under the sun, because however much a man labors to seek it out, yet he won't find it. Yes even though a wise man thinks he can comprehend it, he won't be able to find it. 9:1 For all this I laid to my heart, even to explore all this: that the righteous, and the wise, and their works, are in the hand of God; whether it is love or hatred, man doesn't know it; all is before them. 9:2 All things come alike to all. There is one event to the righteous and to the wicked; to the good, to the clean, to the unclean, to him who sacrifices, and to him who doesn't sacrifice. As is the good, so is the sinner; he who takes an oath, as he who fears an oath. 9:3 This is an evil in all that is done under the sun, that there is one event to all: yes also, the heart of the sons of men is full of evil, and madness is in their heart while they live, and after that they go to the dead. 9:4 For to him who is joined with all the living there is hope; for a living dog is better than a dead lion. 9:5 For the living know that they will die, but the dead don't know anything, neither do they have any more a reward; for the memory of them is forgotten. 9:6 Also their love, their hatred, and their envy has perished long ago; neither have they any more a portion forever in anything that is done under the sun. 9:7 Go your way--eat your bread with joy, and drink your wine with a merry heart; for God has already accepted your works. 9:8 Let your garments be always white, and don't let your head lack oil. 9:9 Live joyfully with the wife whom you love all the days of your life of vanity, which he has given you under the sun, all your days of vanity: for that is your portion in life, and in your labor in which you labor under the sun. 9:10 Whatever your hand finds to do, do it with your might; for there is no work, nor device, nor knowledge, nor wisdom, in She'ol, where you are going. 9:11 I returned, and saw under the sun, that the race is not to the swift, nor the battle to the strong, neither yet bread to the wise, nor yet riches to men of understanding, nor yet favor to men of skill; but time and chance happen to them all. 9:12 For man also doesn't know his time. As the fish that are taken in an evil net, and as the birds that are caught in the snare, even so are the sons of men snared in an evil time, when it falls suddenly on them. 9:13 I have also seen wisdom under the sun in this way, and it seemed great to me. 9:14 There was a little city, and few men within it; and a great king came against it, besieged it, and built great bulwarks against it. 9:15 Now a poor wise man was found in it, and he by his wisdom delivered the city; yet no man remembered that same poor man. 9:16 Then said I, Wisdom is better than strength. Nevertheless the poor man's wisdom is despised, and his words are not heard. 9:17 The words of the wise heard in quiet are better than the cry of him who rules among fools. 9:18 Wisdom is better than weapons of war; but one sinner destroys much good. 10:1 Dead flies cause the oil of the perfumer to send forth an evil odor; so does a little folly outweigh wisdom and honor. 10:2 A wise man's heart is at his right hand, but a fool's heart at his left. 10:3 Yes also, when the fool walks by the way, his understanding fails him, and he says to everyone that he is a fool. 10:4 If the spirit of the ruler rises up against you, don't leave your place; for gentleness lays great offenses to rest. 10:5 There is an evil which I have seen under the sun, the sort of error which proceeds from the ruler. 10:6 Folly is set in great dignity, and the rich sit in a low place. 10:7 I have seen servants on horses, and princes walking like servants on the earth. 10:8 He who digs a pit may fall into it; and whoever breaks through a wall may be bitten by a snake. 10:9 Whoever carves out stones may be injured by them. Whoever splits wood may be endangered thereby. 10:10 If the axe is blunt, and one doesn't sharpen the edge, then he must use more strength; but skill brings success. 10:11 If the snake bites before it is charmed, then is there no profit for the charmer's tongue. 10:12 The words of a wise man's mouth are gracious; but a fool is swallowed by his own lips. 10:13 The beginning of the words of his mouth is foolishness; and the end of his talk is mischievous madness. 10:14 A fool also multiplies words. Man doesn't know what will be; and that which will be after him, who can tell him? 10:15 The labor of fools wearies every one of them; for he doesn't know how to go to the city. 10:16 Woe to you, land, when your king is a child, And your princes eat in the morning! 10:17 Happy are you, land, when your king is the son of nobles, And your princes eat in due season, For strength, and not for drunkenness! 10:18 By slothfulness the roof sinks in; And through idleness of the hands the house leaks. 10:19 A feast is made for laughter, And wine makes the life glad; And money is the answer for all things. 10:20 Don't curse the king, no, not in your thoughts; And don't curse the rich in your bedchamber: For a bird of the sky may carry your voice, And that which has wings may tell the matter. 11:1 Cast your bread on the waters; For you shall find it after many days. 11:2 Give a portion to seven, yes, even to eight; For you don't know what evil will be on the earth. 11:3 If the clouds are full of rain, they empty themselves on the earth; And if a tree falls toward the south, or toward the north, In the place where the tree falls, there shall it be. 11:4 He who observes the wind won't sow; And he who regards the clouds won't reap. 11:5 As you don't know what is the way of the wind, Nor how the bones grow in the womb of her who is with child; Even so you don't know the work of God who does all. 11:6 In the morning sow your seed, And in the evening don't withhold your hand; For you don't know which will prosper, whether this or that, Or whether they both will be equally good. 11:7 Truly the light is sweet, And a pleasant thing it is for the eyes to see the sun. 11:8 Yes, if a man lives many years, let him rejoice in them all; But let him remember the days of darkness, for they shall be many. All that comes is vanity. 11:9 Rejoice, young man, in your youth, And let your heart cheer you in the days of your youth, And walk in the ways of your heart, And in the sight of your eyes; But know that for all these things God will bring you into judgment. 11:10 Therefore remove sorrow from your heart, And put away evil from your flesh; For youth and the dawn of life are vanity. 12:1 Remember also your Creator in the days of your youth, Before the evil days come, and the years draw near, When you will say, "I have no pleasure in them;" 12:2 Before the sun, the light, the moon, and the stars are darkened, And the clouds return after the rain; 12:3 In the day when the keepers of the house shall tremble, And the strong men shall bow themselves, And the grinders cease because they are few, And those who look out of the windows are darkened, 12:4 And the doors shall be shut in the street; When the sound of the grinding is low, And one shall rise up at the voice of a bird, And all the daughters of music shall be brought low; 12:5 Yes, they shall be afraid of heights, And terrors will be in the way; And the almond tree shall blossom, And the khagav shall be a burden, And desire shall fail; Because man goes to his everlasting home, And the mourners go about the streets: 12:6 Before the silver cord is severed, Or the golden bowl is broken, Or the pitcher is broken at the spring, Or the wheel broken at the cistern, 12:7 And the dust returns to the earth as it was, And the spirit returns to God who gave it. 12:8 Vanity of vanities, says Kohelet; All is vanity! 12:9 Further, because Kohelet was wise, he still taught the people knowledge. Yes, he pondered, sought out, and set in order many proverbs. 12:10 The Preacher sought to find out acceptable words, and that which was written blamelessly, words of truth. 12:11 The words of the wise are like goads; and like nails well fastened are words from the masters of assemblies, which are given from one shepherd. 12:12 Furthermore, my son, be admonished: of making many books there is no end; and much study is a weariness of the flesh. 12:13 This is the end of the matter. All has been heard. Fear God, and keep his mitzvot; for this is the whole duty of man. 12:14 For God will bring every work into judgment, with every hidden thing, whether it is good, or whether it is evil.

manifestations of the high-pitched arrogant demand – “I know how it was and why it is so!” (and will be.)”. Faugh! Spiritualness, spirituality... We mustn´t

Sing in the brain, my dear.

claim any Faith!!!, no faith can be politically institutionalised, we mustn´t create any new churches!!!, no existing churches may have any connection to state power, they must be financed exclusively by their own communities, must have solely not-for-profit legal status, since they draw the borders, but not those in the sense of a wall in a room, that protects us against heat, or frost... That type of nothing-protecting borders must cease en bloc, as well as those of the church.

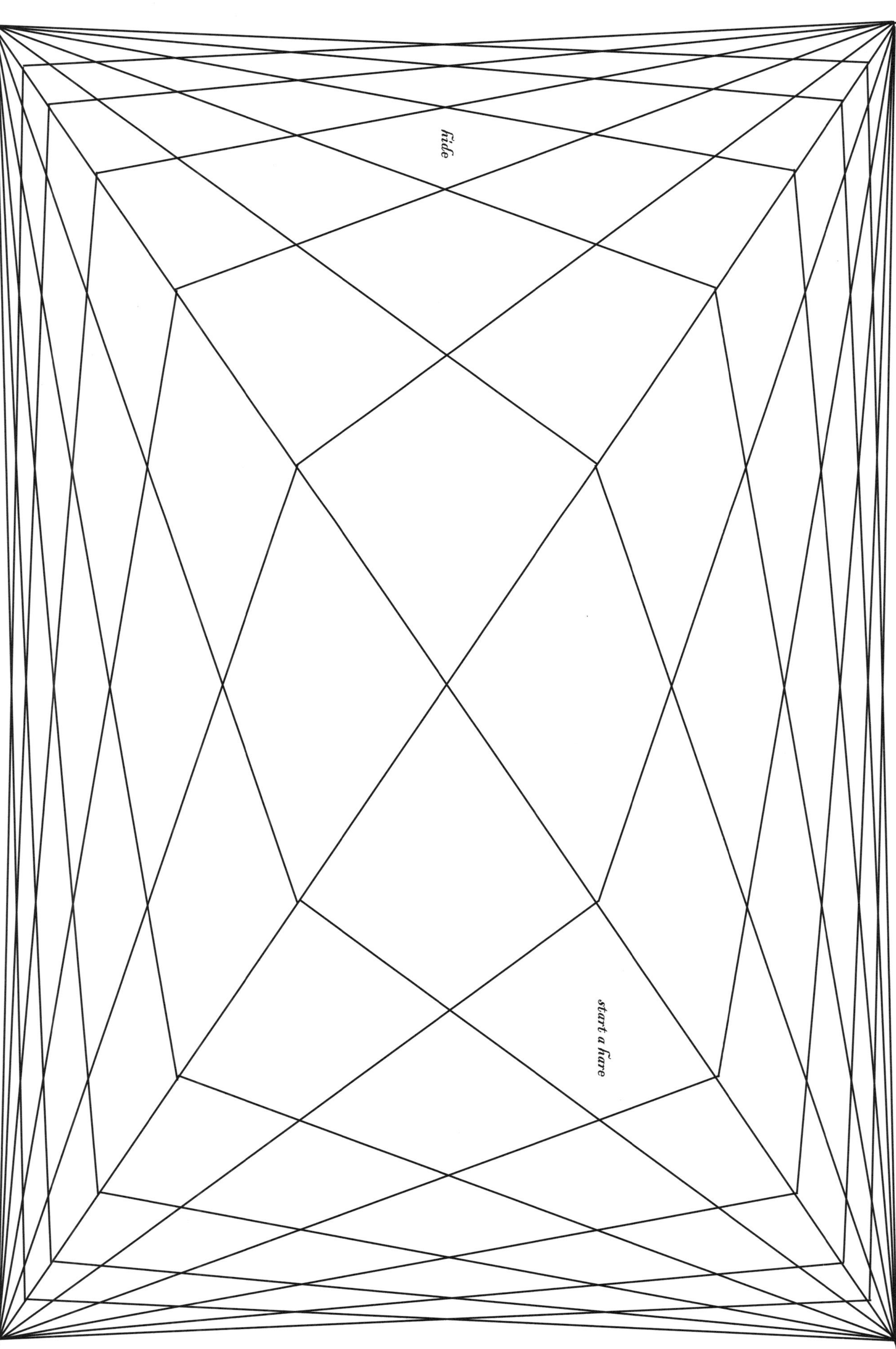

No Greater Hungary – just Great World, where there is enough room even for Hungarians! We must constantly remind ourselves that the truth, which we are

inclined to rely on, is only human, hence consequently fallible (we cannot
measure everything), and / but – that a man is not the only what there is here and

> he has been eating beans

> he meets her
> they start to talk
> he moves himself carelessly
> he farts*
> he runs away

> > they'll never talk to each other again

> > they'll never kiss

> > they'll never have sex

> > they'll never marry

> > they'll never have kids

> > they'll never divorce

> >

*one second

too early

there. It is crucial to talk and cooperate! And if, in spite of it all, we can not find a way to each other (reason and will) (BIOMATH >> SOCMATH / BIOMATH

<< SOCMATH; BIOMATH >> SOCMATH / SOCMATH >> BIOMATH), and, truly, we really cannot, because we all are exhausted from our jobs up to the

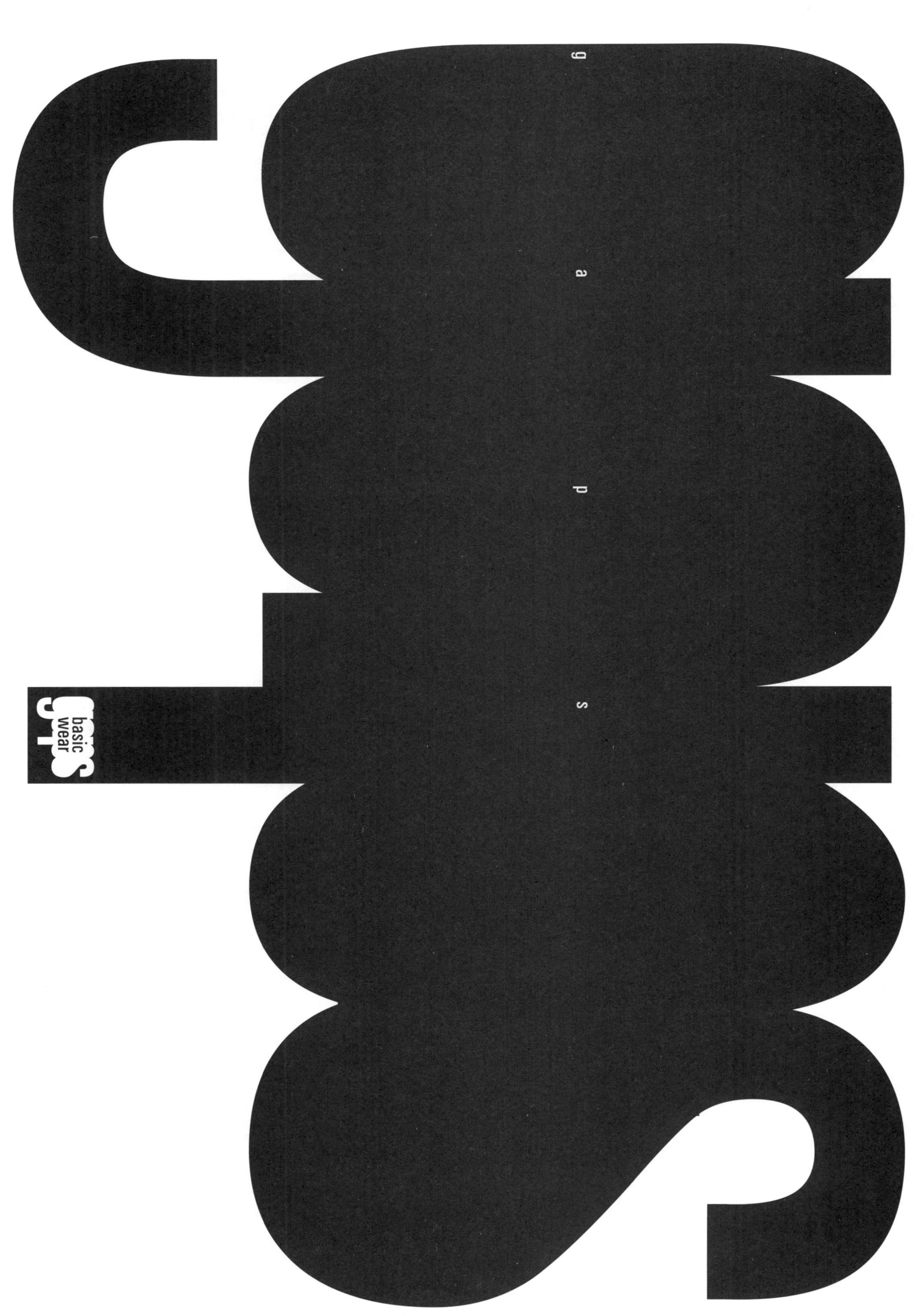

surface of the family ego skeleton, the family, which primarily must eat and be in warmth, because a film director does not go to concerts and an actor doesn´t read books and a writer will not come to an exhibition, about which a journalist will not write, because he is just looking at the convex bottom of some Jennifer

Why am I so tired?

Cause I was dreaming about falling asleep.

Lopez somewhere at the Nouvelle Cousine / Societé Croulant banquet after the award-giving of the so-called Academy, then / THEREFORE I propose the urgent foundation of an AGENCY OF INITIATION AND MEDIATION OF INTERDISCIPLINARY DIALOGUE (A.I.M.I.D. – “that doesn´t sound bad,

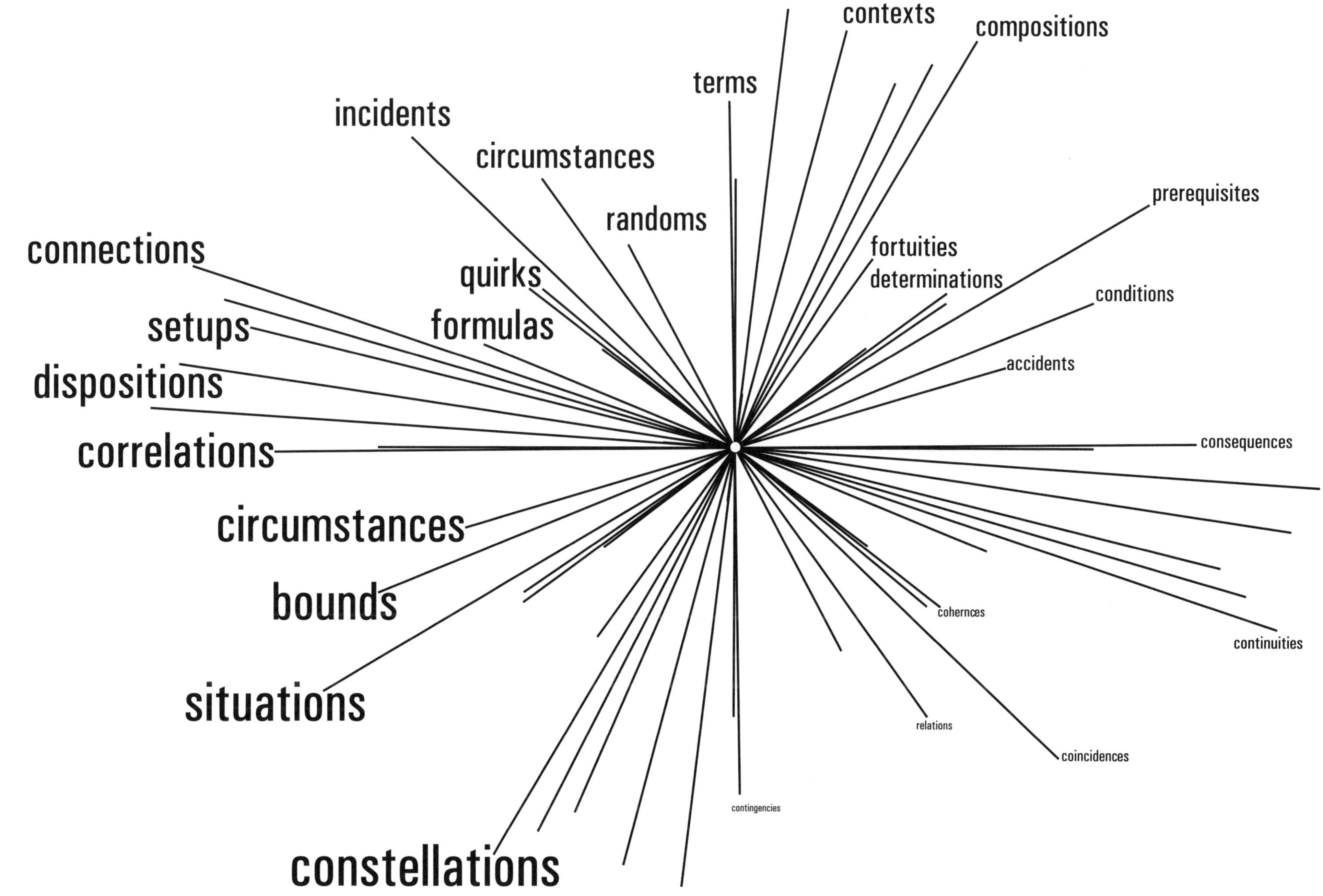

does it?") a national agency ABOVE the level of UNESCO, ABOVE the level of the UN! This "apolitical", pacifist, non-profit association (also both the so-called

left wing and right wing, both religiously-based and atheist...) would in its core
consist of an inter-disciplinary staff of brilliant minds; first, it would define

to two too

to two too

totwotoo

totwotoo

the sum All (and in accordance with All, widen its rows) and then it would generate the closest (themselves the first audience to themselves) and further discourse priorities. It would formulate them and concentrate the persons involved, motivate, moderate, do post-production processing, evaluate and

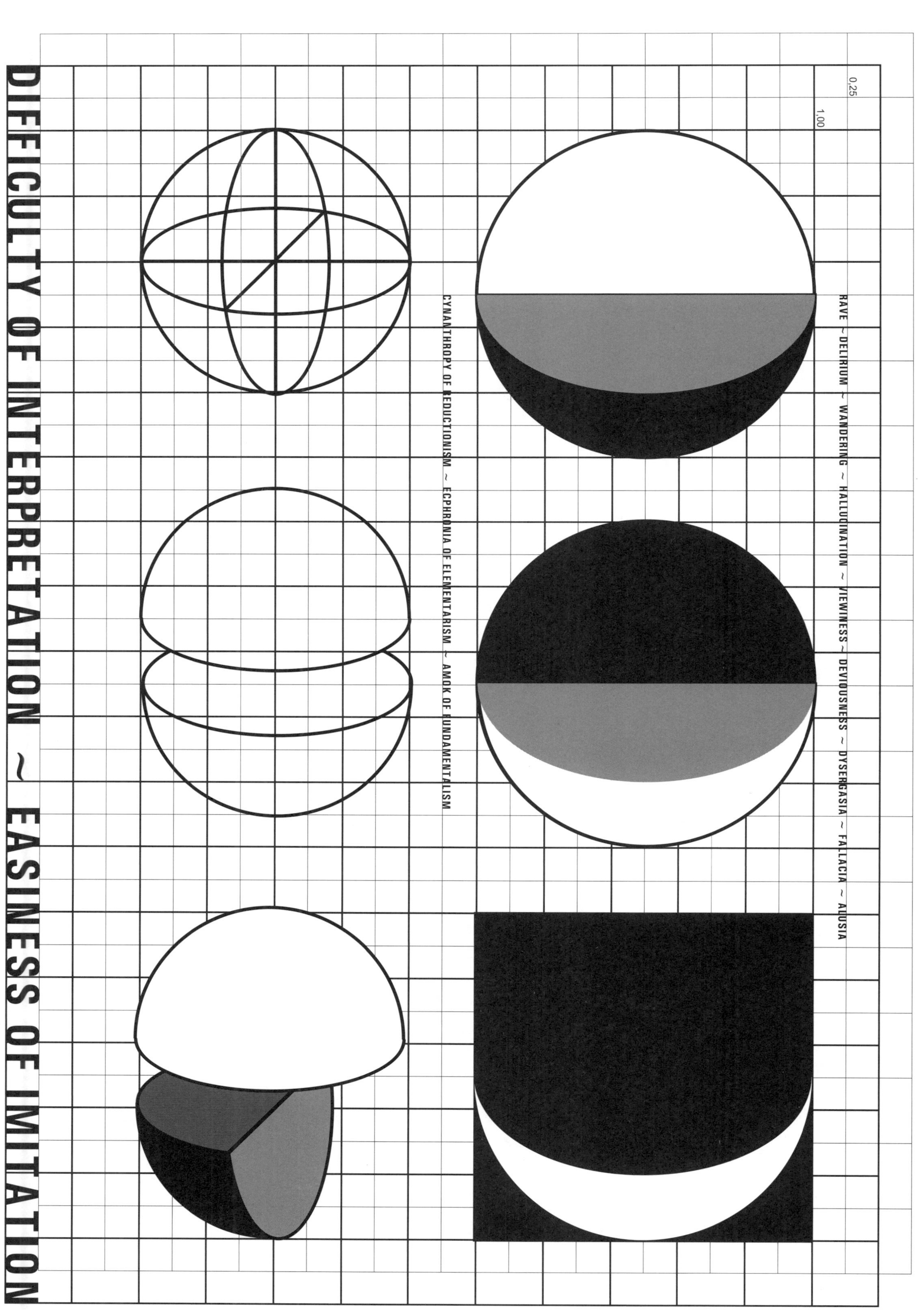

spread the discourse, spread the meaning of such a discourse and give birth to an authority of a new type, which would unconditionally not expose merely IQ (this distinguishes it significantly from elite clubs like Mensa International / mens = mind, mensa = table...) (I don´t choose the person to spend time with this

ONE WAY DEAD END

evening according to his/her IQ), as it often and dangerously paralogically happens, but would deal exactly with the revaluing, redefining of WHAT

Exhausted Herror Mélanchö entered Misanthropolis. The city was empty.

But it was only the human dimension of death. Always subjagated to belief of sensual comprehention of reality, illusion of knowledge.

HER
TENTACLES RUSTY
OF MEN-
STRUATION HONEY.

Yes, there are worms and microbes down there in corpses and other gutters. They do not wait for you. They have enough time, space and peace to begin a new story - Shestory.

Mélanchö

"TODAY" MEANS "THE KNOWLEDGE"! Its sole ideology would be
"THE KNOWLEDGE", i.e., something that is only illusionary = ultra

processual, temporal, ephemeral only in more cases, but not losing poignancy! A.I.M.I.D. methodology would be adjusted to this ultra processuality, logically

its aim wouldn´t be the final defining of Knowledge, it would refuse
the resignation to the definite defining of Knowledge. This authority would arise

DEMO-

from independence (that´s one of the reasons for its “apolitical nature”) – it would not have any ambition to dictate (like the mentioned impuissant

Wash each mm(!) of your body seriously, carefully, my dear.

formalistic UN tries to declare with helpless dumbness), but it would attempt it by that very Knowledge, so that its conclusions were generally accepted, in the

Boris Ondreička, *T. P. #13*

sense of equality, liberty and love, and then spontaneously applied in everyday practice (so, something like Doctors Without Borders, without a red or whatever coloured cross or any other badge of a different colour). Therefore, it would think and delicately communicate within local cultural standards (for example, it

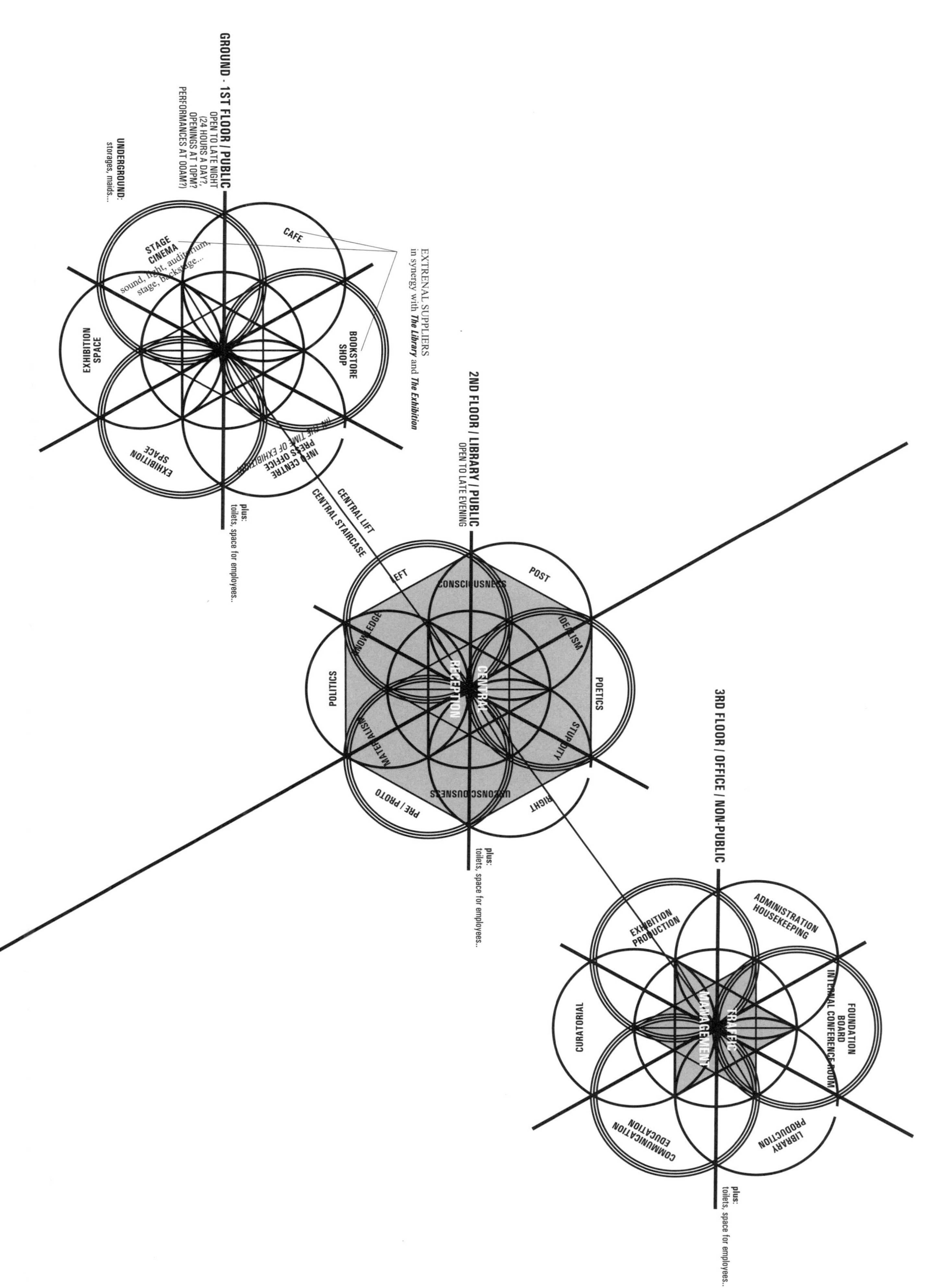

Boris Ondreička, *Strobe series {House}*

would not take notice of the contextual situation of Roma in Europe en bloc, but it would study regional specifics in detail...) and “it would try” not to be west-centric. Financing would be correlatively multi-sourced, since it would cover all disciplines – that means, consequently of all possible types of grants

TRANSPARENCY:

the color of
abstract friendships,

ph neutral hugs,

sugarless kisses,

fat-free sex

(innovation, creativity, science and research and art and culture and media and education and local development and social and health care and minorities and communities and cross-border cooperation and environment and civic society and informational society and public administration and defence and security

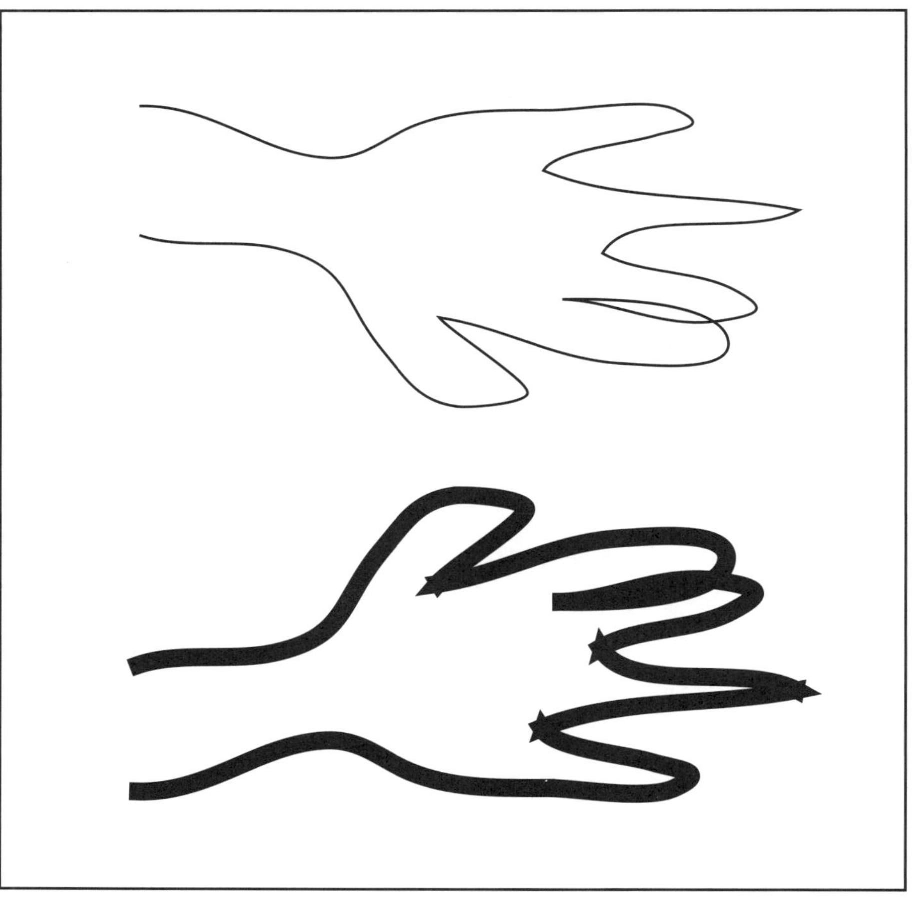

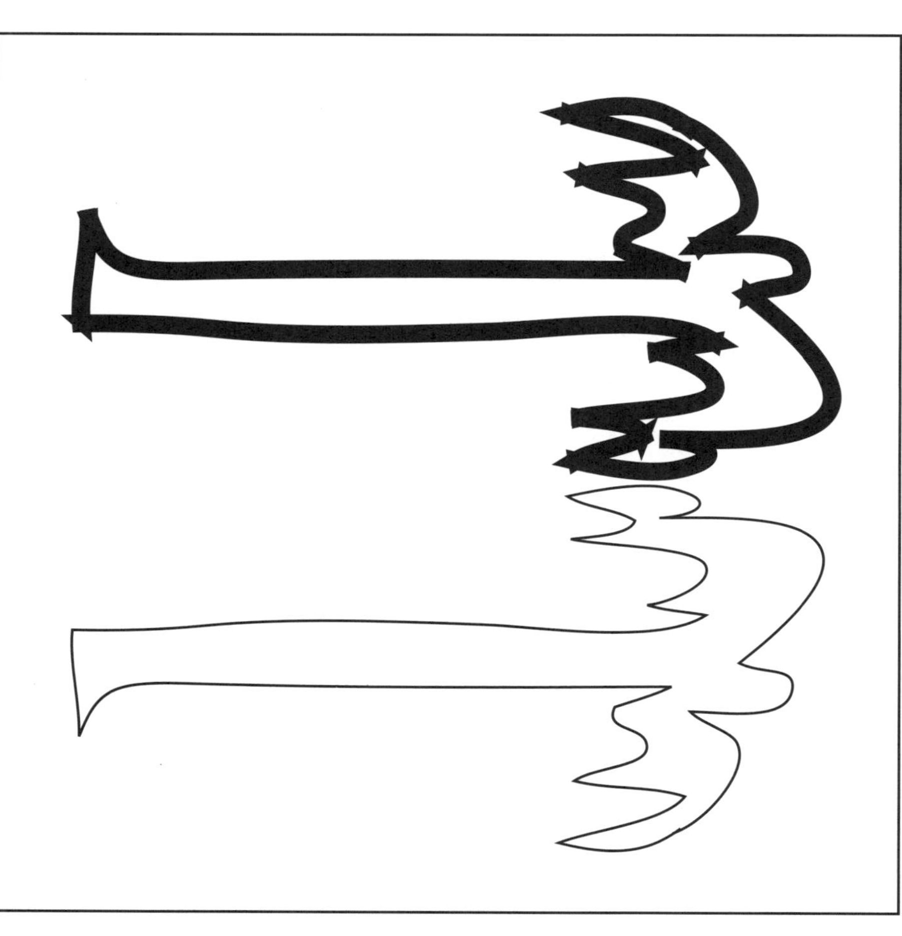

and the future and economics and currency and the power industry and business
and work and competitiveness and mobility and freedom and equal opportunities

Boris Ondreička, *4 palms*

Connect holes of your head together (1:1 / 15 poss. ...).

You can connect more holes together in one time of course, and / or all.

You can connect holes of the rest of your body as well, of course.

Use shoe-lace, for example, my dear.

and social responsibility... – illustrative examples taken from structures of the official division of the European Union grant section – bureaucratically pre-

Boris Ondreička, *T. P. #14*

defined types of grants aid the thematisation of problematic / problem areas, i.e., clarify the contemporary political viewing of what should be supported, and that is very interesting, but they have to undergo serious criticism, because by their categorisation they themselves paralyse inter-disciplinarity to a great extent,

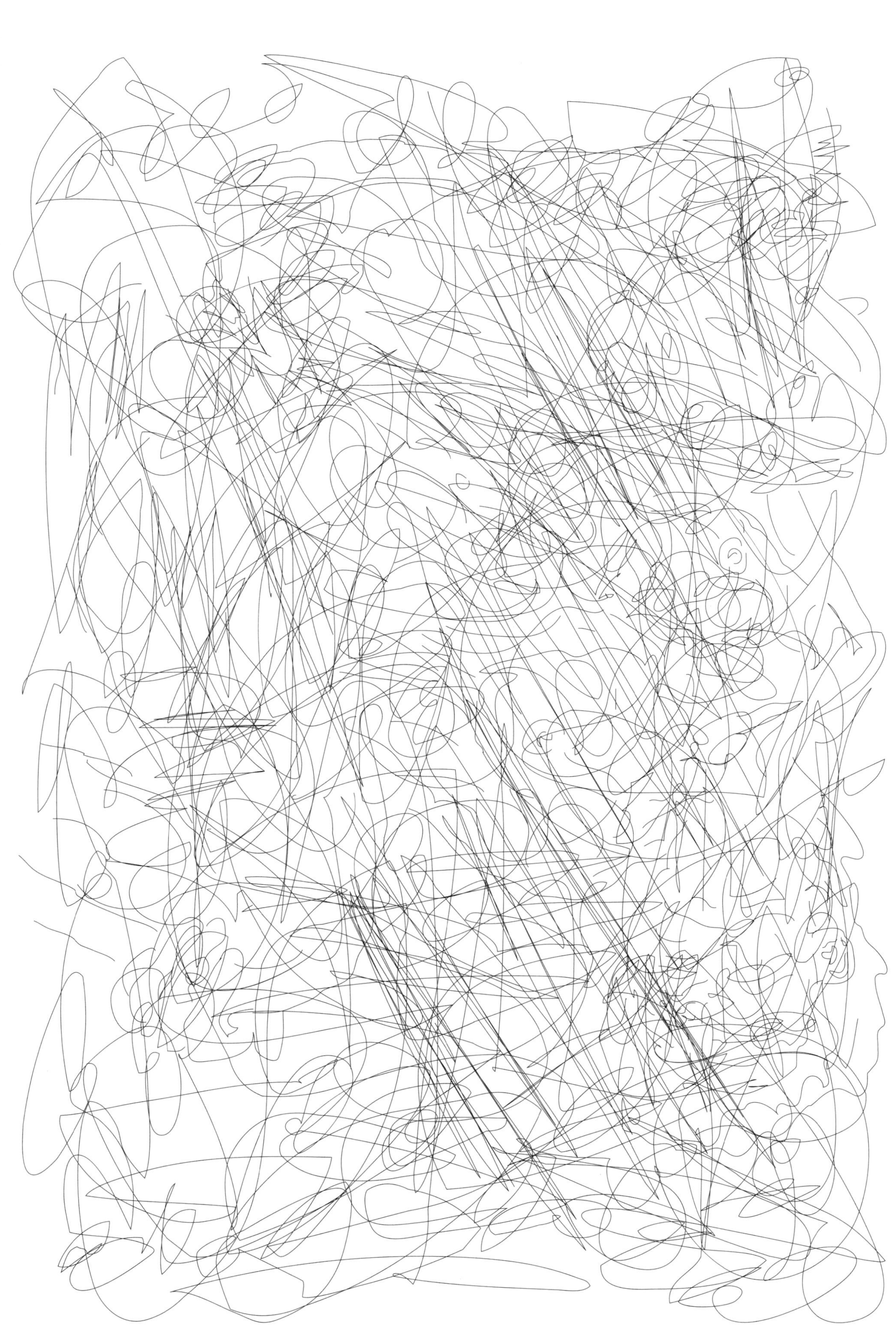

they build those nothing-protecting walls). A.I.M.I.D. would operate in parallel, on the full area of the whole world. It would have branch offices in each capital of the world, plus others, chosen due to their specific significance in representative locations (i.e., not only in Moscow, but also in the "artificial

WE HAVE PROGRAMMED:

truth.ai,
truth.ait,
truth.at
truth.be
truth.bmp,
truth.cdr,
truth.cgm,
truth.ch
truth.com
truth.cz
truth.de
truth.dft
truth.dib,
truth.dk
truth.dll,
truth.doc,
truth.dwg,
truth.dxf,
truth.edu
truth.emf,
truth.enu
truth.eps,
truth.epsf,
truth.fh,
truth.fin
truth.gif,
truth.hu
truth.icb,
truth.indd,
truth.indt,
truth.iss
truth.it
truth.jpe,
truth.jpeg,
truth.jpf,
truth.jpg,
truth.jpx,
truth.lst
truth.mov,
truth.mpeg,
truth.mui,
truth.nl
truth.ocx,
truth.orf,
truth.org
truth.pdf
truth.pjl
truth.png,
truth.psf
truth.pxr,
truth.pcd,
truth.pct,
truth.pcx,
truth.pdd,
truth.pdf,
truth.pic,
truth.ps,
truth.psd,
truth.raw,
truth.rle,
truth.rtf,
truth.tiff,
truth.sav,
truth.sct,
truth.sk
truth.svg,
truth.svgz,
truth.tif,
truth.tiff,
truth.txt,
truth.uk
truth.vda,
truth.vst,
truth.vxd
truth.wmf,
truth.xcl,
truth.xdr,
truth.xml,
truth.etc.

town” of Novosibirsk, which itself has such a remarkably high IQ..., so, not only in Santiago de Chile, but also in Ciudad Abierta de Ritoque, which belongs to

Catholic university...). A.I.M.I.D. global headquarters would be on "neutral" grounds, e.g., in Genève. (Neutra, apart from being a name of a marvellous

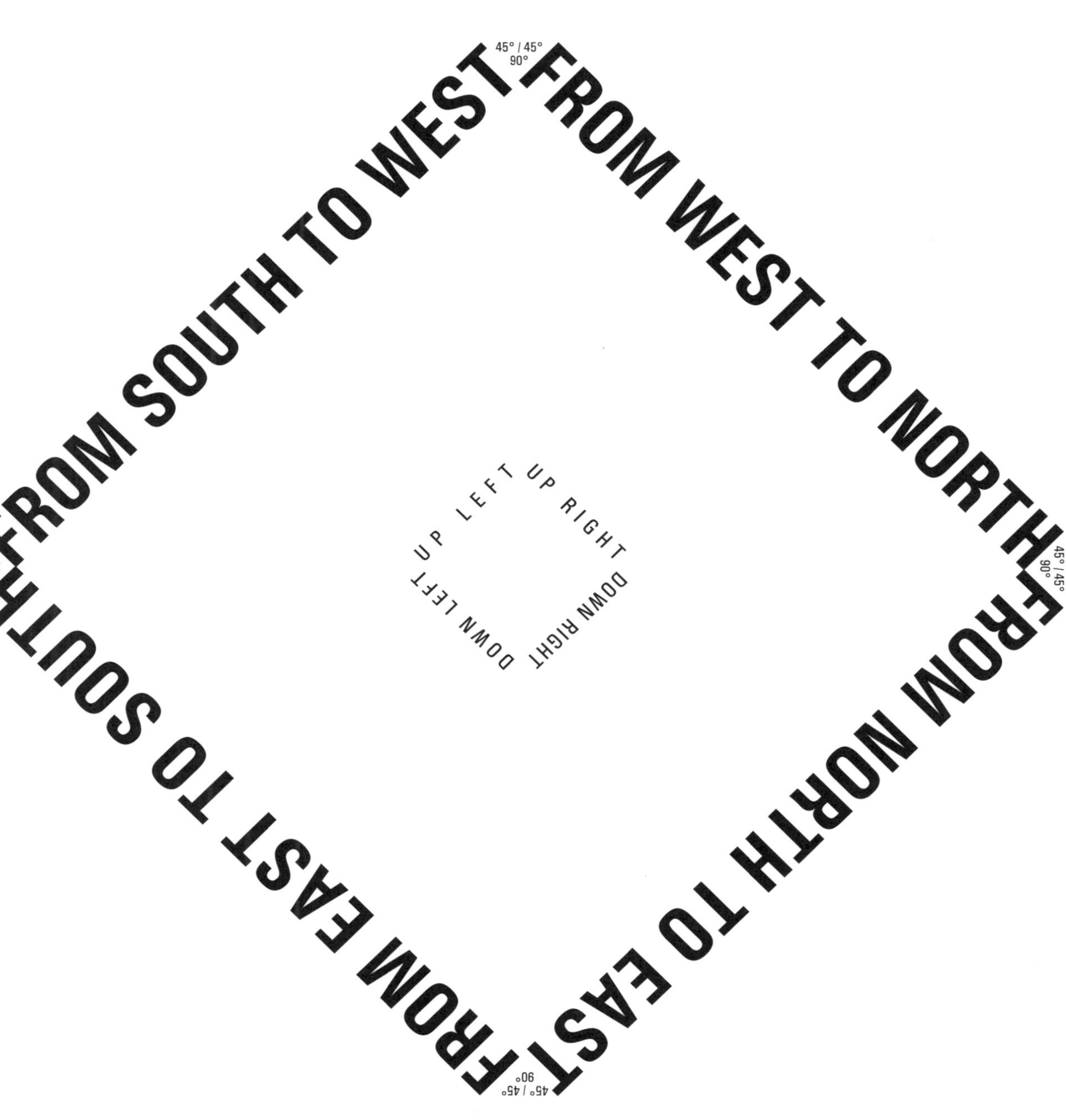

architect of Austrian origin, is also the Latin name for the Slovak town of Nitra, which Germany has been using up to now, and his family will probably come from there.) A.I.M.I.D. could initiate global issues (with the "quiet" objective of a global "state", faugh, what am I talking about, more precisely, massive

I am empty as a room in parents' house left over by daughter married the right man.
I am waiting for reorganisation of my interior to get the new function.
But as same as when parents are asked what they dream about to buy a present for their anniversary I remain superfluous.
They always used to answer:

"We have everything."

whispering about the cessation of the state as such, churches, political parties, clowns, armies... as such; that, however, wouldn´t be part of its official statutes

☻,☺, probably...) of such type as e.g.: A.I.M.I.D.-Q.-No.000001969) How to secure the honesty and solidarity of all involved in geo-cultural space with 0-%

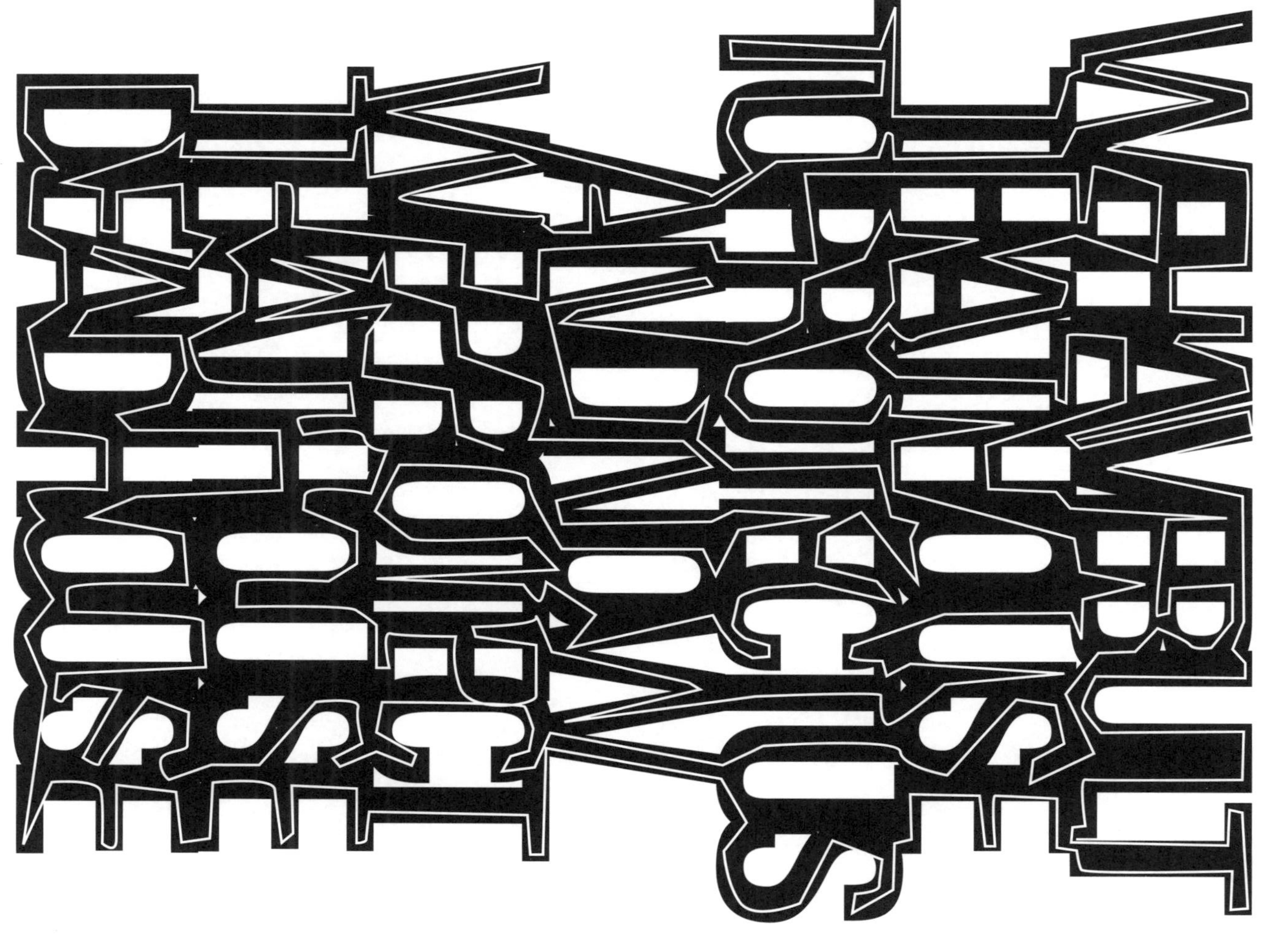

authoritative involvement of the state, without collective proprietorship ("literary" reference to Murray Newton Rothbard and Austrian School) (layman-illustrative contents), with a non-party principle. Based on the fact that democracy, which is still today accepted in the West (and forced upon the rest of

HÜSKER DÜ

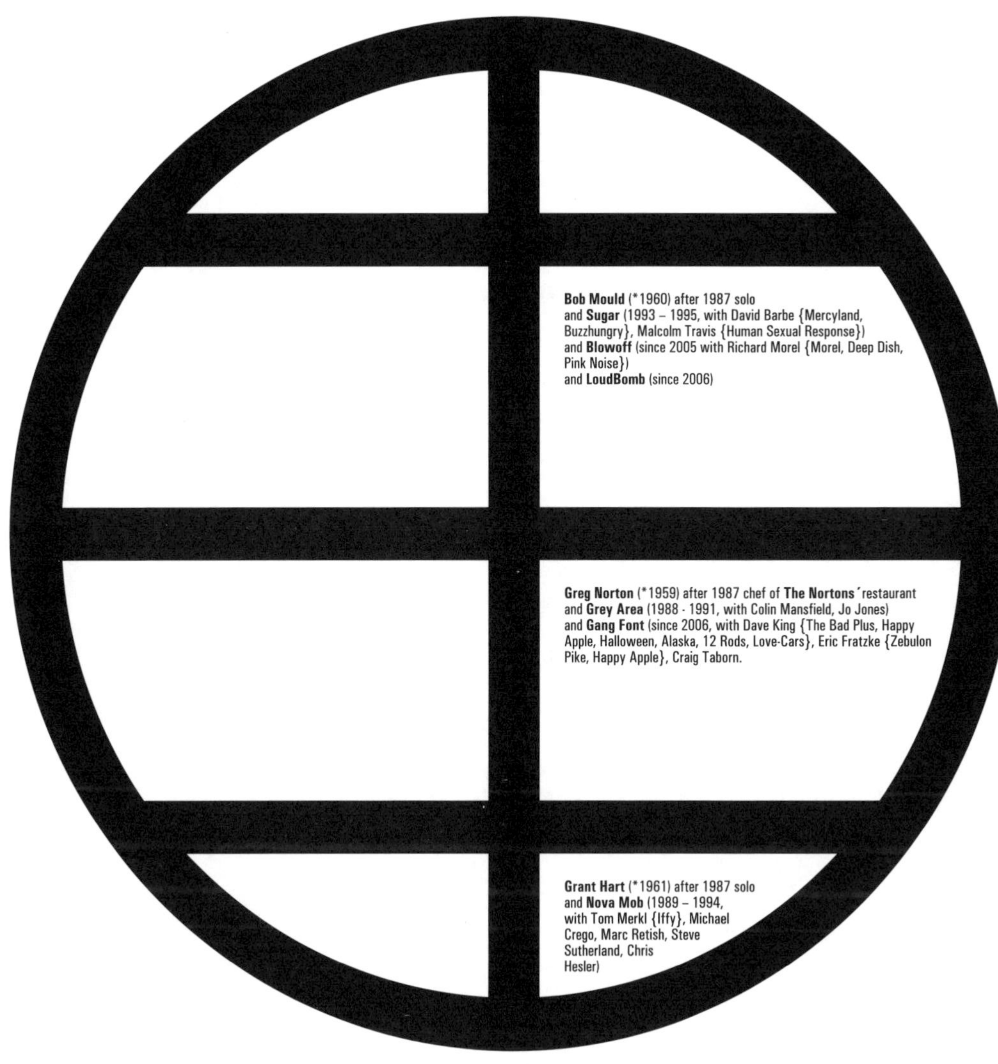

Hüsker Dü (1979 – 1987)

"The circle is the band, the three lines across are the members, and the intersection is the common train of thought." {Bob Mould}
"Hüsker Dü" means "Do you remember?" in Danish and Norwegian {after 1970s popular game}.

ALBUMS

1982 **LAND SPEED RECORD**

"All Tensed Up" (Mould) – 2:02
"Don't Try to Call" (Mould) – 1:30
"I'm Not Interested" (Hart) – 1:31
"Guns at My School" (Mould) – 0:55
"Push the Button" (Hart) – 1:48
"Gilligan's Island" (Hart) – 1:23
"M.T.C." (Norton) – 1:09
"Don't Have a Life" (Norton) – 2:09
"Bricklayer" (Mould) – 0:53
"Tired of Doing Things" (Hart) – 0:58
"You're Naive" (Mould) – 0:53
"Strange Week" (Hart) – 0:57
"Do the Bee" (Hart) – 1:49
"Big Sky" (Mould) – 0:57
"Ultracore" (Mould) – 0:47
"Let's Go Die" (Norton) – 1:26
"Data Control" (Hart) – 5:28

1983 **EVERYTHING FALLS APART**

"From the Gut" – 1:36 (Mould/Norton)
"Blah Blah Blah" – 2:09 (Mould/Norton)
"Punch Drunk" – 0:29 (Mould)
"Bricklayer" – 0:31 (Mould)
"Afraid of Being Wrong" – 1:21 (Mould)
"Sunshine Superman" – 1:56 (Donovan)
"Signals from Above" – 1:38 (Mould)
"Everything Falls Apart" – 2:15 (Mould)
"Wheels" – 2:08 (Hart)
"Target" – 1:45 (Mould)
"Obnoxious" – 0:53 (Mould)
"Gravity" – 2:37 (Mould)

Everything Falls Apart and More CD bonuses

"In a Free Land" – 2:53 (Mould)
"What Do I Want?" – 1:15 (Hart)
"M.I.C." – 1:10 (Mould)
"Statues" – 8:45 (Hart)
"Let's Go Die" – 1:54 (Norton)
"Amusement" – 4:57 (Mould)
"Do You Remember?" – 1:55 (Mould)

1983 **METAL CIRCUS**

"Real World" (Mould)
"Deadly Skies" (Mould)
"It's Not Funny Anymore" (Hart)
"First of the Last Calls" (Mould)
"Lifeline" (Mould)
"Diane" (Hart)
"Out on a Limb" (Mould)

1984 **ZEN ARCADE**

"Something I Learned Today" (Mould) - 1:58
"Broken Home, Broken Heart" (Mould) - 2:01
"Never Talking to You Again" (Hart) - 1:39
"Chartered Trips" (Mould) - 3:33
"Dreams Reoccurring" (Hüsker Dü) - 1:40
"Indecision Time" (Mould) - 2:07
"Hare Krsna" (Hüsker Dü) - 3:33
"Beyond the Threshold" (Mould) - 1:35
"Pride" (Mould) - 1:45
"I'll Never Forget You" (Mould) - 2:06
"The Biggest Lie" (Mould) - 1:58
"What's Going On" (Hart) - 4:23
"Masochism World" (Hart/Mould) - 2:43
"Standing by the Sea" (Hart) - 3:12
"Somewhere" (Hart/Mould) - 2:30
"One Step at a Time" (Hart/Mould) - 0:45
"Pink Turns to Blue" (Hart) - 2:39
"Newest Industry" (Mould) - 3:02
"Monday Will Never Be the Same" (Mould) - 1:10
"Whatever" (Mould) - 3:50
"The Tooth Fairy and the Princess" (Mould) - 2:43
"Turn on the News" (Hart) - 4:21
"Reoccurring Dreams" (Hüsker Dü) - 13:47

1985 **NEW DAY RISING**

"New Day Rising" (Mould, Hüsker Dü)
"The Girl Who Lives on Heaven Hill" (Hart)
"I Apologize" (Mould)
"Folk Lore" (Mould)
"If I Told You" (Hart, Mould)
"Celebrated Summer" (Mould)
"Perfect Example" (Mould)
"Terms of Psychic Warfare" (Hart)
"59 Times the Pain" (Mould)
"Powerline" (Mould)
"Books About UFOs" (Hart)
"I Don't Know What You're Talking About"
"How to Skin a Cat" (Mould, Hüsker Dü)
"Whatcha Drinkin'" (Mould)
"Plans I Make" (Mould, Hüsker Dü)
"Erase Today" (Mould)

1985 **FLIP YOUR WIG**

"Flip Your Wig" (Mould)
"Every Everything" (Hart)
"Makes No Sense at All" (Mould)
"Hate Paper Doll" (Mould)
"Green Eyes" (Hart)
"Divide and Conquer" (Mould)
"Games" (Mould)
"Find Me" (Mould)
"The Baby Song" (Hart)
"Flexible Flyer" (Hart)
"Private Plane" (Mould)
"Keep Hanging On" (Hart)
"The Wit and the Wisdom" (Mould)
"Don't Know Yet" (Mould)

1986 **CANDY APPLE GREY**

"Crystal" (Mould)
"Don't Want to Know If You Are Lonely" (Hart)
"I Don't Know for Sure" (Mould)
"Sorry Somehow" (Hart)
"Too Far Down" (Mould)
"Hardly Getting Over It" (Mould)
"Dead Set on Destruction" (Hart)
"Eiffel Tower High" (Mould)
"No Promise Have I Made" (Hart)
"All This I've Done for You" (Mould)

1987 **WAREHOUSE: SONGS & STORIES**

"These Important Years" (Mould)
"Charity, Chastity, Prudence, and Hope" (Hart)
"Standing in the Rain" (Mould)
"Back from Somewhere" (Hart)
"Ice Cold Ice" (Mould)
"You're a Soldier" (Hart)
"Could You Be the One?" (Mould)
"Too Much Spice" (Hart)
"Friend, You've Got to Fall" (Mould)
"Visionary" (Mould)
"She Floated Away" (Hart)
"Bed of Nails" (Mould)
"Tell You Why Tomorrow" (Hart)
"It's Not Peculiar" (Mould)
"Actual Condition" (Hart)
"No Reservations" (Mould)
"Turn It Around" (Mould)
"She's a Woman (And Now He Is a Man)" (Hart)
"Up in the Air" (Mould)
"You Can Live at Home" (Hart)

1994 **LIVING END**

"New Day Rising" (Mould/Hart/Norton)
"Girl Who Lives on Heaven Hill" (Hart)
"Standing in the Rain" (Mould)
"Back from Somewhere" (Hart)
"Ice Cold Ice" (Mould)
"Everytime" (Norton)
"Friend, You've Got to Fall" (Mould)
"She Floated Away" (Hart)
"From the Gut" (Mould/Norton)
"Target" (Mould)
"It's Not Funny Anymore" (Hart)
"Hardly Getting Over It" (Mould)
"Terms of Psychic Warfare" (Hart)
"Powerline" (Mould)
"Books About UFOs" (Hart)
"Divide and Conquer" (Mould)
"Keep Hanging On" (Hart)
"Celebrated Summer" (Mould)
"Now That You Know Me" (Hart)
"Ain't No Water in The Well" (Mould)
"What's Going On" (Hart)
"Data Control" (Hart)
"In a Free Land" (Mould)
"Sheena Is a Punk Rocker" (Ramones)

SINGLES

1981 "Statues", "Amusement"
1982 "In A Free Land", "What Do I Want?", "M.I.C."
1984 "Eight Miles High", "Masochism World"
1984 "Celebrated Summer", "New day Rising"
1985 "Makes No Sense At All", "Love Is All Around"
1986 "Don't Want To Know If You Are Lonely", "All Work and No Play", "Helter Skelter"
1986 "Sorry Somehow", "All This I've Done For You", "Flexible Flyer", "Celebrated Summer", "Fattie"
1987 "Could You Be The One?", "Everytime", "Charity, Chastity, Prudence, And Hope"
1987 "She's A Woman (And Now He Is A Man)" "Ice Cold Ice, "Charity, Chastity, Prudence And Hope", "No Reservations"
1987 "Ice Cold Ice", "Gotta Lotta Medley", "The Wit And The Wisdom", "What's Going On?", "Green Eyes"

VIDEOS

1985 "Makes No Sense at All", "Love Is All Around"
1986 "Don't Want to Know If You Are Lonely"
1987 "Could You Be the One?"

DVDS

1985 / 2007 Live from the Camden Palace (Live from London UK TV show on 1985, released on DVD on 2007)

COMPILATIONS / Song(s):

1982 The Blasting Concept "Real World"
1983 Underground Hits 2 "Deadly Skies", "Lifeline"
1985 A Diamond Hidden in the Mouth of a Corpse "Won't Change"
1986 The Blasting Concept Vol. 2 "Erase Today"
1990 Duck and Cover "Eight Miles High"
1991 Never Mind the Mainstream: The Best of MTV 120 Minutes vol. 2 "Could You Be the One?", SST Acoustic "Never Talking to You Again"
1993 Cash Cow - The Best of Giorno Poetry Systems
1965-1993 "Won't Change", Faster & Louder: Hardcore Punk, Vol. 1 "Statues"
2000 Gimme Indie Rock, Vol. 1 "Pink Turns to Blue"
2003 All That Rock "Hardly Getting Over It"
2004 Left of the Dial: Dispatches from the '80s Underground "Don't Want to Know if You Are Lonely"
2009 Adventureland Original Motion Picture Soundtrack "Don't Want to Know if You Are Lonely"

the world) as the only possible state system just because of necessity because we cannot establish anything more functional (and the best in disposition does not

Create (in written form) the band:
title, members (names), bio and bios, discography..., my dear.

have to mean sufficiently good!), is based on election returns, which are extra-fragilely dependent on the (bi)polarisation of feelings (meaning emotions!!!)

Boris Ondreička, *T. P. #15*

of majorities, which are mostly so very uneducated (which political parties use for strategic calculations) that they build preferences only from the most vulgarly accessible sources, such as pre-election media campaigns inclined to simply-glossy 5-word colourfully-monumental forte-promises of retouched-

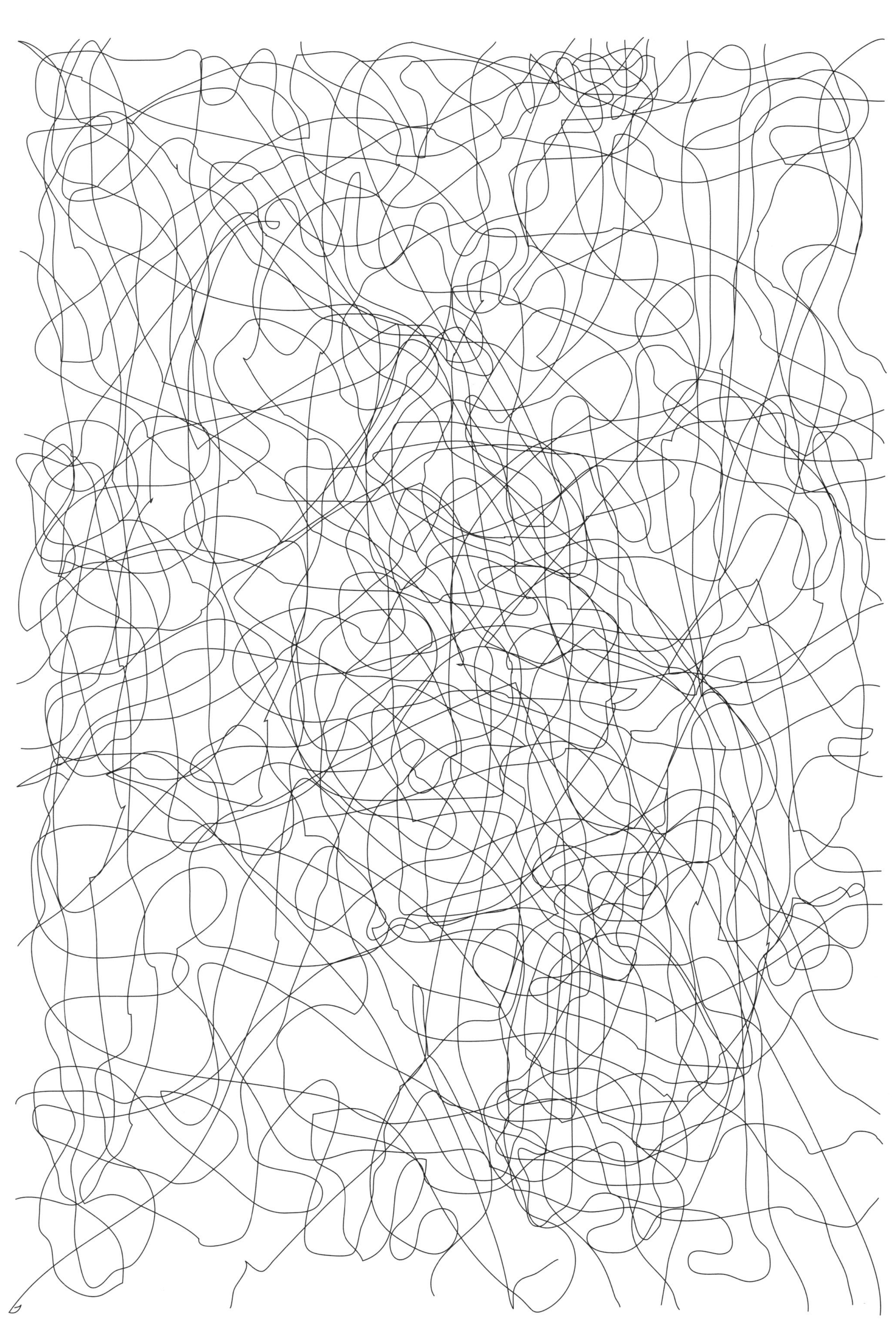

smiling faces of the right age and sex ("Give her glasses!" "No, that frame is too thick, shit!"), then perform choices without seriousness of the act, with scepticism and unconscious cynicism..., where demo-cracy mutates in fact into parto-cracy (any political party is a regular business subject soliciting us –

Lovers

0,25

"The fact that you can see her doesn´t mean that she can see you."

1,00

What are the most beautiful moments of life? Is it every day (?) some I would rather not experience, skip them. I would like to turn back time and right all the wrongs. I would like to have learned to ski and skate when I was 4, or taken better care of my body, exercise. I would like to have been a better student at grammar school, and learned English, Hebrew, German, Russian, French, Spanish, Latin, Greek, Arabic, etc. I would like to have learned to play the guitar and the piano when I was around 10, so that I, myself could compose. I would like to have read many more texts and books, mainly philosophical and historical ones, and poetry. I would like to have learned to better master a camera and PC when I was 15, or so, to be able to edit my texts. I would like to be able to make money easier and faster. I would like to be straightforward, disciplined, reliable, neat, attentive, more courageous, wiser, more sensitive. But I don´t want to go back, because then this daughter of mine would not have been born. Only "would" remains.

They are * Christmas or birthday presents, the first jump into the sea and the view from the top of a mountain, the first love, the following loves, the first sex and the following sex, marriage, the birth of a child, friendship, and when your partner and your child is happy, and when she is successful, and healthy, when a thrilled audience applauds you.

I said: "May this moment never end." And then others like that came. Those in love think, I thought so too, that there is nothing more beautiful and they fear ageing, disappearing from relationships, marriages, but now I would no longer exchange my wife for any falling in love, because love and falling in love are not the same, and all those films and songs about cheating (Daniel Jurado, "What Were The Chances", And Now That I´m in Your Shadow Secretly Canadian, 2006)

are only catharsis for the feeling of guilt, the inability to be moderate, the justification of lies and deception through romance.

Separation, divorce should be a joyful, liberating occasion, since the process of getting acquainted (with oneself and each other) is not terminated by any marriage, although marriage should be / is a beautiful thing. Cheating is a mean hiding away of one´s own feelings, and then, at parting, divorce, one is happy and the other is unhappy; that´s not fair. Trust means also being able to say: "I don´t feel good with you anymore." This, however, requires sincere self-discovery, will, in order to be able to recognise in time that something is going on with me, that I have ceased to be happy. And maybe those songs and books and films and comic operas

hellp!

actually want to provide us with the courage to be able to decide to finally set off on our own journey. To be able to recognise and admit ignorance, mistakes. To stop looking back and blaming partners, whose binds allegedly, morally prevent us from acting autonomously and truthfully.

Thus, we cruelly hurt the partners and double-deceive, ourselves and them into believing that "there is no other way..."

To separate in such a situation is the very right and ethical, a true proof of love, and if it has really disappeared somewhere, then at least a genuine act of responsibility – evidence that we care about that person and we should care about each and every human.

And maybe those films and song, elegies, odes and books want to show us how not to do it, by interpreting the mirror of experience of others.

Cheating , infidelity is also about the lack of faith in the person, the relationship with the person with whom we are cheating on our partner. We hurt both. However, above all, infidelity is mainly about the lack of faith in oneself. Hence, we also hurt ourselves - all three involved.

And if we (all parties) have children, then them as well. And if our lover has a partner, – we also hurt him/her.

Infidelity is the loss of reason and courage, of sobriety, because there are millions of beautiful people in the world, but that doesn´t mean that all should (or can) mutually "exchange" (even if it´s not such a revolting idea). We stop thinking with the brain, but let ourselves be led (or misled) by our dick (or cunt), because, mostly, we are not led by feelings, but by libido, instinct, which also comes to power thanks to the fact that it is a representative of deeper problems.

On the contrary, true faith is also for my wife to be able to say that she is not happy with me anymore when she feels it, and since I love her dearly, I will try to help her, even to leave me, if we both realise that it is indeed best for her, because, at the end of all these days and those days, what is best for her is best for me as well.

plebeiance for a relatively lucrative deal called “state leadership”. Elections are actually half-public tender, and that doesn’t have to be negative, if such a service of a regular business subject would be clearly made pragmatic to the sponsor, client, which is the society, citizenry) where theory becomes corrupted in

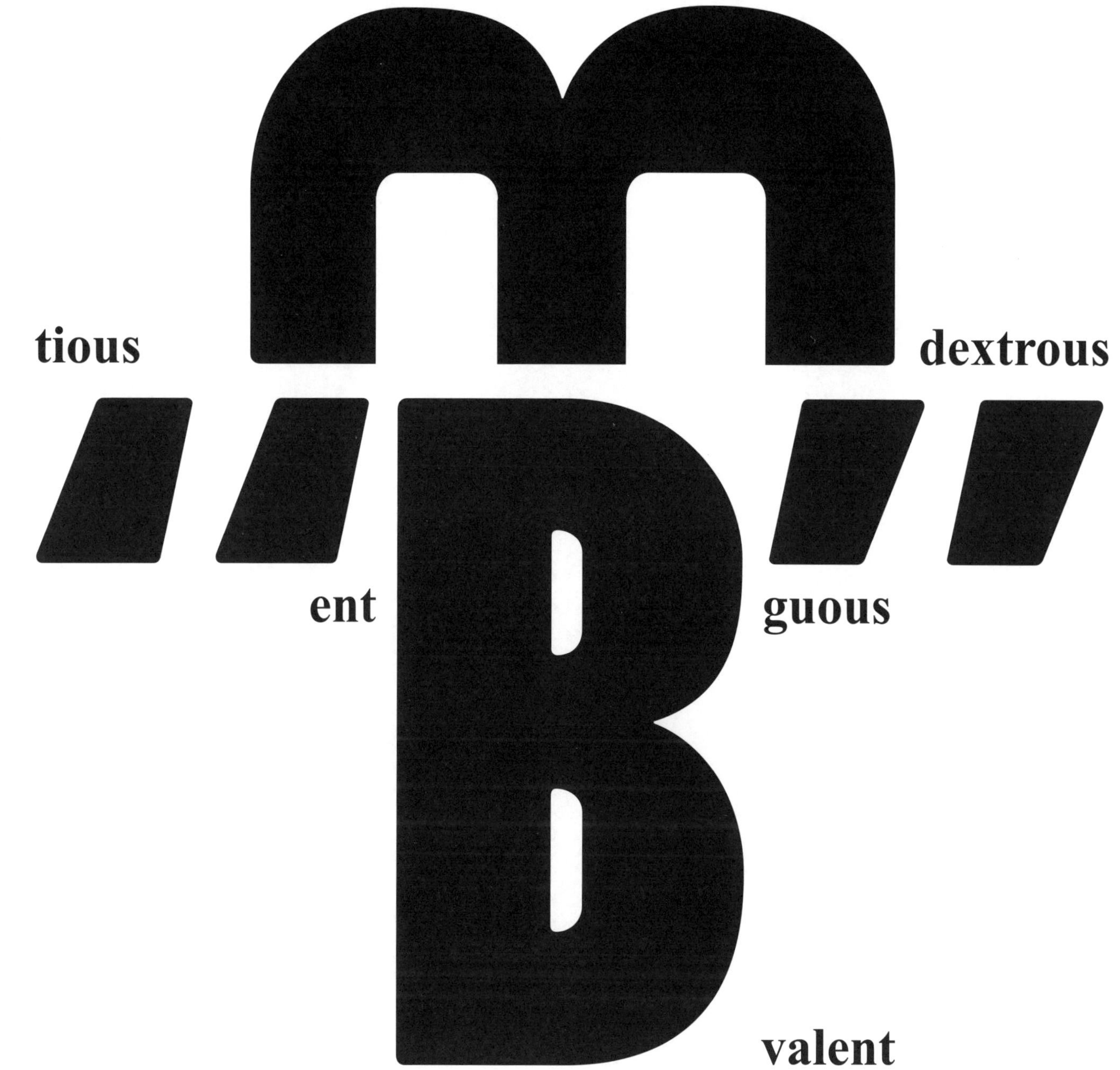

practice, transforms / returns to half-empty proclamation???; What would be the result of the first democratic election in North Korea? What would the logic of repressive forces (police and such, since to eliminate poverty and resultant criminality is not “so easy” as to eliminate states) look like in such

open rooms
astrided apartments
straddled corridors
crotched houses

open windows
mauled curtains
broken cupboards
supined vases

a Worldspace? Or, not so tremendously bombastic: A.I.M.I.D.-Q.-No.000848894)
XX (pianist): “One of the most frequent inter/devices of self/expression –

communication is the keyboard. Telephone, PC, ATM... When I think of future keyboards, I will have to keep talking about fingers anyway. Will the future

amors

keyboard still be connected / restricted to the size of fingertips? How will the size of fingertips develop (how is it developing) in relation to the increase of frequency of such usage in relation to the entire evolution of homo sapiens (in terms of the backbone erection process through labour... – the usage of sms

C1)

inside out,
outside in,
front backwards,
back frontwards

C1) is an originally 100% plural – a compound of 50% of A1) the mother and 50% of B1) the father {while A1) together with B1) can conceive another C1), or with other(s) B) other D), E)...}. In continuation of this to-extent-limited reflection these facts are already irrelevant due to the rationalisation of the limitation.

{Ignoring the fact that both A1) and B1) have predecessors, ...}

C1X) is plural (physical, the "body") – a compound of individual organs and their mutual symbiosis

C1Y) is plural (mental, the "soul") – a compound of sub -

C1Ya) "as I see myself" {inside in view}
- C1Ya1) "unlimited vision", {ahead}
- C1Ya2) "critical C1Ya1) retrospection" {behind}

C1Yb) "who I want to be" {inside out view}
- C1Yb1) "unlimited visions", {ahead}
- C1Yb2) "critical C1Yb1) retrospection " {behind}

C1Yc) "critical C1Ya) and C1Yb) retrospection" {inside both in and out view}

C1Yd) "as others see me" {outside in view}, {ahead}

C1Ye) "critical C1Yc) and C1Yd) retrospection" {both outside and inside and in and out view}, {both ahead and behind}

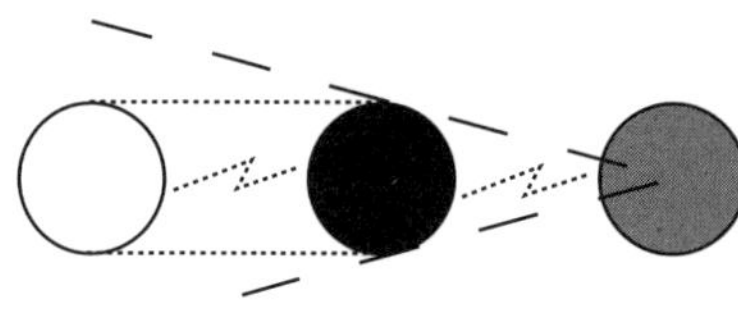

§1}:
I don´t know
I am not sure
I don´t want to know
I am afraid
I know

§2}:
I don´t wa t
what
I would want

Separation of C1) into C1X) and C1Y), i.e., the physiognomy from the psyché is schematic, because from a natural point of view, they are not separated – the brain is also viscera, one of the body organs, like the heart, sex organs, liver, kidneys... Plurality and singularity are also only schematic since they function together inseparably (in this case within the integrity of the personality).

So, C1X) is a superior quantity because it contains C1Y). C1Y) is subordinate to C1X). C1Y) is a result of a necessary separation in terms of capacity. C1X) = C1)!

Among individual sub-C there can occur conflicts (as indicated in §1 and §2). E.g.: C1 a) and C1b), or C1 a) and C1d). Often, there arises a paradoxical clash between C1X) and C1Y). The neglect of these conflicts can have serious consequences. The correct diagnosis of the nature of these conflicts is crucial since they can also be of a physiognomic character (brain dysfunction, insufficient liver function, 5HT, etc.), and in order to choose the appropriate remedy.

The influence of C1Y) on C1X) is inseparable from the influence of C1X) on C1Y): the psyché influences the physiognomy and the physiognomy influences the psyché.

Separation is the economy of wholeness. Without separation we can not ascertain wholeness (simply due to its ungraspable format). Without permanent awareness of wholeness we cannot correctly diagnose the conflicts of separation (the psyché doesn´t work as it should, because the liver doesn´t work as it should...), so we will not be able to execute any appropriate remedy (if we cure one, the other will rally "by itself" / what is first and what is second?).

verifiably influences the development of the fingertips of today´s generation mainly those under-25), to its future genetics? I know that fingers are not indispensable, since there has already for some time beensimilar inter/devices not counting with touch, but operating e.g. with voice. Will future technologies

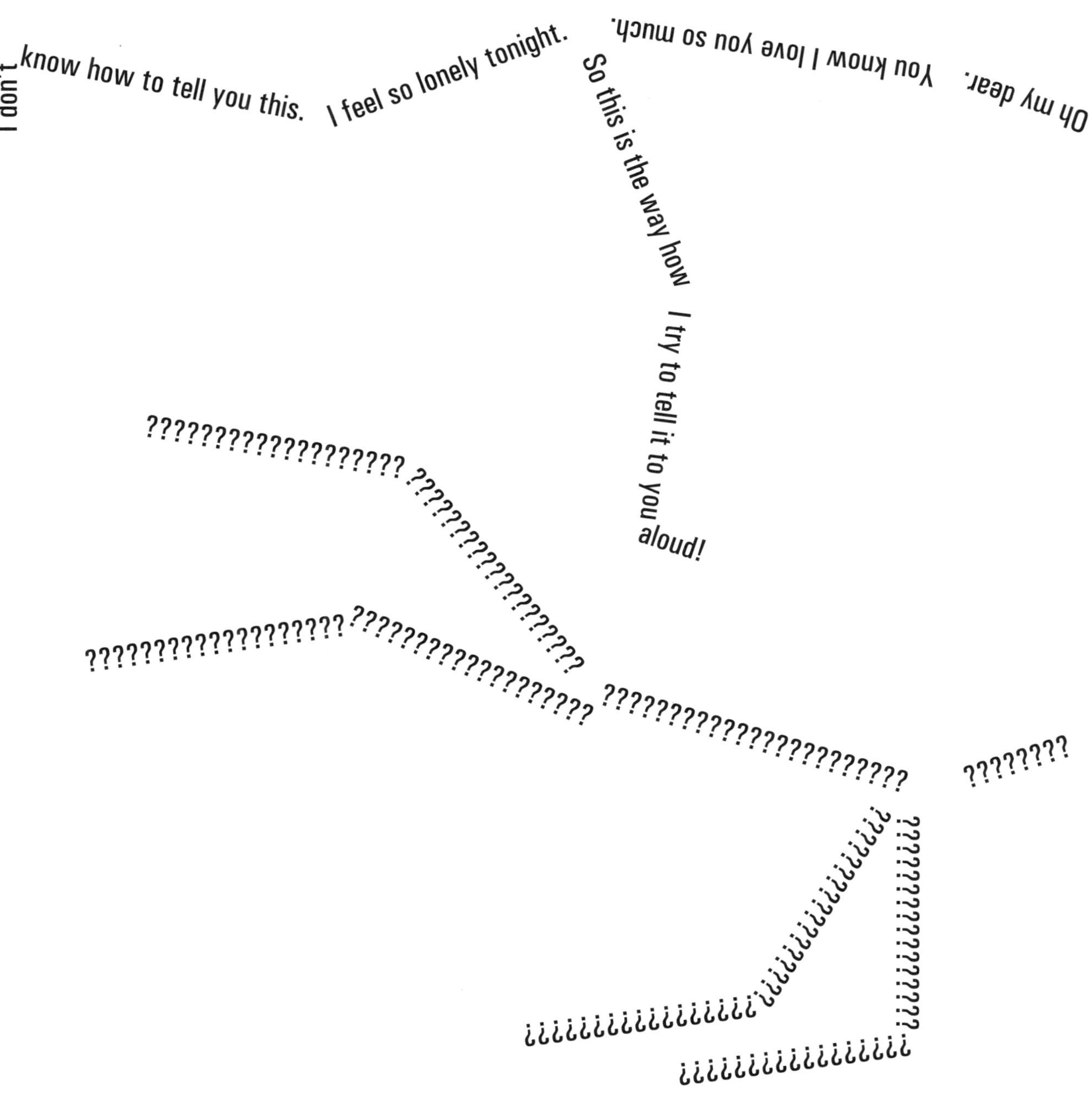

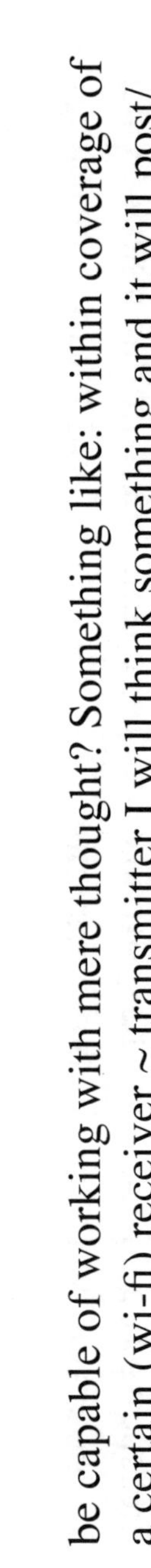
be capable of working with mere thought? Something like: within coverage of
a certain (wi-fi) receiver ~ transmitter I will think something and it will post/

produce itself (even without my voice instruction) in the product of my desired intention... But, HOW will that technology differentiate between Spontaneous

The River without solidarity.

The River without principles.

The River without belief.

The River which lacks banks.

The Journey without surety of getting to the place which was planned before.

and Intentional, when not even I, myself can control it now and then, when even that I is sometimes incapable of doing so? Will it ever be possible to create such a delicate technology of mental space interior sorting? YY (a neuro-physician, let´s say): ,,Yy yyy yyyy yyy yy yyyyy - ∞. ZZ (a cyber-engineer, let´s say):

second, minute, hour, day, week, month, year, decade, century, millenium

second	minute	hour	day	week	month	year	decade	century	millenium
	60 seconds	60 minutes 3600 seconds	24 hours 1440 minutes 86400 seconds	7 days 168 hours 10080 minutes 604800 seconds	4 weeks 28 days 168 hours 10080 minutes 604800 seconds	12 months 4 weeks 28 days 168 hours 10080 minutes 604800 seconds	10 years 120 months 4 weeks 28 days 168 hours 10080 minutes 604800 seconds	10 decades 100 years 1200 months 4 weeks 28 days 168 hours 10080 minutes 604800 seconds	10 centuries 100 decades 1000 years 12000 months 4 weeks 28 days 168 hours 10080 minutes 604800 seconds

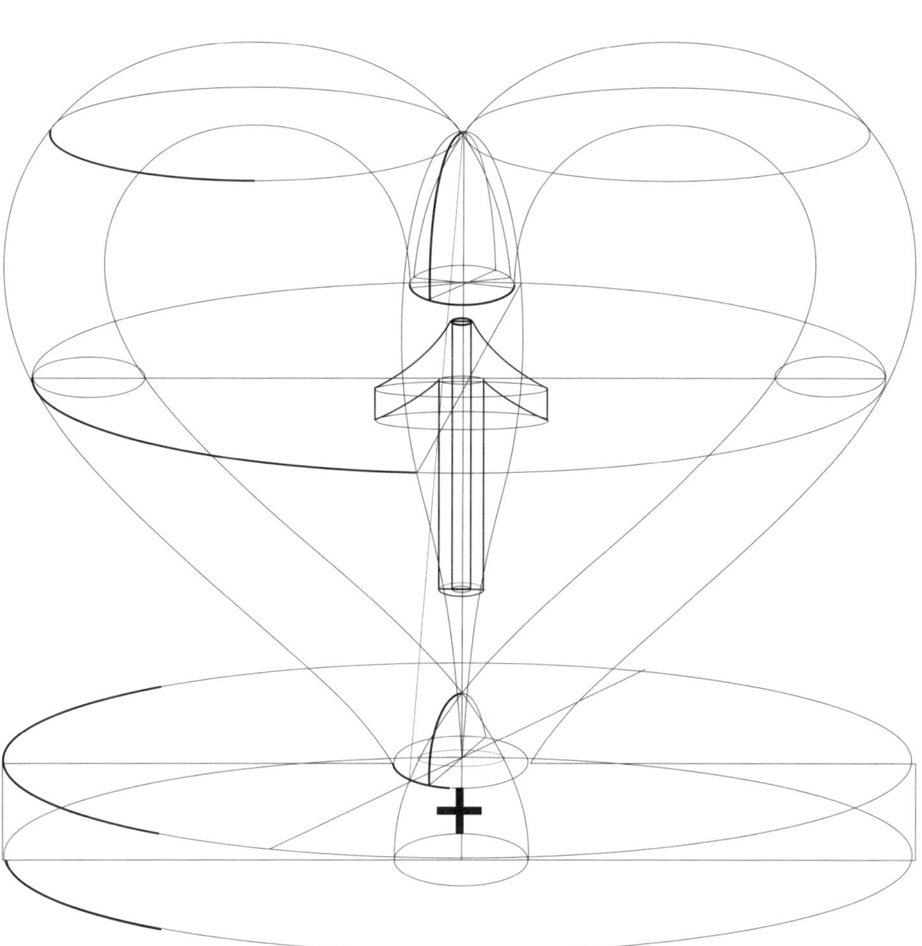

"Judith!"
"You did what?"

„Zz zzz zzzz zzz zz zzzzz - ∞." . . . Thereafter, A.I.M.I.D. would reformulate the outputs of these dialogues into understandable language (by testing the reading

Use spouting shower as a microphone, my dear.

of samples of the educationally weak, different cultural and world-view samples
and so on) in the widest possible language mutations and publish them in

Boris Ondreička, *T. P. #16*

the form of free online downloads. WWW.AIMID.COM would be worldwide promoted by global media partners, although Wikipedia, which has overrun all previous encyclopaedias, not only in terms of quality of data, but also in relevance of information, has achieved a general knowledge even without that,

Nancy Black [64 years of age, grand-mother of John Black]: *I see,Johnny,you brought your friend with you.*

John Black [8 years of age, grand-son of Nancy Black]: *Yes, Nancy,it is George White, my best school mate.*

George White [8 years of age, friend of John Black]: *Nice to see you, Mrs. Brown.*

Nancy Black: *Pleasure on my side,George. Okey, I leave you boys.*

John Black: Bye, Nancy.

£0,-

over 18

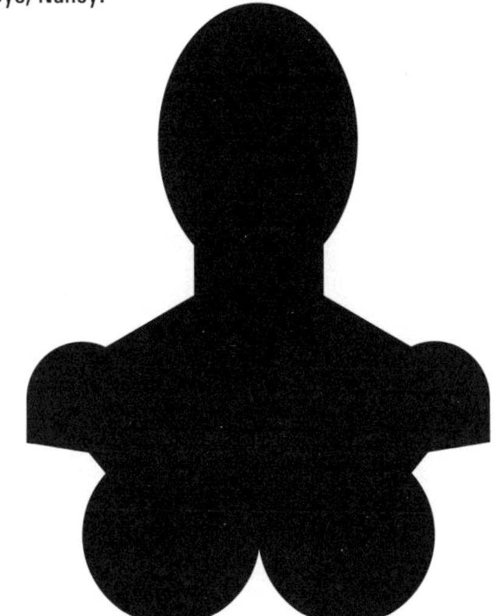

tuesday:

free entrance

LEFTIST DANCEFLOOR

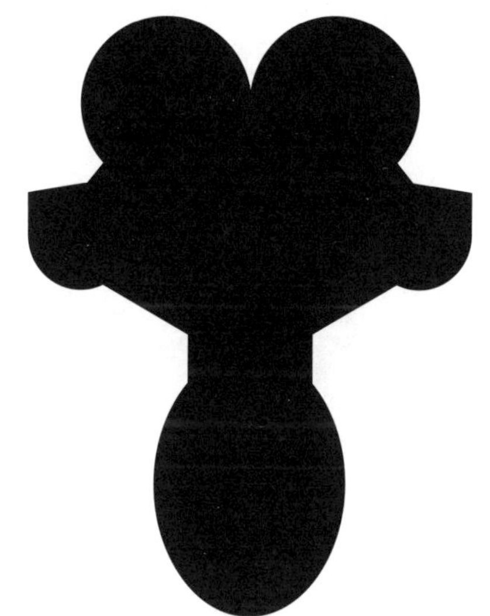

wednesday:

RIGHTIST DANCEHALL

entrée gratis

George White: *That's weird. Why do you call your grandma Nancy?*

John Black: *I do not know really. She wants so.*

over 21

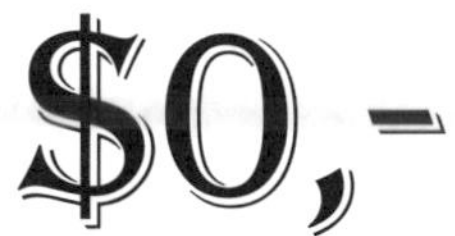

pm/am

just on the basis of practicality, quality, enrichment of users. At the same time, fundamental retrievals would be chosen from the sum of dialogues, and

generalising, “leading” texts of crucial importance would be compiled.
WWW.AIMID.COM would be constructed so that the degree of entry profundity

I write texts (also) on

abasement, abashmend, abb, abeyance, abhorence, abjection, abnegatio, abomination, abortion, absurdity, accidie, ache, acratia, actuating, addiction, ado, adversity, affliction, agony, agressivity, ailment, akathisia, alarm, alas, algos, aloofness, ambiguity, amok, amphibolia, anger, angor, anguish, animosity, annoyance, antagonism, anticlimax, antilogy, antinomy, antipathy, anxiety, apathy, apepsy, apery, apprehension, arrears, askance, assault, astrocity, attrition, aversion, awe, awfulness, awkwardness, badness, baldness, bale, bankruptcy, bannitio, barbarity, bareness, baseness, bdelygmia, beastliness, beguilement, bedlam, beggary, belly, bellyache, besetment, bile, bilge, bish, bitterness, blackness, blague, blame, bleakness, block, blouder, blubber, bluff, blunder, blur, bogus, boner, boodle, boof, bop, bother, breakaway, breakdown, breakup, breeziness, bunco, bungle, bur, burdensomeness, cacoethes, caducity, calamity, callousness, canaille, cancer, canker, carelessness, caristia, carrion, castigation, cataclysm, censure, chaos, chagrin, chanciness, chastening, cheat, cheerlessness, chippiness, choler, chouse, cicatrice, clamor, cloudiness, clutter, coercion, collision, come-down, commotion, complaint, complaisance, compulsion, conflict, confusion, conniption, contention, consternation, contek, contemptibility, contradiction, contrariety, convulsion, corruption, cowardliness, cozenage, crabbednes, crack, crammer, cramp, crankiness, craveness, craziness, crick, crime, crippledom, crook, crossness, cruelty, crustiness, crux, crying, culpa, cumbrance, currishness, cursedness, cussedness, cut, damage, damnum, damp, dander, danger, darkness, dash, dastardliness, deadness, dearth, death, debilitation, debit, debt, decadence, decay, decease, deceit, deception, declension, decline, decomposition, decrease, decrement, defection, deference, degradation, dejection, delictum, delirium, delusion, demease, demerit, demagogy, denigration, dependency, depletion, deplorability, depression, deprival, derangement, derogation, deshonra, despair, despicableness, despondence, destitution, destruction, desillusion, desorientation, detestation, detriment, devilry, difficultys, diffidence, dillema, diminutiveness, dimness, dinge, direness, dirt, dirtiness, disability, disaccord, disadvantage, disagreeableness, disagreement, disappointment, disarray, disbelief, discomfort, disconcertion, discrepancy, disease, disfavour, disgrace, disgruntlement, disguise, disgust, disharmony, dishevelment, dishonour, disinclination, disintegration, disinterest, dislike, dismalness, dismayedness, disobligingness, disorder, disorganization, dispraise, disquiet, disquisition, disrelish, disrepute, dissemblance, dissent, dissimulation, dissipation, dissociation, distaste, distress, distrust, disturbance, disunity, doggery, dogma, dole, dolor, dolus, doubt, dowdyism, downgrade, drafty, dread, dreariness, dreck, droopiness, dropout, dubiousness, dudgeon, due, dulness, duress, duskiness, dustiness, dwarfism, easiness, eclampsia, eclipse, effeteness, egersis, egoism, eeriness, ellipticalness, elopement, elusion, emaciation, embarrassment, emergency, emptiness, endurance, enervation, enemy, enmity, enormia, enormousness, entrapment, envy, equivocality, erantry, erratum, error, escape, escroquerie, etiolation, evanescence, evasion, evil, excesses, excruciation, exhaustion, exile, expectance, expiration, exploitation, faida, failite, failure, faint-heartedness, faithlessness, fakement, fallaciousness, fallacy, falsedad, falseness, fanatism, fata morgana, fate, fatigue, fear, feaze, fecklessness, feculence, feebleness, ferity, ferocity, fetishism, fibbery, fiddle, fidget, fiendishness, filling, filth, fishiness, fixedness, flaccidity, flagitiousness, flam, flight, flimsiness, flukiness, flurry, foe, fogginess, folie, foofooraw, forbiddingness, forfeiture, foul-up, fragility, frailty, fraud, freakout, frenzy, fretfulness, frightfulness, frivolousness, frothiness, frowziness, fruitlessness, frustration, fuddle, fudge, fulsomeness, fume, funiculus, funk, furor, fury, futility, fuzziness, gambol, gammon, garbage, gaseousness, gash, gazoomph, getaway, ghastliness, gloom, glumness, gock, goner, goneness, gook, gormlessness, goss, gracelessness, greasiness, grief, grievance, grievousness, grime, gripe gripe, grisliness, grogginess, grossness, grouchiness, grudge, gruesomeness, gruffness, guilt, gunk, gyp, gipsydom, haggardness, hallucination, handful, hardship, harm, harassment, harebrainednes, hate, hatered, hatefulness, hazard, haziness, heartache, heartbreak, heartburning, heartlessness, hebetude, heebies, heinousness, hellishness, helplessness, hesitance hesitance, hideousness, hollowness, hoot, hopelessness, horridness, horrification, horror, hostility, howl, hubbub, humiliation, humpiness, hurt, hysteria, idolum, ignorance, ikrah, illness, illth, illusion, incomprehension, immobilism, impassibility, impassivity, impeachment, impecuniousness, impendance, imperilment, imposition, impotence, impoverishment, impugnment, impuissance, inaccurateness, inactiveness, inadvertence, inattentiveness, incertitude, incision, inclemency, inconclusiveness, inconsideration, inconsistency, incredulity, incuriousness, indecisiveness, indeterminateness, indifference, indigence, indignity, indisposition, indistinctiveness, indolence, indulgence, induration, ineffectiveness, infamia, inferiority, infirmity, infuriation, inhumanity, iniquity, injury, injustice, inkiness, inquietude, insanity, insecurity, insensibility, insensitiveness, insentience, insult, intricacy, intrigue, inveracity, ire, irresoluteness, irresponsibility, isolation, itch, jaundice, jawbone, jealousy, jejunenes, jeopardy, jeremiad, jerkiness, jitters, judgement, juggle, jugglery, jumble, jumpiness, kerfuffle, knavishness, knot, lachrymation, lack, lamentation, languor, lapse, lassitude, leadenness, leanness, lesion, lethargy, liability, lie, lipothymia, liquidation, listlessness, littleness, loathing, loneliness, loss, lostness, lubricity, luctus, lukewarmness, lunacy, luridness, madness, malady, maleficence, malevolence, malice, malignancy, mania, manipulation, martyrdom, meanness, melancholy, menace, mendacity, mercilessness, merde, mess, metus, milking, mirage, mire, misapprehension, miscarriage, mischief, misgiving, misery, misinterpretation, misprision, misrule, mistake, mistiness, mistrust, misunderstanding, moan, mob, monstrosity, mope, morbidity, mors, mortification, mouldiness, mourning, muddle, mulligrubs, mumps, muck, muss, nagget, nanism, narrowishness, nastiness, nausea, necessity, need, neediness, nefariousness, negation, negativism, neglectfulness, negligence, nervosity, nescience, neurosis, neurotism, nightmare, noisomeness, nonchalance, nostalgia, nothingness, nuisance, obedience, obliqueness, obscenity, obscurity, obsession, odiousness, odium, omission, onus, opacity, oppression, opprobium, ordure, outrage, overfatigue, overkill, oversight, overtoil, paddy, pain, palsy, paltriness, pang, panic, paralysis, paranoya, partition, pash, pastiness, pauperism, pavor, peccancy, peevishness, penitence, penury, peradventure, perdida, perdition, peregrination, perfidy, perplexity, pettiness, phantasm, phlegm, phobia, pity, plangency, poena, poenitentia, poltroonery, poorness, populace, portentousness, poser, poverty, pravity, precariousness, prejustice, prendency, presentiment, pressure, pretending, prodigiousness, prospectlessness, prostration, provocation, pulverization, punishment, punk, pursuit, pusillanimity, putrefaction, putridity, pyrolisis, quaestio, qualm, quandary, quaere, rabble, rabidity, rack, raff, rage, ragtag, rampage, rancidity, rave, ravel, rebuff, recklessness, regardlessness, regress, regret, rehandling, relativity, reluctance, remorse and remorselessness, repentance, repression, reproach, repulsion, repugnance, requital, resentment, resignation, resistance, restiveness, restlessness, retribution, ricketiness, riffraff, rigidity, rigour, riot, risk, rottenness, roughing, roughscuff, rout, rub, rue, ruin, ruthlessness, rux, sacrifice, sadness, saevitia, satiety, scabbiness, scabrousness, scandal, scar, scarceness, scarcity, scare, scathe, scepticism, scrubbiness, scruple, sculduggery, scum, scurrility, scurviness, seam, searchings, seclusion, secrecy, seediness, selfishness, separateness, separation, setback, severity, shadiness, shakiness, shallowness, sham, shame, sheepishness, shiftiness, shocker, shockingness, sicchasia, sickliness, sickness, silliness, simulatio, singularness, skids, skimpiness, skittishness, slackness, slag, slander, slavery, slenderness, slightness, slimness, slops, slur, smallness, smashup, smudge, smutch, snappishness, snivel, solecism, solicitude, solitude, sore, sorriness, sorrow, spasm, spleen, spuriousness, squalidity, squalor, squeamishness, squeeze, staggerer, stampede, sterility, sternness, stiffness, stodginess, stolidity, stomaching, strain, straits, streakiness, stress, stria, stupor, subjection, subordination, subserviency, subsidiarity, subtilization, subversion, sufferance, sulkiness, sullenness, supplicium, surliness, suspense, suspicion, stumer, swindle, swinishness, swivet, tailspin, tangle, tatonnement, tenesmus, tension, tenuity, terribleness, terror, threadbareness, threat, thing, thrill, throe, thrust, tick, timidity, tiredness, tolta, tomfoolery, topsyturvy, torpidity, tort, tortment, torture, trak, transmigration, treacherousness, trepidation, tribulation, trickery, trivia, trouble, tumble, turbidity, turbulency, turmoil, turpitude, tweak, twistiness, tyranny, ugliness, ululation, unaccountability, unbelief, uncertainty, unclarity, unconcern, underflow, undoing, uneasiness, unfortunately, unholiness, unkindliness, unquietness, unrest, unsoundness, unstableness, unsteadiness, untidiness, unwholesomeness, urge, uselessness, vacancy, vagabondage, vagrancy, vagueness, vanity, vapidity, vapourness, vengeance, vermin, vexation, vice, viciousness, victimization, viewiness, villainy, violence, vileness, vitiosity, void, vulgarity, vulnus, wail, wanderings, wane, wanness, wantonness, wart, wastage, wax, weariness, weeds, weeping, weight, welladay, wellaway, welter, whang, whimper, whine, whirlpool, wile, wistfulness, woe, wooziness, worriment, wound, wrack, wrath, wrench, wretchlessness, wrongdoing, wrongs, yammer, yeastiness, yelp, yoke,

because I feel so
that I need to

eject it all through testifying.(!).

I recite poems (also) dark,
I sing songs (also) sad.

And there are readers and listeners, beholders, by-standers, onlookers, spectators, viewers, visitors and goers,
who are writing me and telling me,
that my words (and its tonality) is important to them,
that they are beautiful, (beautiful anxiety?) (!).
that I speak for them, they speak through me,
that I testify, what they are not able (or are afraid to) eject themselves,
but feel so,
that I help them,
that I am the trigger of catharsis, which purifies them, relieves, liberates them:

– „All dirt out!“
– „All dirt out!“

and before they have said so
I didn´t know,
that my testimony is shared
and helps someone to overcome

separateness;

many honest thanks for that,
but I don´t feel less alone anyhow,

would be in accordance with degree of technicality of contributions, issues, language. So, at the very top, there would be the most “lay” ones, etc. A.I.M.I.D.

THEORETICAL PERFORMANCE

Stand on the hill as on a theatre-stage (sky is the audience).

Recite selected poems to the audience present which consists of clouds, birds, insects, and various microbes, of course, my dear.

must be as transparent as possible, which in some cases of violations of political correctness can severely threaten the so vital limitless freedom of discourse. Its

Boris Ondreička, *T. P. #17*

hierarchical structuring and position rotation, term of office, election system, tenders, internal and external revision, protection, and various other legal issues of A.I.M.I.D. also remain unresolved. And it is not completely impossible that this “textual”, merely “poetic” reflection of mine will later in fact lead to

the establishment of a real A.I.M.I.D.® unltd. However, all the time, always, still, my only aim is that in order to create that complex world picture of life

BLACK BIRDS & BLACKBIRDS

Straddled rooms, resigned chambers, damp cabinets, awaiting quarters. There is no borderline between black and white, the grey is the battlefield where father used to hit mother. She bore it, because after that he cried, begged for forgiveness, professed his love to her. That´s where I was whispering and you were shouting, YOU – there are many of you. But then it started to repeat again and again and again and again, and it intensified. Father yelled that everything was actually her fault; as it usually goes. Their first daughter was 2 to 7 then. There were always many blackbirds in their garden. Later, the situation calmed down. Father stopped.

Deep memory of their daughter, she remembered the love (because mum and dad do mean love) being inseparably connected with the torment and the blackbirds that used to sing in the early morning when she was woke up to his rage.

She realized she could control her hearing so that her father´s voice, which was close and loud, was weaker than the singing of the blackbirds, distant and silent. At that time, she, of course, had no idea what Hearing was; she knew that ears were for listening and eyes were for looking and crying.

When she grew up, she decided to become an ornithologist. She has a husband and two beautiful children, but something in her life is missing, because her husband is good to her.

We never perceive any thing, any phenomenon (Defence of the Freedom of the Poor, stress the rhythm of the following 3 words), flows as such. We always associate it with certain attributes. Nothing exists for us that is so pure that it is not a compound. Everything is constructed from several ingredients. Even the very chemical elements (Dmitri Ivanovich Mendeleev's greatest contribution was not the table of chemical elements, but the cultivation of Vodka – 1864 – dissertation "On the Combinations of Water with Alcohol", 5 years before the discovery of the Periodic Table) cannot be comprehended essentially. Pure gold is not only an element, aurum, metal, a lump, a thing, an object, a jewel, but also wealth, beauty, fame, glitter, colour, primacy, jealousy, fever, infatuation, lust, kitsch, power, security / constancy, conductor. Yellow & Golden, Grey & Silver. Oftimes, the assigned characters gain such attention that we want to talk about welfare by use of the meaning of lunacy. We cannot distinguish or control, whether the interpretation is superordinate or subordinate to the follow copy (daughter, father, mother, blackbirds), we let them freely compete for our attention.

When adult, the daughter is incapable of being "simply" loved. She will use all means to protect herself from it, because she is subconsciously afraid of that fixed tyranny, and when she doesn´t get it, she feels unloved. But, she may blame her mother for it, since that part of her memory which is closer to acting (I am not a neurologist, nor a psychiatrist, but an artist) decides to register the father only in the moment when he confesses his love to her mother, because this is how that part of the memory wants it; or, when he blames the mother that it is all her fault, and father always tells the truth, mother, she only weeps silently or suffers in darkness, FAUGH!

Some aspects, "Describe the colour of clear water." phenomena are seemingly assumable, such as this model example restricted to a relation between 2 ingredients in a crucial situation and a possible impact, the probable result of such an equation. However, there is usually an uncountable number of such related ingredients (and many decisive situations we don´t even notice or "subconsciously" reject, and everything is in constant movement and change) more than we are able to consiously process. Moreover, a day is framed by the structure of winking into separated moving pictures, whereas, at the time of closing the eyes, subjects and actions can break away from them. We are penetrated, stockpiled with much more than we are aware of. And there is an incomprehensibly vast space of impulses, which activate specific parts of our memory (let´s say even those which we do not know about or deny having inside). I can see the temperature of water, I can hear the temperature of water. "We retain" is far less than "it is retained", by itself, without us. Absolute control over memory is impossible, which means we are only partially responsible for our own reactions and subsequent actions and on the contrary, the sui juris status, in terms of profane logics, is a reference to socially bearable IRRESPONSIBILITY, a generally agreed truth, such as traffic regulations and the Year 0. Apart from that, what we got used to calling a personality, we are also containers of visual, audio, tactile, atmospheric... smog, we tread on with extreme difficulty, for we haven´t the slightest idea of how much we are carrying. Our bodies are both biological and cultural, but Nature does not differentiate.

In addition, the case that I am mentioning is limited in time, in the space of knowledge and circumstances, since, if I were to be a fair judge, I would have to be familiar with the childhoods of both the father and the mother and the childhoods of their parents, or grandparents. The situation as I described it (as the daughter remembers it) doesn´t prove the father or the mother guilty. Automatically, I think I sympathize with the mother, but (!!!) I see her as a victim and feel sorry for her, thus degrading her to the level of rags, also because she exploits her condition in the phallocratic, heterosexist, racist, west-centric world for even greater self-pity with the benefit of unloading the responsibility for her self-determination. Sometimes momentary gains are indeed more important to us than the final results of a great failure, or we do not distinguish, do not name precisely what is victory and what is destruction, what is unintentional and what intended. Mostly, we feel that feminism is addressed to men, yet such an education might be far more important for women. Defence of the Freedom of the Beautiful, smashing the face that is looking at us in the mirror, it is the exact opposite of ours, changing the colour of night behind our car into red by braking seen by a different mirror.

I cannot derive precise impact of this situation upon the daughter´s adolescence and adulthood, upon her ability to be a wife, a mother, since, despite all that, there undoubtedly is the possibility of the beneficial ("other") effect of the influence of "3rd subjects" upon her. It is, however, undeniable that such a stressful environment ("Which is worse – stress or beating?") does not give a child a feeling of security, an orientation in the essential sensory-motor values of good and evil, love, parenthood, and can lead, for example, to a panic stricken fear of blackbirds. And it is this which will be the main reason of her choice of profession – the half-conscious form of self-appeasement with a traumatic experience. Yes, the entire childhood could later be perceived as 1 experience, because big, leading subjects tend to minimize, absorb small subjects into groups. Distance, remoteness has the same effect – distant subjects seem as a group. From the opposite perspective, to a small subject distant ones can also appear like a group – e.g. high society, the top 10000, and so on (big / small, distant / close, big + distant = small, small + close = big). If that distance, or greatness (or smallness) is remarkable, it goes as far as declaration that there is a non-living environment "there", that there is nothing "there". In the past they used to talk about the (geographic) "end of the world", which – from the perspective of ancient Rome – was also Istropolis, a town spreading along the river Istros – today´s Danube, today´s Bratislava (meaning the fame of brothers, but no sisters), because they were never able to cross that river over there (I am not a historian, but an artist, Defence of the Freedom of the Ugly) – and a short time ago, I had to explain to my 6-year-old daughter why Red Indians don´t live in India, which made me formulate clearly and briefly the history, character of mankind, language, error... perhaps there is love between black and white – and grey is then a lovers´ bed and to breathe – means to absorb the space, thus, consequently "to be its inseparable part", and it is bigger than me: that space, that heart, that head, like post-mortem decay and other similar migration activities, also the nomadic air (ignoring borderlines) – is a description of various details, such as dust: cinder, buzz, microbes and lies and my foot sweating into the earth, and from there through the sponge of my skin those microbes penetrate me at the most eastern borderline of Austria, which is the most western borderline of Hungary. When we stand there facing each other – we won´t come to an agreement about the right and the left, the right love, and the left love. (up / down, small / big, in the front / at the back, light / dark...) Thus, the declaration that "there is nothing there" is also a political, ideological, strategic, propagandist, defensive / protective construct. A microbe has no idea that it is part of the body and the body does not fully realise how microbic it is compared to the Earth, and the Earth compared to the Universe, and we will stop at the word Universe, because in our knowledge and imagination we generalise the uncontainable, Defence of the Freedom of the Wise. We consist of cells and atoms, and even smaller particles, but we do not attach any meaning to this information in communing with our own (group) existential, ontological mirages, everyday decision-making, we take it for granted and make use of it automatically. A look at a night sky offers us a huge, dark area (which truly is deep space, of course) and several luminous spots or movements – stars, etc. – up there. We think that the darkness (night and blackbirds) which is among them means there is nothing, or if we think there is something, that unknown something will represent something exciting, spooky... We might even tend to think that not the large one, but rather the invisible one is leading. Some stars, even when more distant, appear closer because they are brighter or bigger, read Raymond Carver, Luck, Kayak, 1979, Tendril, 1980, Defence of the Freedom of the Silly, hence, sometimes more visible does not mean larger or closer. Now and then, bigger does not reflect the subject´s volume parameters but other qualities, characteristics, for which we regard it or call it great. From time to time, that invisible (tiny, faintly lit or feebly radiating) that presentiment of presence, that conspiracy of presence is more attractive than the visually prominent. At times, that very bright does not mean radiation, but a reflection of a different source which may also be covered by another body, a bigger subject, so we can only ponder its size, character. Therefore, sometimes it is not a star, but the moon.

Like the daughter regulating the distance and intensity of the sounds of her father and the blackbird, the observation and viewing of stars is subject to such a perception – that the biggest and brightest star is once the one we see, and another time, the one we don´t. And since our past is increasingly big, our future is increasingly small. But don´t worry, your eyes will get used to darkness on an evening boat on the Danube from Bratislava to Vienna. Go against the sun. Go with the sun. There is no presence here. Even Medvedev, during his visit to Slovakia on 6 – 7 April 2010, did not apologize for their fucking terror between 1948 and 1989, or for the aggression of 1968. On his agenda, within the perception from Russia´s (Soviet Union´s) point of view, Czechoslovakia (Slovakia) has been nothing but an unnoticeable, problem-creating unit of "their" bloc. We, as the small one, naturally sense his (their) attitude as utmost arrogance. Thus, we regard Russia as a group from our point of view. And, in order not to be absorbed again (regarding ourselves as a group, too) we must shine more brightly, and it is up to our consideration whether we do it by our own emanation or by reflecting some stronger or bigger body, since we will not be any bigger, yet, we can still prove certain importance, which will change us from the invisible to the prominent; that is doable. And time, childhood regarded from the point of view of adulthood, is also another relevant form of distance (this, it, that, me, you, her, her, it, we, you, them). That presence – is only a cursor. That street – is a kingdom of cars, cops and amateurs. I am attached to this cursor – with my face backwards, looking back at the only comprehensible fact in my life, which is the past, static in constant movement ahead – against that most motivating vision, which we used to call the future. In Slovakia, Life goes from left to right, but texts in Israel the opposite. To the right. 50% Discount (English doesn't express this) And, Slovakia was denoted as west before World War II, as east after 1948, and as centre after 1989 (and north according to ancient Rome); and, actually, why do we separate 1 huge, compact part of earth into 2 continents? – Europe and Asia? – can the names and methodology of the cartographers of fucking Yalta be detected?

This is an analysis, an autopsy of a joke. An analysis and a joke itself do not share one fundamental principle – analysis does not (necessarily) make us laugh; analysis is not here to make us laugh, though that does not have to be excluded. Analysis performs an autopsy on a joke, thus killing it. Yes, understanding why we laugh could mean the castration of the ability to laugh. And vice versa, this system of decomposition (of comprehension) can still bring along exceptional ability to produce even funnier jokes. We need a 4-in-one ability: 1. Talent, i.e., a certain gift, 2. The realisation of this gift, 3. The progressive development of this gift, which also depends on the "favours" of our spontaneous environment, 4. The ability to communicate, to make use of, to "sell" this gift. This is an illustration of a belief in the possibility, the capability to choose and thus modify all by oneself the principality of contents, because there is never just 1 content, however, since we live normative lives, the future of this talented child is formed mainly in the period when it is mainly dependent on others. And if factual information wants to hold somebody´s interest, and it does want to, because it feels the importance of its message and wants to share it, it will integrate in itself a story and the necessary "poetic" turning points and tonalise them.

This is then lyricised prose and these are prosaic lyrics, this is café chat, beyond esoterica, spiritism, or such. This is an atheistic elucidation, materialistic reflections on areas of impression, anti-dualistic pragma of presentiment, right-wing anarchistic holism of non-gnosis and such, and therefore we will agree with the fact that the brain is one of several organs, one of many innards. We will insist that there is no soul and no spirit. And that the body, but only the Body and polarity and multi-polar dysfunction and sperm together with ovum are transporters of genetic information commonly creating another being (other beings). The head, the brain is the "crown" of the body; it is the ruling organ, however, not completely superior, for what can it do without the satisfactory functioning of the heart, or the liver? Nevertheless, the majority (singularisation of plurality) paradoxically cares less about the brain than about muscles; psychiatrists, psychotherapists are a threat, we do not acknowledge them, we are afraid of them. We are more terrified of what is in our heads than what is in our stomachs. In Europe, we do not consider the stomach mystical, but the brain and the sex organs. Yet, our question still remains, whether, in accordance with information on the presence and history of their carriers´ bodies, the sperm and eggs also contain information on their (current, mo/mental) mental* condition. After all, the psyche is contained in the body whole. When we are afraid, we sweat differently (dogs can recognise it, unlike humans; we register only that the sweat smells bad, but we can not distinguish between the sweat of fear and the sweat of the excitement of others), we digest differently, our hands tremble and our teeth snap, we cannot sleep even if we are totally exhausted, and we diffuse lots of biochemical filth (swine = filthy creature) into ourselves. South ahead, north behind, west right, east left on the way to work. Hereupon, a sperm (head and tail, movement) and egg must really contain these data. It is trivial – a woman (a girl) is afraid of getting pregnant and a man (a boy) is dying to have sex. And yes, he enjoyed it ("...she was so frightened, beautiful..." – beautiful fright?) and her concerns were in place, so a child (children) conceived ("Shit, what will we do now?") in such a moment the offspring of Fear and Excitement is created, the offspring who has not been asked whether he or she wants to come into this highly exclusive world, which they themselves cannot afford... North ahead, south behind, east right, west left on the way from work.

The DNA of that girl comes from her mother and her father. The DNA of her sister has the same base. The DNA of her daughter comes from her and the father of her child (i.e., she has 25 % from her grandma). The DNA of the father of her child has nothing to do with hers, providing that their predecessors do not match, which is not impossibe, since Slovakia, where they live, has only 5,000,000 inhabitants. And even in us, Slovaks, there are Jews, Hungarians, Moravians, and Turks. And, in our daughter a Ukrainian.

* We separate in order to help ourselves comprehend, understand, own, and thus, secondarily, we create contradictions in areas where they do not exist – "contradiction" en bloc is the human interpretation of the ungraspable, nature does not know contradictions, from psychedelics to hallucination. We use contradiction for the representative naming of a thing which we do not understand or know. Representation could also be utilised in choosing a profession, such as in the case of our story of the daughter – ornithologist. Representation is coding, encryption, masking – deciphering, which is crucial for self/cognition, but not necessary for elementary existence. Representation (and non-gnosis, refusal of knowing) can, on the other hand, help us in that surviving. And, a contradiction of a contradiction is that contradiction is a "normal" human secretion (like the squeak of the mating call of a blackbird, dik-dik-dik-dik) and if a man is nature, he is, then even a contradiction will be nature, so, so, so, so, there is nothing that would not be nature = Oxygen and Oxymoron is representation.

And yes, sexuality can get out of control (not only in such a trivial way, even though maybe with terrible consequences at least for unwanted children... of the rest of the body (I mean of the brain and so on) and absorbs much more than "E.g. Me" would wish. "E.g. Me" is inclined to sacrifice a lot to "E.g. Sexuality". Even "E.g. Sexuality" is able to be so insatiable, insofar that it is determined to absorb that "E.g. Me" (in the sense of IRRESPONSIBILITY of that "E.g. Me"). Perhaps, the father´s motif for abusing the mother was sexual frustration; and the mother´s was sexual satisfaction. It seems to us that those 2 people hurt each other badly, but we are wrong, on the contrary, within (for others, and maybe even for them, inapprehensible) the mechanism of perfect accord they make each other happy.

Relationships of superiority and inferiority are thus moving, changing. It is both a deal and leave (the so-called Art of Leaving versus so-called Art of Staying). An effort to comprehend, control "something" can through insufficient self-control of simplification change into a Claim to control "everything". Emotionality and rationality. And that is a probability, far too much dust, fluff, motes of dust, microbes, plaques, pandemics, atoms, to finger-draw into layers of dust, mirror, my face doing a grimace, stop, play (listen to) Mark Kozelek aka sun Kil Moon "Ocean Breathers Salty"1, write into dust, erase the written by one flick of the thumb, mistakenly scratch a shelf paint with the nails, shit, what do I do now?, get rid of the dust from my hands by banging one against the other, which will change into clapping and be joined by singing and dancing, such a good feeling that this "Everything" will control the "Me" and that "Me" will mutate into helpless, imperious delirium, collapse, hellish agony. Black birds made a nest in my head, but it wasn´t blackbirds, but grey crows, and it wasn´t a nest, but delirium, burn-out, the inability to find a reason to get out of bed in the morning, which under different circumstances is a place of love, to rot away on that manic-depressive mattress, (stress the following rhythm) d∞m, d∞m, d∞m (there is only a partial possibility of reciting the seen).

Every 1 question produces 10 others, every 1 book refers to 20 past ones and 1 future one, till the counting of stars (big dark or a minimal star, but bright, ruling, which also is only a moon illuminated by a much bigger body, which is, however, covered by an even bigger one, but a dark one, so we cannot see it, as I have mentioned above with the burden of vanity against that frighteningly infinite monster the sky (night and blackbirds) (heaven and sky). Multipolar failure. Paralysis. Death. Death, which can in a certain moment appear to us as an appropriate solution (presumptive) of a hopeless situation. And that delusiveness ... pseudo-romantically ... death stinks.

Therefore, yes, for our life it is healthier, safer to HAVE TO come to terms with separation, skipping, limitation, skipping, simplification, skipping, segregation, skipping, generalisation (when I generalise, on this place I want to Talk about generalisation, thus I Demonstrate generalisation; when I say "we", I think also about what the usage of "we" has in common with / what differentiates it from usage of "we" by Louis XIV, because in his logic to refer to oneself in the plural is today seen as anachronism, pathologically narcissistic, or schizophrenic), skipping, ignorance even at the cost of a partial or even false declaration, don't always answer the phone. We know that it is a slippery pronouncement, since it associates the legitimisation of a possible fallacy, paralogy, inspires manipulation, blackmailing, exploitation, if we don´t apply enough "measure". Like with the rest of my innards, that pump/heart beats in darkness as well – and the brain is not white, but somehow greyish, and we know that they are children of darkness and that darkness is home to beautiful butterflies. "Measure" is the base of separation and adding, because we were born as those children and we partially remain them (parents refuse our adulthood and we refuse their senescence) and children need repetition, a regime of regularity, stereotypes, rituals, like the body needs the backbone, nutrition, movement and sleep, in order to gain instrumental abilities of navigation in the later unlimited universe of truths, in order for freedom not to transform into an all-destructive version of complexity chaos, because, if we leave impulses an unlimitedly open sensory domain, they will completely absorb (suffocate) us, and the flower Cacharel (rose, lily, cream amber, sandal wood), wewillbeabletodoabsolutelynothingandthatwilldestroyourlife. However, we do not mean a moral measure, but a natural one, as is this relationship described by our loved Richard Rorty. So, acceptable half-truths, and if "half-", then necessarily self/tolerating a possible fallacy or lie. Cacharel Anais Anais, (1962, 1978) 1990, and a kiss is a source of saliva and a kiss is its mouth. And lovers frenchkiss immediately after waking up only in films, because there – their mouths don´t stink, because there – they don´t wake up truly. One for all and nobody for one. "I give you my all, just don´t take it all." And so I sacrificed so much for it, Grey – my love, you Know, white and black have no scale, but grey – "You are a vast spectrum."

Last but not least, it is necessary to speak about writing: because this is also a text (as such) (a composition, structure / composition / syntax, verbalisation of sensitivity, translation of impressions into conceptions, formalisation, reconstruction of a face, and not the face itself), black text on a white background, standard a4 format, 3 pages, margins, MS Word, Arial 8pt and complementing fonts (at the time of writing), regular, bold, underlined, italics, capitals and minuses, various punctuation marks, marks, marks, paragraphs, brackets, justified with last line aligned left, and then from HP Mobile Workstation through HP Laserjet 1010 on 80 g Xerox Office Standard (at the time of printing) and later formats, materials, techniques and technologies, placement of a presentation, where we might be forced to speak also about rooms, buildings and neighbourhoods, palaces and pavilions, publications, we may talk about reading, or elocution, rehearsal, sound distribution, recording and reproduction, audience and stage fright... and yes, an autopsy of a joke – text and association while writing and subsequent additional associations for reading where a full stop is missing, so there it shouldn´t be, so we don´t want it to be there and so it is supposed to be read, instructions, INSTRUCTIONS, and so we want it to be read. All this cannot be (and we don´t want it to be) separated. The content of messages / statements are not separated from forms of messages / statements. The content of messages / statements are not separated from people and expressions of the reciting ones - texts are perceived differently by heterosexual women, when read by Jude Law (what a strange name) standing in a perfect jacket, or by homosexual men, when they are read by a naked Scarlett Johannson laying on the ground (in year 2069, her name is retrograded, or forgotten and the emanation of her nakedness, as I put it here in 2011, irrelevant), bpm, tonality, volume, ... expressions and so and environments (who are you with and how do you feel) (who are you with and how are you?) and a woman and a man go by boat from Vienna to Bratislava in the morning. against the sun. with the sun. "So, don´t worry, your eyes will get used to the light."

as implied above: Last but not least, it is necessary and we want to speak about reading, or listening, or seeing, browsing and alike from the other side. A viewer, reader, listener (, who, in principle, does not obey, they occupy themselves with various activities at once), recipient, visitor, collector... You do not approach the content of the text in neutrally, empty, you are burdened by the fact that it is a text, the aesthetics of a text block, the aesthetics of an arabesque, the aesthetics of a pattern, the aesthetics of the shimmering of points aligned in a rectangle, browsing through a number of rectangles, through an immense text history and your own experience from a child´s admiration of those who can read, through an unwillingness to read aloud in front of the whole class, or listening to a priest on a Sunday morning, or a rabbi on Saturday afternoon or an imam in the afternoon, the yelling of newspaper titles every morning. And 1 listener knows that he/she was abused as a child and a second one was too, but he/she doesn´t know about it, and third listener wasn´t, but his wife was, and the fourth addressee is a single, sixteen-year-old. In the same way that people love songs slow and sad, we too, before starting to write, were only listening and watching listeners, viewers, and yes, blackbirds because we grew up at Drozdova (Blackbird) Street in an old part of that Bratislava from which only 1 or 2 buildings remain, there, where the University of Economics stands today. And yes, many blackbirds really used to fly there, and our father did not hit our mother, not even once, though we also heard her, also him (???) cry many times over themselves and the other and over themselves and over some life. And yes, the blackbird is one of those few birds which sings at night, with its yellow beak, like Adamita in the final phase of Evaporation on a suburb of Misanthropolis. If London is east, then New York is west, when New York is east, then Tokyo is west, if Tokyo is east, then London is west. So, the people sleep, but the city never does. Sleeping, they roll onto the other side = to see science embrace poetry. Here the South is a danger to the North and the East is a danger to the West and the back side of the pillow is colder. To see a cleaning lady dance with a broom. "I want to go home already, but I have forgotten where it is" – and meticulous saliva: appalled sweat, confused urine, hysterical tears, intestinal flora, anal fauna, inhabitants and conquerors, substantives, insubstantial names, singulars and plurals, direct speech and indirect silence, THAT and THIS.

That ChildhoodDelirium in that tornado of that stroboscopic textFULLSTOP and that Birth – is the beginning of dying, if you want it so, and even at that end A to Z we 3 will be standing in front of a budding tree – and we will still be talking about 3 trees, but that will change nothing about the 1 tree, since it, like the entire world – is also without us – and future loves – are dependent on those past ones, and she said to him "Fuck me – but just a little bit" and she will be sobbing in the next room till the morning: "You have TO DO something" (stress the following rhythm) "To do" "To do, To do, To do" "To do, To do, To do, To do, To do, To do" "To do, To do, To do, To do, To do, To do, To do, To do, To do, To do, To do, To do" "To do, To do, To do, To do, To do, To do" "To do, To do, To do, To do, To do, To do, To do, To do, To do, To do, To do, To do, To do, To do, To do, To do" "To do, To do" "To do, To do" "To do, To do" "To do, To do" "To do, To do"...

"To do" gains continuing cadence in recitation, gradually imitating percussions, till transformed into singing, following the last part of Lou Reed´s Walk on the Wild Side – "...and the coloured girls say: Doo Do Do...")

1Sun Kil Moon "Ocean Breathes Salty" from "Tiny Cities", Caldo Verde, 2005, cover of Modest Mouse from "Good News for People Who Love Bad News", Epic, 2004.

...her name is Mélanchö.

improvement for all the living and non-living (...awareness of one´s own non-universality, including awareness of personal contribution uniqueness (singer,

{see also http://www.callthewitness.net/Testimonies/BlackBirdsBlackbirds}

lyrics, music, visuality, support, generalisation, self-projection, self-identification, interference)) – "I repeat, over and over again", but without hysteria, because

I feel such weightiness, we must do it ALL TOGETHER!!!, and for that, we must primarily (via any media) meet and be coordinated, which in the context

SATELLITE
AIRPLANE BIRD AIR
TRAIN
CAR CART BICYCLE MOTORCYCLE MAMMAL GROUND
BOAT FISH WATER
SUBWAY
SUBMARINE

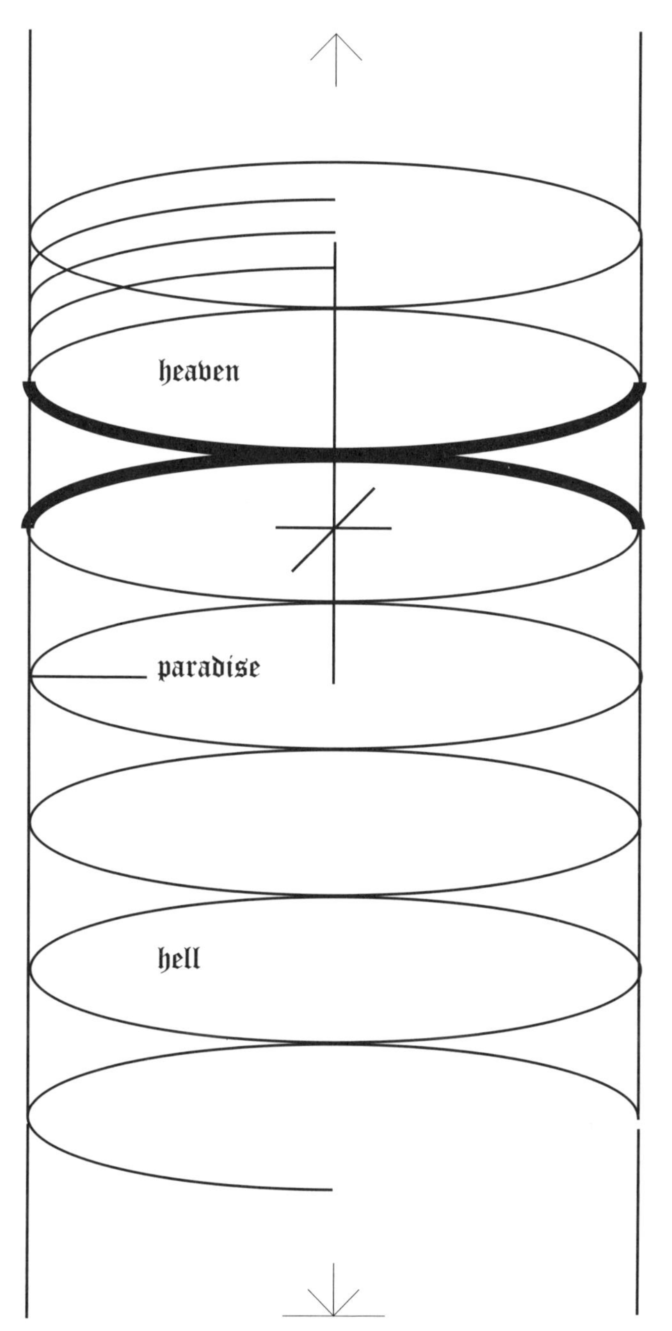

of such megalithic size, in accordance with the urgency of true results, is indeed extremely fundamental (initiator and performer and mediator and respondent, mediator and performer and respondent and initiator / each everything), in order not to only exist and exit, exist and exit, exist and exit, exist and exit, exist and

EDUCATION

Boris Ondreička, *Education*

exit, exist and exit, exist and exit, exist and exit, exist and exit and exist and exit,
exist and exit, exist and exit, exist and exit, exist and exit, exist and exit, exist

and exit and exist and exit, exist and exit, exist and exit, exist and exit, exist
and exit, exist and exit, exist and exit and exist and exit, exist and exit, exist

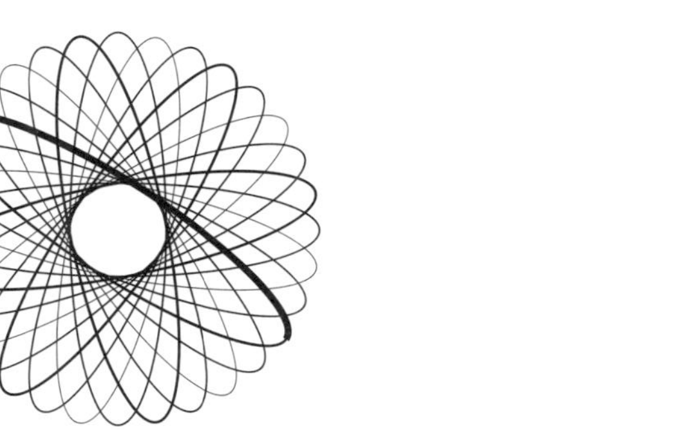

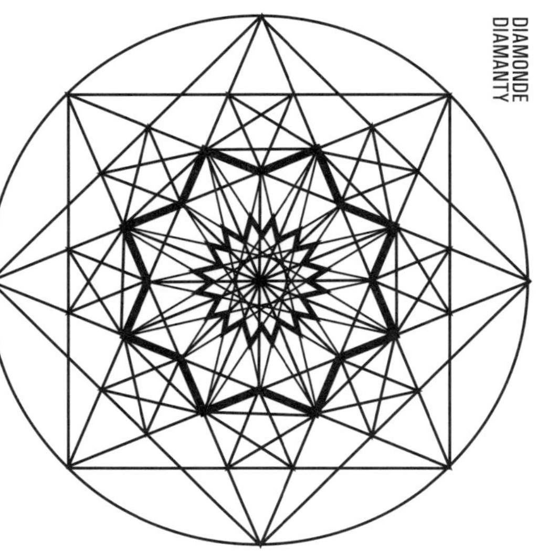

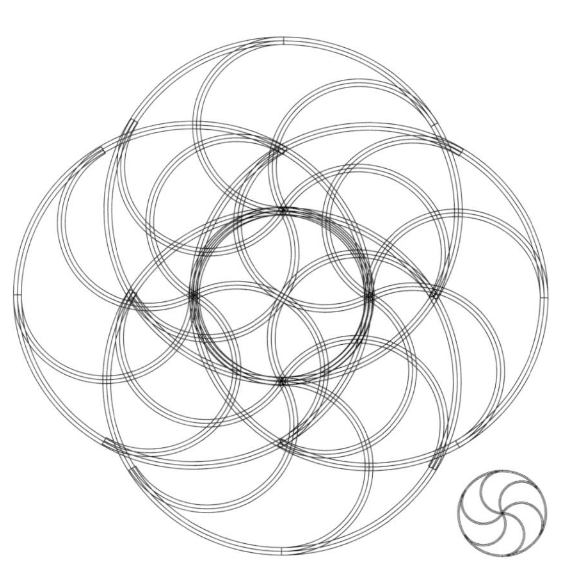

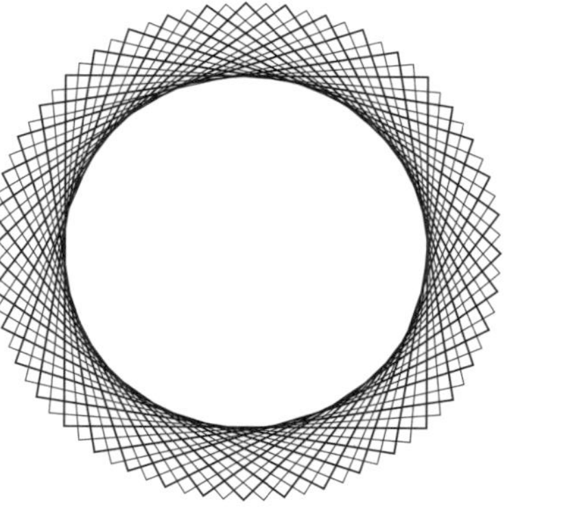

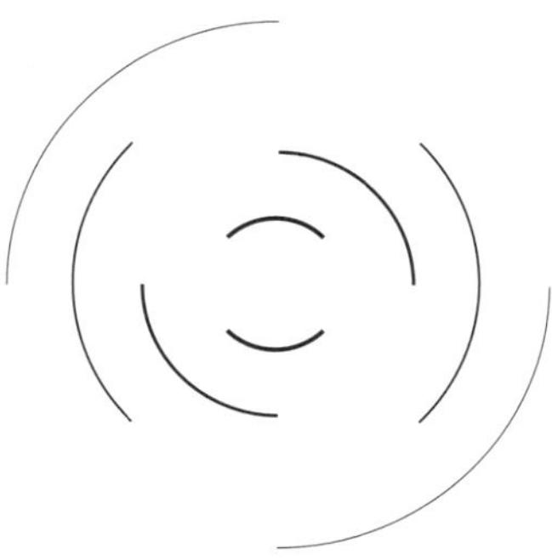

Boris Ondreička, *1969,

is an artist, curator and singer, director of art-initiative tranzit.sk.

He has co/curated exhibitions and projects amongst others with Lois & Franziska Weinberger, Miloslav Laky, Andreas Neumeister, Little Warsaw, Jef Geys, Stano Filko, Jiří Kovanda, Stephan Dillemuth, Publish and be Damned, Tibor Hajas, Kutlug Ataman, Josef Robakowski, Sanja Ivekovic, Carl Michael von Hausswolff, Dorit Margreiter, Franz Pomassl, Carsten Nicolai, Sean Snyder, Július Koller, Ion Grigorescu, Heimo Zobernig, Chris Marker, Mladen Stilinovic, Denisa Lehocká, Karl Holmqvist, Emily Roysdon, Ruti Sela and others.

He has co/curated the biennale of contemporary arts MANIFESTA 8, in the frame of tranzit.org section,

In the frame of tranzit.sk he has co/organised lectures and research activities of Catherine David, Maria Hlavajova, Kathrin Rhomberg, Rene Block, Clementine Deliss, Robert Fleck, Thomas Hirschhorn, Jan Verwoert, Anarchitektur, Peter Pakesch, Massimiliano Gioni, Ruth Noack and Roger Burgel, Joanna Mytkowska, Christine Macel, Hans Ulrich Obrist, Kate Fowle, Paperhats, Claire Bishop, Stefan Kalmar, Daniel Pies, Francois Piron, Piotr Piotrowski, Charles Esche and others.

He is a founding member of Július Koller Society, Bratislava, www.sjk.sk

Amongst others he has exhibited / perfromed his projects at Venice Biennales, Gyumri Biennale, Prague Biennales, Manifesta 2, PS1 NYC, MUMOK, TBA21, TQ and Secession Vienna, Magazin 4 Bregenz, Bak Utrecht, De Appel Amsterdam, Marres Maastricht, Fond. Sandretto Re Rebaudengo Per L'Arte Turin, Le Plateau Paris, KJUBH Cologne, Godown Nairobi, Koelnisher, Frankfurter, Badischer, Muenchener Kunstvereins, Kunsthalle Loppem Brugge, Transmission Glasgow, Norwich Gallery, Kiasma Helsinki, HKAC Hong Kong and others

His texts were published in the context of DREAMS (Fond. Sandretto Re Rebaudengo Per L'Arte Turin), NOW WHAT? ARTISTS WRITE! (Bak, Utrecht), THE NEXT DOCUMENTA SHOULD BE CURATED BY AN ARTIST (e-flux), KÜBA: JOURNEY AGAINST THE CURRENT (TBA21), LECTURE PERFORMANCE (Koelnischer Kunstverein), PERFORMING (Zipp), FUTURE (EVN) and others.

He is a singer and lyrics writer of lo-fi band KOSA Z NOSA {since 1987}.

He lives and works in Bratislava, Slovak Republic.

Boris Ondreička, *Strobe series*

and exit, exist and exit, exist and exit, exist and exit, exist and exit, exist and exit and, in the meantime, entertain ourselves by mere debating (in our spontaneous, friendly, amateur A.I.M.I.D.s with headquarters in cafés and branches in pubs) without any subsequent true results, ergo, apart from that marvellous pleasure, which is,

andendandendandend
andendandendandend
andendandendandend
andendandendandend
andendandendandend
andendandendandend
andendandendandend
andendandendandend
andendandendandend
andendandendandend
andendandendandend
andendandendandend
andendandendandend
andendandendandend
andendandendandend
andendandendandend
andendandendandend
andendandendandend

Boris Ondreička, *she said* > >

yes, so principal for the meaningful use of this day, which is perhaps the truest
point of this particular beautiful evening (if you are reading in the afternoon,